I0015003

DEMYSTIFYING LARGE LANGUAGE MODELS

UNRAVELING THE MYSTERIES OF LANGUAGE
TRANSFORMER MODELS, BUILD FROM GROUND UP,
PRE-TRAIN, FINE-TUNE AND DEPLOYMENT

JAMES CHEN

Published by James Chen, 2024

ISBN: 978-1-7389084-8-6 (Paperback)

ISBN: 978-1-7389084-7-9 (Hardcover)

Preface

In recent years, Large Language Models (LLMs), based on transformer architectures such as the well-known ChatGPT by OpenAI, have taken the world by storm, revolutionizing fields as diverse as natural language processing, content generation, and even code writing. These powerful models, capable of understanding and generating human-like texts, have opened up new frontiers in technology, exploring realms that were once considered the exclusive domain of human cognition.

However, despite their widespread adoption and impact, the inner workings of LLMs often remain in mystery, leaving many users and practitioners with a superficial understanding of these remarkable systems. This book aims to demystify LLMs, providing a comprehensive and accessible guide to their underlying principles, architectures, and practical applications.

Since introduced in 2017, the Transformer architectures have set a new benchmark in machine learning tasks, particularly Natural Language Processing (NLP). Given their impact, it's essential to understand their inner workings and not view them as black boxes.

This book was crafted with a simple yet audacious goal: to equip you with the knowledge and confidence to construct and utilize LLMs, irrespective of your background. Through this book, readers will embark on a journey that explores the intricacies of the Transformer architecture step by step, diving deep into the construction of these models from the ground up.

You do not need a PhD in computer science or experiences in machine learning to start this journey. We will be addressing fundamental topics, such as the mathematics that power these models and the basics of PyTorch -- an open-source machine learning library, before diving into advanced topics. However, we do assume some basic knowledge of Python programming and general computer science principles.

In addition to the theoretical and technical aspects, this book offers hands-on practices, equipping readers with the skills and knowledge necessary to pre-train transformers from scratch, leveraging state-of-the-art techniques and best practices. Furthermore, we will delve into the art of fine-tuning, covering both traditional methods and cutting-edge approaches such as Parameter Efficient Fine-Tuning (PEFT) and Low-Rank Adaptation (LoRA).

As we navigate the vast potential of LLMs, we will also confront one of the most imperative challenges in this field: the presence of biases and toxic content generated by these models. This book will provide insights and strategies for detoxifying pre-trained or fine-tuned models by introducing the Reinforcement Learning with Human Feedback (RLHF), ensuring that these powerful tools are used responsibly and ethically.

Finally, we will explore the deployment of LLMs, offering practical guidance on integrating these models into real-world applications, from chatbots, web UI, and content generation systems to more specialized use cases.

All the source codes in this book are readily available on GitHub for a comprehensive educational experience that combines theory and practice. By the completion of reading this book, you will have a solid foundation and an invaluable toolset with which to implement cutting-edge language models.

Whether you are a seasoned practitioner, a curious researcher, or simply someone fascinated by the incredible capabilities of LLMs, this book will serve as your comprehensive guide, empowering you to unlock the full potential of these transformative technologies. As you embark on this journey, remember: every expert was once a beginner. Revel in the process, and don't be disheartened by initial roadblocks. In the end, the journey is as enriching as the destination itself.

The ideas around artificial intelligence evolves rapidly, and things are changing week by week, what is state-of-the-art at the time of this writing may soon become commonplace. However, the fundamental concepts, approaches, and challenges remain consistent. It's these enduring elements that this book seeks to illuminate.

Welcome to the adventure in unraveling the mysteries of Language Transformer Models!

Table of Contents

1. Introduction

O ur world is becoming smarter each day thanks to something called Artificial Intelligence, or AI for short. This field of technology, from being a future concept to a tangible reality, is infusing and changing many parts of our lives. This book is an invite to learn about exciting parts of this bright new world.

Everything started with an idea named Machine Learning (ML). It's like teaching a computer to learn from data, just like we learn from our experiences. A lot of the tech magic we see today like autonomous driving, voice assistants or email filters would not be possible without it.

Then came to Deep Learning (DL), a special kind of Machine Learning (ML). It's like imitating how our brain works to help computers recognize patterns and make predictions.

On taking a closer look at Deep Learning, we find something called Language Models. Particularly, Generative AI and Large Language Models (LLM) have a unique place, they can create text that looks like written by human, which is really exciting!

At the heart of these changes, there are Transformer models designed to work with language in unique and powerful ways. The magic of the Transformer model is its incredible ability to understand language context, which makes it perfect for tasks like language translation, text summarization, sentiment analysis, and creating conversational chatbots like ChatGPT, where the Transformer model works as the backbone. This is the main topic of this book.

To explore the amazing world from AI to the language models, there are some tools that experts love to use, two of them are Python and PyTorch.

Python is a programming language that many people love, because it's easy to read, write and understand. It's like the friendly neighborhood of programming languages. Plus, it has a lot of extra libraries and packages that are specifically designed for Machine Learning, Deep Learning and AI. This makes Python a favorite for many people in these fields.

One of these extra libraries and packages is called PyTorch, like a big cabinet filled with useful tools just for Machine Learning and Deep Learning. It makes creating and training models like Transformer models much easier and simpler.

When we're working on such complex tasks like training a language model, we want tools that make our work easier and faster. This is exactly what Python and PyTorch offer. They help streamline complex tasks so we can spend more time on achieving our goals and making progress.

Therefore, this book is all about taking this exciting journey from the big world of AI to the specialized area of Transformer models, and this book will use Python and PyTorch to help you learn how to build, train, and fine-tune transformer models.

Welcome aboard and get ready to learn about how these technologies are helping to shape our future.

1.1   What is AI, ML, DL, Generative AI and Large Language Model

AI, ML, and DL, etc. — you've likely seen these terms thrown around a lot. They shape the core of the rapidly evolving tech industry, but what exactly do they mean and how are they interconnected?

Let's clarify. As a very high-level overview as shown in Figure 1.1, Artificial Intelligence (AI) includes Machine Learning (ML), which includes Deep

Learning (DL). The Generative AI is a subset of Deep Learning, the Large Language Mode is inside Generative AI. There are also some other things included inside the Generative AI, such as Generative Adversarial Network (GAN) and so on.

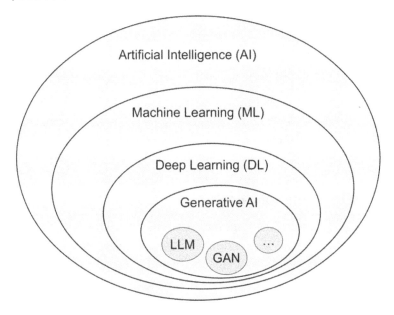

Figure 1.1 AI, ML, DL, Generative AI and Large Language Model

Artificial Intelligence (AI)

Artificial intelligence is to create the machines and applications that can imitate human perceptions and behaviors, it can mimic human cognitive functions such as learning, thinking, planning and problem solving. The AI machines and applications learn from the data collected from a variety of sources to improve the way they mimic humans. The fundamental objective of AI is to create systems that can perform tasks that usually require human intelligence. This includes problem-solving, understanding the natural human language, recognizing patterns, and making decisions. AI acts as the umbrella term under which ML and DL fall.

As some examples of artificial intelligence, autonomous driving vehicles like Google's Waymo self-driving cars; machine translation like Google Translate; chatbot like ChatGPT by OpenAI, and so on. It's widely used in the areas such as image recognition and classification, facial recognition, natural language processing, speech recognition, computer vision, etc.

Machine Learning (ML)

Machine learning, an approach to achieve artificial intelligence, is the computer programs that use mathematical algorithms and data analytics to build computational models and make predictions in order to resolve business problems.

ML is based on the concept that systems can learn from data, identify patterns, and make decisions with minimal human intervention. ML algorithms, also known as models, are trained on a set of data (called training sets) to create a model. When new data inputs come in, these models then make predictions or decisions, without being explicitly programmed to execute those tasks.

Different from traditional computer programs where the routines are predefined with specific instructions for specific tasks, machine learning is using mathematical algorithms to analyze and parse large amounts of data and learn the patterns from the data and make predictions and determinations.

Deep Learning (DL)

Deep learning, as a subset of machine learning, uses neural networks to learn things in the same, or similar, way as human. The neural networks, for example artificial neural network, consist of many neurons which imitate the functions of neurons of a biological brain.

Deep learning is more complicated and advanced than machine learning, the latter might use mathematical algorithms as simple as linear regression to build the models and might learn from relatively small sets of data. On the other hand, deep learning will organize many neurons in multiple layers, each neuron takes input from other neurons, performs the calculation, and outputs the data to the next neurons. Deep learning requires relatively larger sets of data.

In recent years the hardware is developed with more and more enhanced computational powers, especially the graphics processing units (GPUs) which were originally for accelerating graphics processing, and they can significantly speed up the computational processes for deep learning, they are now an essential part of the deep learning, and new types of GPUs are developed exclusively for deep learning purpose.

Generative AI

Generative AI is a type of artificial intelligence systems that have the capability to generate various forms of contents or data that are similar to, but not same as, the input data they were trained on. Generative AI is a subset of Deep Learning (DL), meaning it uses deep learning techniques to build, train, understand the input data, and finally generate synthetic data that mimic the input training data.

It can generate a variety of contents, such as images, videos, texts, audio and music and so on.

My book of "*Machine Learning and Deep Learning With Python*[3]", ISBN: *978-1-7389084-0-0, 2023,* or [3] in the Reference section at the end of this book, introduced the Generative Adversarial Network (GAN) which is a typical type of generative AI, it consists of two neural networks, a generator and a discriminator, which are trained simultaneously through adversarial training. The generator produces new synthetic images, while the discriminator evaluates if it's real or fake. Through the iterative training process the generator is trained to create the synthetic images that close enough to the original training data. That book also includes a hands-on example of how to implement the GANs with Python and tensorflow library.

Large Language Model (LLM)

The Large Language Model is a subset of Generative AI, it refers to the artificial intelligence systems that are able to understand and generate human-like languages. The LLM models are trained on vast amounts of textual data to learn the patterns, grammar, and semantics of human language, this huge amount of text may be collected from the internet, books, newspaper and other sources. In most cases, extensive computational resources are required to perform the training on the huge amount of data, therefore the graphics processing units (GPUs) are widely used for training the LLMs.

There are some popular LLMs available as of today, including but not limited to:

- **GPT3, and 4**: developed by OpenAI, it can perform a wide range of natural language processing tasks.
- **BERT**: (Bidirectional Encoder Representations from Transformers): developed by Google.
- **FLAN-T5**: (Fine-tuned LAnguage Net, Text-To-Text Transfer Transformer), also developed by Google.
- **BloombergGPT**: developed by Bloomberg and focus on the languages and terminologies in financial industry.

The Large Language Model (LLM) is the focus of this book.

1.2   Lifecycle of Large Language Models

When an organization decides to implement Large Language Models (LLMs), there is a typical process that includes several stages of planning, development, integration, and maintenance throughout the lifecycle of LLMs. It's a comprehensive process that encompasses various stages, each crucial for the successful development, deployment, and utilization of these powerful AI systems, as shown in Figure 1.2.

1. Objective Definition and Feasibility Study:

The organization should define the clear goals for what to achieve with the LLMs, identify the requirements, and understand the capabilities they could provide.

The organization should also conduct feasibility research to analyze the technical requirements and the potential return on investment (ROI), examine the available computational resources, data privacy policies, and whether the chosen LLMs can be effectively integrated into current infrastructures.

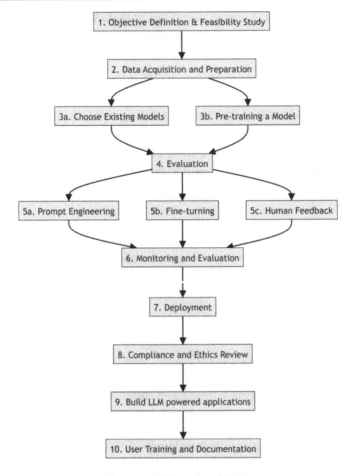

Figure 1.2 Lifecycle of LLMs

2. Data Acquisition and Preparation:

The organization should collect a large, diverse, and representative dataset, pre-process the dataset which include cleaning, annotating, or augmenting the data. This step is very important to ensure data quality, diversity and volume to train or fine-tune the model.

3a. Choose Existing Models:

The organization should understand the cost structure for using different LLMs, and consider the total cost of ownership over the lifespan of the LLMs. Section 4.6 of this book introduces some most popular LLMs in the industry, by reviewing the goals and requirements the organization should be able to select a pre-trained LLM that best suits its specific needs.

3b. Pre-training a Model:

Alternatively, if the organizations have their very specific requirements and goals that cannot be addressed by existing LLMs, they might decide to pre-train a LLM from scratch on its own, they should be prepared to invest significant resources and follow a structured process. Completing this process successfully requires careful planning and a significant commitment of resources not only the hardware devices but also the talents.

Chapter 4 of this book goes through the steps of pre-training a LLM model with a machine translation task, which is a hands-on practice.

4. Evaluation:

After pre-training the model, or selecting an existing pre-trained model, the organization should evaluate the model's performance using validation datasets, and identify the areas that need to improve.

5. Prompt Engineering, Fine-turning and Human Feedback

There are a few ways to fine-tune the model, which include Prompt Engineering, Fine-tuning and Human Feedback, they are used together to make the LLM performs as desired.

Prompt engineering is to create input prompts to effectively communicate with the model and derive the desired outputs. It will be introduced later in this book.

Fine-turning is a process after the pre-training of a LLM, further train the model on task-specific datasets. It's a supervised learning and allows the model to specialize in tasks relevant to the organization's needs.

As the model is becoming more capable, it's very important to ensure it behaves well and in a way that align with human preferences by the reinforcement learning with human feedbacks.

6. Monitoring and Evaluation

It's important to perform regular evaluation on the model during the fine-turning phase, monitoring and testing the model on various benchmarks and against established metrics to ensure it meets the desired criteria. Chapter 5 will introduce a variety of benchmarks and metrics for evaluating the LLMs.

7. Deployment

After the LLMs are confirmed to work as desired, deploy them into production on the corporate infrastructure where it can be accessed by the user acceptance testing. The deployment of LLMs is a complex and multifaceted process that requires careful consideration of various factors, Chapter 6 discusses the considerations and strategies for deployment.

8. Compliance and Ethics Review

In order not to expose the organization to legal or reputational risks, make sure to conduct periodic reviews and assessments to ensure the LLMs comply with all relevant regulations, industry standards, corporate policies and ethical guidelines, especially with regard to data privacy and security. Chapter 6 also discusses this topic.

9. Build LLM powered applications

After implementing an LLM, the organization might consider building LLM-powered applications to leverage its capabilities to enhance products, services, or internal processes. They may automate tasks related to natural language such as customer service inquiries, or enhance productivity by providing tools for summarization, information retrieval, etc., or improve the user experiences by providing human-like interactions with personalized and conversational AI. Chapter 6 will discuss this together with some practical examples.

10. User Training and Documentation

Provide comprehensive documentation and train end-users on how to interact effectively with the LLMs and the LLM-powered applications.

In conclusion, the lifecycle of LLMs is a multifaceted and iterative process that requires careful planning, execution, and continuous monitoring. By adhering to best practices and prioritizing a wide array of considerations, organizations can harness the power of LLMs while mitigating potential risks and ensuring responsible and trustworthy AI development.

1.3   Whom This Book Is For

This book is a treasure for anyone who is interested in learning about language models, it's written for people with different computer programming levels, whether you're just starting out or already have experiences. No matter you're taking your first steps into this fascinating world, or looking to deepen your understanding of AI and language models, you will be benefit from this book, which is a great resource for everyone on their learning journey.

If you're a beginner, don't worry! This book is designed to guide you from the basics, like Python and PyTorch, all the way to complex topics, like the Transformer models. You will start your journey with the fundamentals of machine learning and deep learning, and gradually explore the more exciting ends of the spectrum.

If you already have some experience, that's great too! Even those with a good understanding of machine learning and deep learning will find a lot to learn here. The book delves into the complexities of the Transformer architecture, making it a good fit for those ready to expand their knowledge.

This book also serves as a companion guide to the mathematical concepts underlying the Large Language Models (LLMs). These background concepts are essential for understanding how models function and their inner workings. As we journey through this book, you'll gain a deeper appreciation of Linear Algebra, Probability, and Statistics, among other key concepts. This book simplifies these concepts and techniques, making them accessible and understandable regardless of your math background.

By humanizing those mathematical expressions and equations used in the Large Language Models, this book will lead you on a path towards mastering the craft of building and using large language models. This makes the book not only a tutorial for Python, PyTorch and LLMs, but also a friendly guide to the intimidating world of mathematical concepts.

So, whether you're a math-savvy or just a beginner, this book will help you within your comfort zone. It's not just about coding models, but understanding them and, in the process, advancing your knowledge about the theory that empowers ML and AI.

1.4 How This Book Is Organized

This book is designed to provide a comprehensive guide to understanding and working with large language models (LLMs). It is structured in a way that gradually builds your knowledge and skills, starting from the fundamental concepts and progressing towards more advanced topics and practical implementations.

Before diving into the intricacies of LLMs, **Chapter 2** establishes a solid foundation in PyTorch, the popular deep learning framework used throughout the book. It also covers the essential mathematical concepts and operations that underpin the implementation of LLMs. This chapter is the foundation upon which everything else in this book will be built.

Chapter 3 delves into the Transformer architecture -- the heart of LLMs. It explores the various components of the Transformer, such as self-attention mechanisms, feed-forward networks, and positional encoding, etc. This chapter is a practical guide to constructing a Transformer from the ground up, with code examples using PyTorch, you will gain hands-on experience and insights into the mechanics of self-attention and positional encoding, among other fundamental concepts.

Pre-training is a crucial step in the development of LLMs, in **Chapter 4** we explore the methodologies to teach LLMs the subtleties of language, and provide you with the theoretical framework and example codes to pre-train a Transformer model. You'll gain hands-on experience by pre-training a Transformer model from scratch using PyTorch.

Once an LLM is pre-trained, the next step is to fine-tune it for specific tasks. **Chapter 5** covers traditional full fine-tuning methods, as well as more recent innovative techniques like Parameter Efficient Fine-tuning (PEFT) and Low-Rank Adaptation (LoRA). By the end of this chapter, you'll expect to have a toolkit of techniques to implement these fine-tuning approaches using PyTorch code examples.

Bringing theory into reality, **Chapter 6** focuses on deploying LLMs effectively and efficiently. You will explore various deployment scenarios, considerations for production environments, and methods to serve your fine-tuned models to end-users. This chapter is about crossing the bridge from experimental to practical, ensuring your LLM can operate robustly in the real world.

As you progress through the chapters of this book, you'll find a balance of theory and application, including code examples, practical exercises, and real-world use cases to reinforce your understanding of LLMs. Whether you're a beginner or an experienced practitioner in the field of natural language processing (NLP), this book aims to provide a comprehensive and practical guide to demystifying large language models (LLMs).

1.5   Source Code and Resources

This book is more than just an informational guide, it's a hands-on manual designed to offer practical experience. To make this learning journey effective and interactive, we've made all the source code in this book available on GitHub:

https://github.com/jchen8000/DemystifyingLLMs.git

This repository contains a dedicated folder for each chapter, allowing you to easily navigate and access the relevant code examples. This includes PyTorch code examples, implementations of the Transformer architecture, pre-training, fine-tuning scripts, simple chatbot, and more.

By cloning or downloading this repository, you can easily replicate, experiment, or build upon the examples and exercises provided in this book. The aim is to provide a comprehensive learning experience that brings you closer to the state-of-the-art in large language models.

Within each chapter's folder, you'll find well-documented and organized files that correspond to the code snippets and examples discussed in the book. These files are designed to be self-contained, ensuring that you can run them independently or integrate them into your own projects.

All source codes provided with this book is designed to run effortlessly in Google Colab, or similar cloud-based Jupyter notebook services. This greatly simplifies the setup process, freeing you from the typical headaches of configuring a local development environment, and allowing you to focus your energy on the heart of the book—the Large Language Models. These code examples are tested and working in Google Colab environment at the time of writing, a free plan with a single GPU is all you need to run the code.

In addition to the source code, this book references a collection of high-quality scholarly articles, white papers, technical blogs, and academic artefacts as its backbone. For ease of reference and to enable further in-depth exploration of specific topics, all these resources are listed in the References section towards the end of the book. These resources serve as extended reading materials for you to deepen your understanding and gain more insights into the exciting world of large language models.

Leverage these resources, explore the references, experiment with the code, and embrace the fantastic journey of unraveling the mysteries of large language models (LLMs)!

2. Pytorch Basics and Math Fundamentals

PyTorch is an open-source machine learning library developed by Facebook's AI Research lab (FAIR), first officially released in October 2016. Originally Torch library was primarily designed for numerical and scientific computing, but it gained popularity in the machine learning community due to its efficient tensor operations and automatic differentiation capabilities, which laid the foundation of PyTorch. It addressed some limitations of the Torch framework and provided more functionalities for machine learning and neural networks. It's now widely used for deep learning and artificial intelligence applications.

In this book PyTorch is used as the primary tool to explore the world of Large Language Models (LLMs). This chapter will introduce some basics of PyTorch, including tensors, operations, optimizers, autograd and neural networks. PyTorch allows users to perform calculations on Graphics Processing Units (GPUs), this support is important for speeding up deep learning training and inference, especially when dealing with large language model where huge datasets and complex models are involved. This chapter will focus on this aspect as well.

The Large Language Models (LLMs) are built on various mathematical fundamentals, including concepts from linear algebra, calculus, and probability theory. Understanding these fundamentals is crucial for developing, training, and fine-tuning large language models, which include complex architectures and sophisticated training procedures. A solid foundation in these mathematical concepts is essential in the field of natural language processing (NLP) and artificial intelligence (AI).

But don't scary, this chapter will introduce the key mathematical concepts from very basic and focus on implementing them using PyTorch.

2.1 Tensor and Vector

In PyTorch, a tensor is a multi-dimensional array, a fundamental data structure for representing and manipulating data. Tensors are similar to NumPy arrays and are the basic building blocks used for constructing neural networks and performing various mathematical operations in PyTorch. Tensors is most often used to represent vectors and matrices.

This section is to introduce some commonly used PyTorch tensor related functions together with their mathematical concepts. These are very basic operations for deep learning and Large Language Model (LLMs) projects, which are used throughout this book.

A vector, in liner algebra, represents an object with both magnitude and direction, it can be represented as an ordered list of numbers, for example:

$$\vec{v} = \begin{bmatrix} 2 & 3 & 4 \end{bmatrix}$$

The magnitude (or length) of the vector is calculated as:

$$\|\vec{v}\| = \sqrt{2^2 + 3^2 + 4^2}$$

In general, a n-dimensional vector has n numbers:

$$\vec{v} = \begin{bmatrix} v_1 & v_2 & \dots & v_n \end{bmatrix}$$

In PyTorch, tensors are commonly used to represent vectors with a one-dimensional array:

```
1    import torch
2    vector = torch.tensor([2., 3., 4.])
3    print("Vector:", vector)
```

Line 1 is to import the library of PyTorch, and Line 2 is to define a one-dimensional array. The result looks like:

```
Vector: tensor([2., 3., 4.])
```

`torch.norm()` function is used to calculate the magnitude (or length) of the vector:

```
4    torch.norm(vector)
```

The result is:

```
tensor(5.3852)
```

The norm, in linear algebra, is a measure of the magnitude or length of a vector, typically it's called Euclidean Norm, and defined as:

$$\|\vec{v}\| = \sqrt{v_1^2 + v_2^2 + \ldots + v_n^2} = \sqrt{\sum_{i=1}^{n} v_i^2}$$

In Python another library, Numpy, provides the similar functionalities, both PyTorch tensors and Numpy arrays are powerful tools for numerical computations. The Numpy arrays are mostly used for scientific and mathematical applications, although also used for machine learning and deep learning; the PyTorch tensors are specifically designed for deep learning tasks with a focus on GPU acceleration and automatic differentiation, we will discuss it later.

Generate a tensor with 6 numbers, which are randomly selected from -100 to 100:

```
1    rand_vec = torch.randint(-100, 100, (6,))
2    rand_vec
```

The result is something like:

```
tensor([ 82, -97,  53, -79, -74, -90])
```

Create an all-zero tensor:

```
1    zeros = torch.zeros(8)
2    zeros
```

The result has 8 zeros in the array:

```
tensor([0., 0., 0., 0., 0., 0., 0., 0.])
```

Create an all-one tensor:

```
1    ones = torch.ones(8)
2    ones
```

The result:

```
tensor([1., 1., 1., 1., 1., 1., 1., 1.])
```

The default data type for tensors is `float32` (32-bit floating-point), when you create a tensor without explicitly specifying a data type, it will be `float32`. In the above example, the number 0 or 1 is followed by a ".", which means it's a float number.

If you want to specify a data type, say int64:

```
1    tensor_int64 = torch.tensor([1, 2, 3],
2                                dtype=torch.int64)
3    tensor_int64
```

The result is an int64 tensor:

```
tensor([1, 2, 3])
```

The table below shows the commonly used data types that PyTorch supports, which allow users to choose the appropriate precision and storage size based on the specific needs.

Data Type	Descriptions
torch.float32, torch.float	32-bit floating-point.
torch.float64, torch.double	64-bit floating-point.
torch.float16, torch.half	16-bit floating-point. Not all operations are supported.
torch.int8	8-bit integer
torch.int16, torch.short	16-bit integer

`torch.int32,` `torch.int`	32-bit integer
`torch.int64,` `torch.long`	64-bit integer
`torch.uint8`	8-bit unsigned integer.
`torch.uint16`	16-bit unsigned integer.
`torch.uint32`	32-bit unsigned integer.
`torch.uint64`	64-bit unsigned integer.
`torch.bool`	Boolean type representing True or False.
`torch.complex64`	64-bit complex number with 32-bit real and imaginary parts.
`torch.complex128`	128-bit complex number with 64-bit real and imaginary parts.

The data type of a tensor can be specified during its creation, or convert an existing tensor to a different data type, for example:

```
4    tensor_float = tensor_int64.to(torch.float32)
5    tensor_float
```

```
tensor([1., 2., 3.])
```

It's important to choose the appropriate data type based on the nature of the data and the requirements of the computations. For example, using lower precision types (e.g., float16) may reduce memory usage but could lead to loss of precision, while higher precision types (e.g., float64) may provide greater precision but require more memory.

Let's look at some other examples of one-dimensional tensors. An empty tensor:

```
1    empty = torch.empty(3)
2    empty
```

will generate a tensor with uninitialized values:

```
tensor([-3.5547e-09,  3.1619e-41, -3.5996e-09])
```

A tensor with a sequence of numbers:

```
1    arange = torch.arange(start=0, end=5, step=1)
2    # arange = torch.arange(5)
3    arange
```

It generates a tensor with values that start at a specified `start` value and increment by a specified `step` size, up to, but not including, a specified `end` value:

```
tensor([0, 1, 2, 3, 4])
```

`torch.linspace()` function generates a tensor with values that are evenly spaced between a start value and an end value, both inclusive, the number of steps or elements in the tensor is specified by the steps parameter:

```
1   linspace = torch.linspace(3, 10, steps=5)
2   linspace
```

```
tensor([ 3.00,   4.75,   6.50,   8.25, 10.00])
```

Similarly, `torch.logspace()` generates a tensor with values that are evenly spaced on a logarithmic scale.

```
1   logspace = torch.logspace(-10, 10, steps=5)
2   logspace
```

```
tensor([1.0e-10, 1.0e-05, 1.0e+00, 1.0e+05, 1.0e+10])
```

A logarithmic scale is a non-linear way of representing numbers, where the distance between two consecutive values is proportional to their ratio, rather than their absolute difference. In other words, instead of increasing or decreasing by a constant amount, the values are multiplied or divided by a constant factor. For example, the distance between 1 and 10 is the same as the distance between 10 and 100, or between 100 and 1000, because they all represent a factor of 10.

In above code example, the results are: 10^{-10}, 10^{-5}, 10^{0}, 10^{5}, 10^{10}.

2.2 Tensor and Matrix

A matrix (or plural matrices) is a two-dimensional array of numbers, symbols, or expressions arranged in rows and columns. The size or dimensions of a matrix are specified by the number of rows and columns it contains, say if a matrix has 3 rows and 4 columns, it is referred to as a 3 × 4, or 3 by 4 matrix. For example:

$$A = \begin{bmatrix} 1 & 2 & 3 & 4 \\ 2 & 3 & 4 & 5 \\ 3 & 4 & 5 & 6 \end{bmatrix}$$

In PyTorch, Tensors are also used to represent matrices. A tensor is a multi-dimensional array, and matrices are simply 2-dimensional tensors in PyTorch. Here's how to represent a matrix in PyTorch:

```
1    A = torch.tensor([[1., 2., 3., 4.],
2                       [2., 3., 4., 5.],
3                       [3., 4., 5., 6.]])
4    A
```

The result is:

```
tensor([[1., 2., 3., 4.],
        [2., 3., 4., 5.],
        [3., 4., 5., 6.]])
```

`torch.zeros()` and `torch.ones()` can be used to create all-zeros or all-ones matrices:

```
1    zeros = torch.zeros(3, 4)
2    print("zeros =", zeros)
3
4    ones = torch.ones(3, 4)
5    print("ones =", ones)
```

The results are:

```
zeros = tensor([[0., 0., 0., 0.],
                [0., 0., 0., 0.],
                [0., 0., 0., 0.]])
ones  = tensor([[1., 1., 1., 1.],
                [1., 1., 1., 1.],
                [1., 1., 1., 1.]])
```

And similar to the case of one-dimensional tensor, `torch.empty()` is used to create a uninitialized matrix and contains arbitrary values and should be initialized later before use:

```
1    empty = torch.empty(2, 3)
2    print("empty =", empty)
```

The result is:

```
empty = tensor([[-3.1e-35, 3.1e-41, -3.4e-35],
                [ 3.2e-41, 8.9e-44,  0.0e+00]])
```

An identity matrix, often denoted as I, is a square matrix with ones on its diagonal (from the top-left to the bottom-right) and zeros elsewhere. The size of the identity matrix is determined by the number of rows (or columns), and it is always a square matrix.

$$I = \begin{bmatrix} 1 & 0 & 0 & 0 \\ 0 & 1 & 0 & 0 \\ 0 & 0 & 1 & 0 \\ 0 & 0 & 0 & 1 \end{bmatrix}$$

torch.eye() is used to create an identity matrix:

```
1    I = torch.eye(4)
2    I
```

```
tensor([[1., 0., 0., 0.],
        [0., 1., 0., 0.],
        [0., 0., 1., 0.],
        [0., 0., 0., 1.]])
```

A lower triangular or an upper triangular matrix is sometimes convenient in deep learning operations, torch.tril() and torch.triu() are used for this purpose. A lower triangular matrix has values in the lower part below the diagonal, and all zeros above diagonal:

```
1    lower_tri = torch.tril(torch.ones(5, 5))
2    lower_tri
```

```
tensor([[1., 0., 0., 0., 0.],
        [1., 1., 0., 0., 0.],
        [1., 1., 1., 0., 0.],
        [1., 1., 1., 1., 0.],
        [1., 1., 1., 1., 1.]])
```

An upper triangular matrix is opposite:

```
3    upper_tri = torch.triu(torch.ones(5, 5))
4    upper_tri
```

```
tensor([[1., 1., 1., 1., 1.],
        [0., 1., 1., 1., 1.],
        [0., 0., 1., 1., 1.],
        [0., 0., 0., 1., 1.],
        [0., 0., 0., 0., 1.]])
```

`torch.empty_like()` creates a new empty tensor with the same shape as the given input tensor, the new tensor is uninitialized with arbitrary values:

```
1    a = torch.tensor([[1., 2., 3., 4.],
2                      [2., 3., 4., 5.],
3                      [3., 4., 5., 6.]])
4    empty_like = torch.empty_like(a)
5    empty_like
```

The input tensor `a` is 3×4 matrix, `empty_like(a)` will create a same size but empty (uninitialized) matrix:

```
tensor([[-2.2e-39, 7.0e-45, -2.5e-38, 3.1e-41],
        [ 0.0e+00, 1.1e-38, -2.5e-38, 3.1e-41],
        [ 2.0e+00, 0.0e+00,  3.0e-05, 2.1e-07]])
```

`torch.cat()` function concatenates several tensors along a specified dimension,

```
1    A=torch.ones(2, 3)
2    B=2*torch.ones(4, 3)
3    C=torch.cat((A,B),dim=0)
4    print("A = ", A)
5    print("B =", B)
6    print("C =", C)
```

The result `c` concatenates `A` and `B` along the dimension of `dim=0` (row direction), in this case the other dimension(s) must be same, meaning same columns in this example,

```
A = tensor([[1., 1., 1.],
            [1., 1., 1.]])
```

```
B = tensor([[2., 2., 2.],
```

```
        [2., 2., 2.],
        [2., 2., 2.],
        [2., 2., 2.]])

C = tensor([[1., 1., 1.],
        [1., 1., 1.],
        [2., 2., 2.],
        [2., 2., 2.],
        [2., 2., 2.],
        [2., 2., 2.]])
```

`torch.stack()` is similar to `torch.cat()` but create a new dimension along the specified direction,

```
1   a = torch.tensor([1, 3, 5, 8])
2   b = torch.tensor([2, 6, 7, 9])
3   c = torch.tensor([5, 6, 3, 2])
4   stacked = torch.stack([a, b, c], dim=0)
5   stacked
```

a, b and c are one-dimensional tensor (or vectors), `torch.stack()` will stack them together along the dimension of `dim=0` (row direction), the result is:

```
tensor([[1, 3, 5, 8],
        [2, 6, 7, 9],
        [5, 6, 3, 2]])
```

This is useful in Natural language processing (NLP), where a, b and c are representing three sentences or sequences, each number represent a word in the sentences, the best practice is to stack multiple sequences in the batch blocks for parallel computational processing.

In most cases, the sentences or sequences have different number of words, as the results a, b and c will have different length, then `torch.stack()` will not work. A technique of padding will be used in this case, it adds extra "0" to the end of short sequences so that they all have the same length.

```
1   from torch.nn.utils.rnn import pad_sequence
2   a = torch.tensor([1, 3, 5, 8])
3   b = torch.tensor([2, 7, 9])
4   c = torch.tensor([5, 2])
5   padded = pad_sequence([a, b, c], batch_first=True)
```

```
6    padded
```

The result makes all sequences the same length, and the shorter ones are padded with "0" at the end of sequences:

```
tensor([[1, 3, 5, 8],
        [2, 7, 9, 0],
        [5, 2, 0, 0]]
```

Then a padding mask is normally needed for processing the padded sequences, `torch.eq()` function can be used to generate padding mask based on the padded matrix:

```
7    padding_mask = padded.eq(0)
8    padding_mask
```

The result has the same size as `padded` matrix, the padded value of "0" is represented as `True`, meaning they are paddings. All other elements are represented as `False`, then we can easily identify which are paddings and which are original numbers.

```
tensor([[False, False, False, False],
        [False, False, False, True],
        [False, False, True,  True]])
```

The transpose of a matrix is a new matrix formed by swapping the rows and columns of the original matrix, say there is a matrix A,

$$A = \begin{bmatrix} 1 & 2 & 3 & 4 \\ 2 & 3 & 4 & 5 \\ 3 & 4 & 5 & 6 \end{bmatrix}$$

The transpose of A is denoted as A^T:

$$A^T = \begin{bmatrix} 1 & 2 & 3 \\ 2 & 3 & 4 \\ 3 & 4 & 5 \\ 4 & 5 & 6 \end{bmatrix}$$

It can be implemented using `torch.transpose()` function:

```
1    A = torch.tensor([[1., 2., 3., 4.],
2                      [2., 3., 4., 5.],
3                      [3., 4., 5., 6.]])
4    A_T = A.transpose(-2, -1)
5    A_T
```

The result is:

```
tensor([[1., 2., 3.],
        [2., 3., 4.],
        [3., 4., 5.],
        [4., 5., 6.]])
```

2.3 Dot Product

Dot product, also called inner product or scalar product, is a fundamental operation in linear algebra, and it is extensively used in machine learning and natural language processing tasks.

The dot product of Vectors:

There are two vectors A and B with the same size:

$$A = \begin{bmatrix} a_1 & a_2 & \dots & a_n \end{bmatrix}$$
$$B = \begin{bmatrix} b_1 & b_2 & \dots & b_n \end{bmatrix}$$

The dot product of A and B is calculated as:

$$A \cdot B = a_1 \cdot b_1 + a_2 \cdot b_2 + \dots + a_n \cdot b_n$$

torch.dot() function is used to calculate the dot product for vectors:

```
1    a = torch.tensor([1, 2, 3])
2    b = torch.tensor([4, 5, 6])
3    dot_product = torch.dot(a, b)
4    dot_product
```

The result is always a numerical value, called a scaler. The two vectors are given in the two 1-dimensional tensors a and b, the dot product is calculated as $1 \times 4 + 2 \times 5 + 3 \times 6 = 32$, the result of above code snippets is:

```
tensor(32)
```

The result is a tensor, use `.item()` to convert to a scaler, or a numerical value:

```
5    print("Dot Product:", dot_product.item())
```

```
Dot Product: 32
```

Please note, both tensors should be in 1-dimensional and the size should be same, otherwise the dot product operation will give an error.

Dot Product of Matrices:

There are two matrices A and B, the number of columns of A is the same as the number of rows of B, then there is a dot product $C = A \cdot B$, otherwise the dot product does not exist.

Say the matrix A has the size of ($m \times n$), and B has the size of ($n \times k$), the result of $C = A \cdot B$ has the size of ($m \times k$). Each item of C is calculated as vector dot product of each column vector of A and each row vector of B.

$$C_{(m \times k)} = A_{(m \times n)} \cdot B_{(n \times k)}$$

$$= \begin{bmatrix} a_{11} & a_{12} & \cdots & a_{1n} \\ a_{21} & a_{22} & \cdots & a_{2n} \\ \cdots & \cdots & \cdots & \cdots \\ a_{m1} & a_{m2} & \cdots & a_{mn} \end{bmatrix} \cdot \begin{bmatrix} b_{11} & b_{12} & \cdots & b_{1k} \\ b_{21} & b_{22} & \cdots & b_{2k} \\ \cdots & \cdots & \cdots & \cdots \\ b_{n1} & b_{n2} & \cdots & b_{nk} \end{bmatrix}$$

$$= \begin{bmatrix} c_{11} & c_{12} & \cdots & c_{1k} \\ c_{21} & c_{22} & \cdots & c_{2k} \\ \cdots & \cdots & \cdots & \cdots \\ c_{m1} & c_{m2} & \cdots & c_{mk} \end{bmatrix}$$

Where:

$$c_{ij} = a_{i1} \cdot b_{1j} + a_{i2} \cdot b_{2j} + \ldots + a_{in} \cdot b_{nj}$$

PyTorch provides optimized implementations for dot product operations for both vectors and matrices. `torch.matmul()` function or @ operator can be used for the calculation of matrices.

```
1    a = torch.tensor([[1, 2],
```

```
2                         [3, 4],
3                         [5, 6]])
4    b = torch.tensor([[7,   8,   9],
5                         [10, 11, 12]])
6    # print( a @ b )
7    print(torch.matmul(a, b))
```

Both a and b are 2-dimensional tensors, representing two matrices, the sizes are 3×2 and 2×3, the result will be a 3×3 matrix:

```
tensor([[ 27,   30,   33],
        [ 61,   68,   75],
        [ 95,  106,  117]])
```

Let's look at how the first element (the top-left one) is calculated, it is the dot product of the first row of a and the first column of b, that is the dot product of [1, 2] and [7, 10]:

$$1 \times 7 + 2 \times 10 = 27$$

Then the middle-left element is calculated as dot product of second row of a and the first column of b, that is [3, 4] and [7, 10]:

$$3 \times 7 + 4 \times 10 = 61$$

And so on.

Dot product is a fundamental operation in the large language models (LLMs), used for various computations like attention mechanisms and so on, which will be introduced in the next chapter.

2.4 Softmax

Softmax is a mathematical function that converts a vector of real numbers, also called logits, into a probability distribution. It transforms the input vector of size n to a same size vector and sum up all its elements to 1.

The input numbers in the vector can be positive, negative or zero, the outputs of the Softmax are between 0 and 1 and sum up to 1. If one of the input numbers is negative or small, the output will be a small probability between 0 and 1; if one of the input numbers is large, it will be turned to a larger probability, still between 0 and 1.

It works like this:

Figure 2.1 Softmax Function

The largest number, 5, is turned to the largest probability, while the smaller numbers are turned to smaller probabilities. All outputs are summed up to 1.0.

The Softmax function is widely used in machine learning, especially in deep neural networks, for multi-class classification problems, where the goal is to assign an input to one of several possible categories. Say the three output values are corresponding to three categories -- Blue, Red and Yellow. The middle one has the highest probability corresponding to the Red category, then this input vector of [2 5 3] will be categorized into Red.

Given an input vector:

$$x = [x_1, x_2, \ldots, x_n]$$

The Softmax is defined as:

$$p_i = \frac{e^{x_i}}{e^{x_1} + e^{x_2} + \ldots + e^{x_n}}$$

$$= \frac{e^{x_i}}{\sum_{j=1}^{n} e^{x_j}}$$

PyTorch has `softmax()` function in `torch.nn.functional` library to calculate it:

```
1    logits = torch.tensor([2.0, 5.0, 3.0])
2    softmax = nn.functional.softmax(logits, dim=0)
```

```
3    print("Logits:", logits)
4    print("Softmax:", softmax)
```

The results are:

```
Logits:  tensor([2., 5., 3.])
Softmax: tensor([0.0420, 0.8438, 0.1142])
```

A smaller input value will get a smaller output probability, if the input is minus infinity, or $-\infty$, the output is zero. This is because:

$$e^{-\infty} = 0$$

And we also have:

$$e^0 = 1$$

Then create a matrix like this,

$$A = \begin{bmatrix} 0 & -\infty & -\infty & -\infty & -\infty \\ 0 & 0 & -\infty & -\infty & -\infty \\ 0 & 0 & 0 & -\infty & -\infty \\ 0 & 0 & 0 & 0 & -\infty \\ 0 & 0 & 0 & 0 & 0 \end{bmatrix}$$

Then apply Softmax on it and see what happen.

```
1    A = torch.zeros(5, 5)
2    mask = torch.tril(torch.ones(5, 5))
3    print("mask=\n", mask)
4    A = A.masked_fill(mask==0, float('-inf'))
5    print("A=\n",A)
```

A is a 5 × 5 all-zero square matrix, mask is a matrix with all-ones at its lower triangular part, and all-zeros above the diagonal, then apply mask to A and fill all zero with minus infinity, or $-\infty$, the result is as below:

```
mask=
 tensor([[1., 0., 0., 0., 0.],
         [1., 1., 0., 0., 0.],
         [1., 1., 1., 0., 0.],
         [1., 1., 1., 1., 0.],
         [1., 1., 1., 1., 1.]])
A=
```

```
tensor([[0., -inf, -inf, -inf, -inf],
        [0.,   0., -inf, -inf, -inf],
        [0.,   0.,   0., -inf, -inf],
        [0.,   0.,   0.,   0., -inf],
        [0.,   0.,   0.,   0.,   0.]])
```

Then apply Softmax:

```
6    nn.functional.softmax(A, dim=1)
```

The result looks like:

```
tensor([[1.0000, 0.0000, 0.0000, 0.0000, 0.0000],
        [0.5000, 0.5000, 0.0000, 0.0000, 0.0000],
        [0.3333, 0.3333, 0.3333, 0.0000, 0.0000],
        [0.2500, 0.2500, 0.2500, 0.2500, 0.0000],
        [0.2000, 0.2000, 0.2000, 0.2000, 0.2000]])
```

dim=1 means the Softmax is applied against columns. The result shows all negative infinity ($-\infty$) elements become zeros in the result. In the first row there is only one element 0, and others are negative infinity, then the 0 becomes 1 in the result; in the second row there are two 0's, Softmax makes them equally divided as 0.5 and 0.5; in the third row, three 0's are equally divided by Softmax as 0.333, 0.333 and 0.333. And the remaining rows are similar, all zero elements are equally divided, and each row is summed up to 1.0.

This technique is often used in Large Language Models (LLMs) when processing the sequences. We will use it later when introducing the masks for the self-attention mechanism.

2.5 Cross Entropy

Cross Entropy is a loss function to measure the difference between two probability distributions. It's widely used in machine learning, especially in classification problems where the goal is to minimize the difference between the predicted probability distribution and the true distribution. It is commonly used to evaluate the performance of a classification model whose output is a probability value between 0 and 1. The Cross Entropy loss increases as the predicted probability diverges from the true label.

The Cross Entropy loss function is often used together with Softmax function to evaluate the models' performances. In last section, Figure 2.1 shows the Softmax function that transforms the vector [2, 5, 3] to the probabilities of [0.042, 0.844, 0.111].

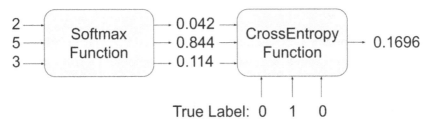

Figure 2.2 Cross Entropy Function

The Cross Entropy function takes the result from Softmax, and compares them with the true label [0, 1, 0], then calculates the difference, or loss, which is 0.1696, as shown in Figure 2.2.

The Cross Entropy between two probability distributions p and q is defined as:

$$H(p, q) = -\sum_{x} p(x) \cdot \log q(x)$$

Where $p(x)$ is the true label of x, and $q(x)$ is the predicted probability.

When talking about the Cross Entropy in the context of Large Language Models, especially in the Transformer model, $p(x)$ is representing the target sentences that we provide to the model and hope the model to generate. While $q(x)$ is representing the actual output from the model. The Cross Entropy is the difference, or loss, between these two, we want to minimize this loss by the training process.

Now let's take at look of how it is implemented in Python.

```
1    import torch
2
3    # Define the Softmax function from scratch
```

```
4    def softmax(logits):
5        exp_logits = torch.exp(logits - torch.max(logits))
6        sum_exp_logits = exp_logits.sum(dim=1, keepdim=True)
7        return exp_logits / sum_exp_logits
8
9    # Define the cross-entropy loss function from scratch
10   def cross_entropy_loss(y_pred, y_true):
11       y_pred_clipped = torch.clamp(y_pred, 1e-9, 1 - 1e-9)
12       return -torch.sum(y_true * torch.log(y_pred_clipped))
```

Line 4 to 7 define the `softmax` function, in last section we used PyTorch provided `nn.functional.softmax()`, now we implement it from scratch.

Line 10 to 12 define the Cross Entropy function, Line 11 makes the data within a min and max range, and Line 12 implements the math expression for Cross Entropy. We implement it from scratch to illustrate the details, while PyTorch provided `nn.CrossEntropyLoss()` function should be used in real projects.

Then prepare some sample data in three classes, and create true label as `[0, 1, 0]`.

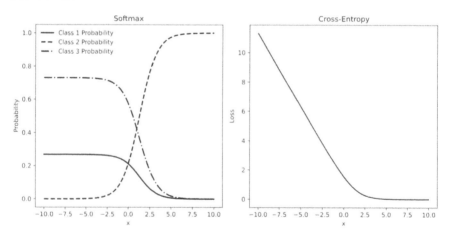

Figure 2.3 Softmax and Cross Entropy

The results are shown in Figure 2.3, the left is the Softmax probabilities of the three classes, and the right is the Cross Entropy loss when compare the probabilities with the true value.

At the very left side when x = -10.0, the Softmax probability of the three classes are [0.269, 0.000, 0.731], the true label is [0, 1, 0], the difference, or loss, between the two is 11.313.

At the middle, when x is around 0, the Softmax is [0.216, 0.196, 0.588], the loss is 1.632, which is much less than the very left point.

At the very right side, when x=10.0, the Softmax is [0.0, 1.0, 0.0], the loss becomes 0.0, because it's the same as the true label.

The Cross Entropy function is used quite often in the book, especially when we build the Transformer model. Please feel free to play with the source code at the Github repository to better understand it.

2.6 GPU Support

PyTorch provide support for GPU (Graphics Processing Unit) which is essential for deep learning and large language model, the computations can be perform on GPUs to speed up the training process. GPUs are designed for parallel processing which allows multiple calculations to be processed simultaneously. Deep learning especially the Large Language Models (LLMs) require massive amounts of data, GPUs can handle them more efficiently than CPUs.

PyTorch supports Nvidia GPUs with CUDA (Compute Unified Device Architecture), which is an API created by Nvidia. Here is how to check whether the GPU (CUDA) is available on a machine:

```
1   if torch.cuda.is_available():
2       !nvidia-smi
3   else:
4       print("GPU is not abailable!")
```

The result should be something like below if GPU is available:

```
+------------------------------------------------------------------+
| NVIDIA-SMI 527.92.01 Driver Version: 528.02 CUDA Version: 12.0   |
|-------------------+----------------------+---------------------+
| GPU Name Persist… | Bus-Id Disp.A        | Volatile Uncorr. ECC |
| Fan Temp Perf …   | Memory-Usage| GPU-U… | GPU-Util Compute M.  |
```

```
|==================+===================+===================|
| 0 Tesla T4    On | 00000000:01:00.0 On | N/A              |
| 34% 45C P8 11W/70W| 223MiB / 15360MiB   | 1% Default      |
...
```

The below code snippets are often used in PyTorch to detect GPU's availability:

```
1    device = 'cuda:0' if torch.cuda.is_available()\
2                     else 'cpu'
3    device
```

If a GPU is available, it shows:

```
cuda:0
```

Now we compare the computation time using GPU vs CPU, create two random tensors of size 10,000 by 10,000, then perform the matrix multiplication operation, and note the time spent:

```
4    tensor1 = torch.randn(10000, 10000).to(device)
5    tensor2 = torch.randn(10000, 10000).to(device)
6
7    start_time = time.time()
8    rand = tensor1 @ tensor2
9    end_time = time.time()
10   print(f"GPU time: {(end_time-start_time):.8f}")
```

`.to(device)` moves the tensors to the specific device, in our case `cuda:0`. However if GPU is not available, `device='cpu'`, then the tensors are sent to CUP. `'@'` operator means matrix multiplication which is equivalent to `torch.matmul()` function. The code captures the start and end time, and shows the time spent for the operation:

```
GPU time: 0.02771497
```

Then do the same thing on CPU:

```
11   tensor3 = torch.randn(10000, 10000).to('cpu')
12   tensor4 = torch.randn(10000, 10000).to('cpu')
13
14   start_time = time.time()
15   rand = tensor3 @ tensor4
16   end_time = time.time()
17   print(f"CPU time: {(end_time-start_time):.8f}")
```

The time spent is:

```
CPU time: 27.39591980
```

0.027s vs 27.39s, GPU is lot faster than CPU, the Large Language Models (LLMs) and complex deep learning models will be benefit from using GPU for the training process. This code is running on Google Colab environment, a Tesla T4 GPU is available for its free plan, it comes with 16GB memory.

2.7 Linear Transformation

A Linear Transformation is a function that maps vectors in one space to another, while preserving the essential linear structure of the input space. In order to explain it, let's start with an extremely simple example:

$$y = Wx + B$$

It's shown as Figure 2.4:

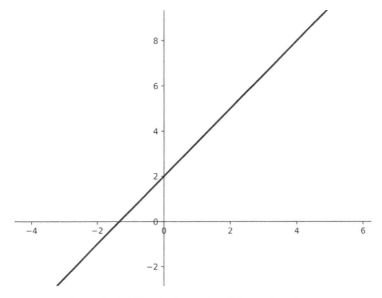

Figure 2.4 A Simple Example of Linear function

W is the weight which is also the slope of the line, and B is called bias which is the value when the line cross y axis. The line will be changing if both W and B are changing. x is the input data and y is the output of the linear function. If the bias is zero, or $B=0$, the line will always pass through the origin point of (0, 0).

Now let's consider both x and y are vectors, say the size of x is 3, and the size of y is 2, then the weight W is a matrix of 2×3, and the bias B is a vector of size 2:

$$W \quad = \quad \begin{bmatrix} w_{11} & w_{12} & w_{13} \\ w_{21} & w_{22} & w_{23} \end{bmatrix}$$

$$B \quad = \quad \begin{bmatrix} b_1 & b_2 \end{bmatrix}$$

Then the linear transformation is defined as:

$$y \quad = \quad x \cdot W^T + B$$

which is:

$$\begin{bmatrix} y_1 & y_2 \end{bmatrix} \quad = \quad \begin{bmatrix} x_1 & x_2 & x_3 \end{bmatrix} \cdot \begin{bmatrix} w_{11} & w_{12} & w_{13} \\ w_{21} & w_{22} & w_{23} \end{bmatrix}^T + \begin{bmatrix} b_1 & b_2 \end{bmatrix}$$

$$= \quad \begin{bmatrix} x_1 & x_2 & x_3 \end{bmatrix} \cdot \begin{bmatrix} w_{11} & w_{21} \\ w_{12} & w_{22} \\ w_{13} & w_{23} \end{bmatrix} + \begin{bmatrix} b_1 & b_2 \end{bmatrix}$$

The above equation can be re-written as:

$$\begin{bmatrix} y_1 & y_2 \end{bmatrix} \quad = \quad \begin{bmatrix} 1 & x_1 & x_2 & x_3 \end{bmatrix} \cdot \begin{bmatrix} b_1 & b_2 \\ w_{11} & w_{21} \\ w_{12} & w_{22} \\ w_{13} & w_{23} \end{bmatrix}$$

A 1 is added to the left of vector x to indicate the bias, then the first row of the weight matrix is the bias. As mentioned earlier, if there is no bias the line will pass through the origin; if the bias is enabled the line will be more flexible and can be moved anywhere in the space.

With a weight matrix, the input vector x is transformed into y, and the bias can be enabled or disabled. This is the Linear Transformation, in this case it will transform x from 3-dimensional space to y in 2-dimensional space.

The linear transformation can be illustrated as Figure 2.5, each arrow is corresponding to an element of W or B. If bias is enabled there is a 1 added to the input.

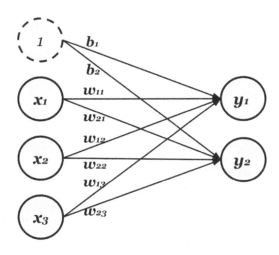

Figure 2.5 Linear Transformation

All elements in W, the weights and biases, are learnable parameters, meaning they will be adjusted during the training process, which iteratively adjusts these parameters based on the difference between the predicted output from x and the actual target values y using an optimization algorithm such as gradient descent.

`torch.nn.Linear()` is the linear transformation function provided by PyTorch, and it's quite simple to use:

```
1    import torch.nn as nn
2    x = torch.tensor([3.0, 2.0, 5.0])
3    linear = nn.Linear(3, 2)
4    y = linear(x)
5    print("Input:", x)
6    print("Output:", y)
```

Line 1 is to import the `torch.nn`, and line 2 to define an input tensor `x`. Line 3 is to define the linear transformation from 3 to 2, meaning the input feature is 3 and output feature is 2. Line 4 is to obtain the output from the function. The results are:

```
Input: tensor([3., 2., 5.])
Output: tensor([-4.9467, -4.3593])
```

We can print out the weight and the bias:

```
7    print(linear.weight)
8    print(linear.bias)
```

```
Parameter containing:
tensor([[-0.5220, -0.0719, -0.5590],
        [-0.4270, -0.4639, -0.4755]],
        requires_grad=True)
Parameter containing:
tensor([-0.4419,  0.2269], requires_grad=True)
```

`requires_grad=True` means this tensor is learnable during the training process, the optimization algorithms like gradient descent will be applied on this tensor in training, and the values are adjusted based on the computations.

The total number of learnable parameters:

```
9    total_parameter = sum(p.numel() \
10                        for p in linear.parameters())
11   print(f"Total Parameters: {total_parameter:,}")
```

The total number of parameters is 8, including the number of weight (6) and bias (2):

```
Total Parameters: 8
```

We can also disable the bias by setting `bias=False` in above Line 3:

```
3    linear = nn.Linear(3, 2, bias=False)
```

In this case the total number of parameters will be 6. As mentioned earlier, the line will always pass through the origin, therefore the flexibility is limited because the linear transformation without bias is only scaling or rotation around the origin.

2.8 Embedding

It's a common practice in natural language processing (NLP) to use embedding to represent words, or tokens. A token is typically a word, a sub-word, a character or special symbol. Each token is represented as an embedding vector, which captures the semantic relationships between words after training process, the words with similar meanings are represented as vectors that are close to each other.

Compared with the traditional one-hot encoding, where each word is represented as a sparse binary vector with mostly zeros, and its size is same as the vocabulary size. When the vocabulary size becomes huge, the one-hot encoding becomes a huge sparse matrix, which is not efficient for computation and difficult capture the semantic relationships between similar words.

Look at an example of how one-hot encoding is working, there are four words: **The sky is blue**, and suppose the whole vocabulary is consist of these four words only, then the one-hot encoding is:

The	sky	is	blue
1	0	0	0
0	1	0	0
0	0	1	0
0	0	0	1

The vector [1 0 0 0] represents the word "The"; [0 1 0 0] represents "sky" and so on. When the size of vocabulary becomes huge, the size of each vector is always same as the vocabulary size, and each vector has almost all zeros. The one-hot encoding is good for categorical classification but is not appropriate for natural language processing (NLP).

Now let's look at how the embedding works, first each word is converted to a token ID which is a numeric index in the vocabulary, as shown below:

Word	Token ID	Embedding Vector (dim=512)

The	15	[-0.3890, -0.3654, 0.4290, ..., -0.4368]
sky	236	[0.5781, 2.0202, 1.5244, ..., 0.4218]
is	21	[0.0907, 0.0958, 1.5828, ..., -0.5666]
blue	1281	[-0.0186, 0.6410, -0.4381, ..., -0.2018]

The vocabulary size can be tens of thousands, the index of 15 is the word "The", the index of 236 is "sky" and so on. Each word is represented by a vector of size 512. The embedding vectors are trainable parameters, the elements are adjusted during training process, and will reflect the similarity between the similar words.

nn.Embedding() in PyTorch will build a lookup table where the key is the token ID, or word index, and the value is the corresponding embedding vector. It takes two parameters, the vocabulary size and the embedding vector size.

```
1   vocab_size = 10000
2   embed_dim = 512
3   embedding = nn.Embedding(vocab_size, embed_dim)
4   sequence = torch.LongTensor([15, 236, 21, 1281])
5   embedded = embedding(sequence)
6   print(embedded.size())
7   print(embedded)
```

In this example, the vocabulary size is 10,000 and embedding vector dimension is 512, line 3 creates the embedding lookup table, line 4 creates a sequence to represent the sentence "**The sky is blue**" with the corresponding token IDs.

Line 5 create the embedded matrix for the sequence, its size is:

```
torch.Size([4, 512])
```

meaning there are 4 vectors each has 512 elements, this is a matrix of 4 by 512. The contents look like:

```
tensor([[-0.3890, -0.3654,  0.4290,  ...,  -0.4368],
        [ 0.5781,  2.0202,  1.5244,  ...,   0.4218],
```

```
        [ 0.0907,   0.0958,   1.5828,   ...,   -0.5666],
        [-0.0186,   0.6410,  -0.4381,   ...,   -0.2018]],
        grad_fn=<EmbeddingBackward0>)
```

Print out the total parameters:

```
8    parameters = sum(p.numel() \
9                      for p in embedding.parameters())
10   print(f"Total Parameters: {parameters:,}")
```

The result:

```
Total Parameters: 5,120,000
```

The total number of parameters of the embedding table is `vocab_size` by `embed_dim`, they are all learnable parameters.

Why Embedding?

The Embeddings are presenting words as vectors, it's possible to group the similar elements together. For example, there are many students in a school, some students like swimming, some like basket ball, some like arts, and some playing chess and so on. If using something like a vector to represent each student, the attributes of swimming, basket ball, etc. are elements of the vector, when the students have higher values in swimming and arts, they can be grouped together, because they are similar in these attributes.

In terms of language processing, the embedding makes it possible to efficiently represent the semantic and contextual information contained in natural language. For example, although the word "*better*" looks similar to "*bitter*", they have totally different meanings; "*better*" is actually similar to "*good*". If represent them in a 3-dimensional space, it looks like Figure 2.6. All the three words are represented in 3-dimensional vectors, "*better*" is similar to "*good*", while "*bitter*" is in totally different direction.

The embedding can capture the semantic meanings of words, the similar words are closer in the embedding space, like "*better*" and "*good*". The embeddings are learnable parameters, at the beginning the vectors are randomly initialized, the similar words are not together, during the training process, the embedded values are adjusted based on the language contexts, the similar words are moved closer and closer gradually.

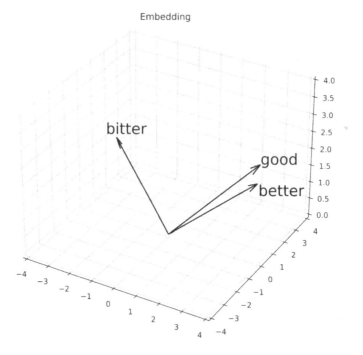

Figure 2.6 Embedding in 3-D Space

Figure 2.6 shows the concept, it's in a 3-dimensional space, in fact the embeddings are in much higher dimensional spaces. In the Transformer mode, which will be introduced in next chapter, the words are embedded in 512 dimensions.

2.9   Neural Network

Neural network is a type of deep learning model composed of inter-connected nodes, called neurons, that work together to process and learn from input data. PyTorch is widely used for building neural networks, it provides the flexible and user-friendly environment for building, training, and deploying neural networks, therefore it becomes a popular choice for many researchers, data scientists and developers in recent years. In this section we will demonstrate how to build a simple neural network with PyTorch.

A neural network, also called artificial neural network (ANN), is one of the deep learning algorithms, which tries to learn things in the same or similar way of human.

In PyTorch, multiple linear transformation layers are stacked together to build a neural network using `torch.nn.Linear()`. An artificial neural network typically includes an input layer, one or multiple hidden layers, and an output layer, as shown in Figure 2.7. There are totally three linear transformation layers in this example, the Input layer to the Hidden Layer1 is a linear transformation layer; the Hidden layer 1 to Hidden layer 2 is another linear layer; the Hidden layer 2 to the Output layer is the third linear layer.

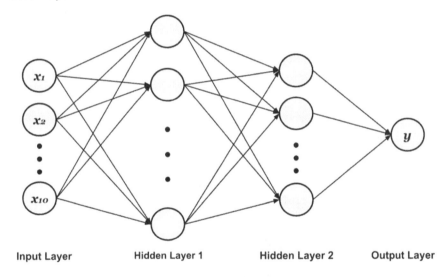

| Input Layer | Hidden Layer 1 | Hidden Layer 2 | Output Layer |

Figure 2.7 Neural Network for Linear Regression

There is an activation function applied to each node in each layer, PyTorch provides variety of activation functions, most commonly used ones are Sigmoid, ReLU (Rectified Linear Unit), Leaky ReLU, Tanh, Softmax and so on. The activation function is selected based on the requirements of the neural network and the nature of the data. In most cases the activation functions are non-linear functions. In this example we choose ReLU as the activation function.

In this section we will build a neural network to perform linear regression on the Diabetes dataset, which comes with scikit-learn (sklearn) package and is commonly used for machine learning regression tasks. This dataset has 10 input variables such as age, sex, BMI, blood pressure and so on, it also has an output variable which is a quantitative measurement of the diabetes progression. The goal of the linear regression is to predict the diabetes progression by providing a new input data like age, sex, BMI, blood pressure, etc. The Diabetes dataset (with 10 input and 1 output variables) is used to train the model by adjusting the weights and bias.

So the Input layer of our neural network has 10 nodes corresponding to the 10 input variables of Diabetes dataset.

The Output layer has one node that correspond to the one output variable of the dataset. Then create two Hidden layers, the first one has 32 nodes and the second one has 16. The architecture of our neural network is shown in Figure 2.7.

First import all required libraries:

```
1    import numpy as np
2    import torch
3    import torch.nn as nn
4    import torch.optim as optim
5    from sklearn import datasets
6    from sklearn.preprocessing import StandardScaler
7    from sklearn.model_selection import train_test_split
8    import matplotlib.pyplot as plt
9    import time
```

Next load the dataset, the Diabetes dataset comes with `sklearn` package,

```
11    device = 'cuda' if torch.cuda.is_available() else 'cpu'
12    # Read data
13    data = datasets.load_diabetes()
14    X, y = data.data, data.target
15    # Standardizing data
16    scaler = StandardScaler()
17    X = scaler.fit_transform(X)
18    # train-test split for model evaluation
19    X_train, X_test, y_train, y_test = \
20            train_test_split(X, y, train_size=0.8, shuffle=True)
```

```
21    # Convert to 2D PyTorch tensors
22    X_train = torch.tensor(X_train, dtype=torch.float32)
23    y_train = torch.tensor(y_train, dtype=torch.float32)
24    X_test = torch.tensor(X_test, dtype=torch.float32)
25    y_test = torch.tensor(y_test, dtype=torch.float32)
26    X_train = X_train.to(device)
27    y_train = y_train.to(device)
28    X_test = X_test.to(device)
29    y_test = y_test.to(device)
30    print(X_train.shape, y_train.shape)
31    print(X_test.shape, y_test.shape)
```

Line 11 detect if GPU is available, if available set `device='cuda'`, otherwise `device='cpu'`, this makes it possible to utilize GPU later.

Line 13 and 14 load the Diabetes dataset, the input variables are loaded in `x`, and the output target variable in `y`. `x` is a matrix of size `(442,10)`, and `y` has the size of `(442,)`. It means this dataset has totally 442 items, each has 10 elements (or 10 input variables) in `x`, and one element (or output variable) in `y`.

Line 16 and 17 scales the data, this is a common and important pre-processing step for any machine/deep learning projects. In most of cases the data in the input variables are in different ranges, say the blood pressure could be from 60 to 160, while the white blood cells count could be in thousands, and some other measurements could be in percentage, and so on. This difference could cause imbalance and inaccurate when performing the mathematical calculations, and sometimes could cause data type overflow in the calculation.

It's always a best practice to scale the data in the pre-processing step. In this example we use `StandardScaler`, which transforms the input variables into a dataset with a mean of 0 and a standard deviation of 1, i.e. it performs the calculation as defined below:

$$X_{scaled} = \frac{X_{raw} - \mu}{\sigma}$$

Where X_{raw} is the original raw data, X_{scaled} is the scaled data. μ is the mean of the raw data, and σ is the standard deviation or the raw data.

After the Standard Scaling, all data elements in x are between 0 and 1, and follow the distribution with mean of 0 and standard deviation of 1. The data looks something like:

```
array([ 0.038,   0.050,   0.061, 0.021, -0.044,
       -0.034, -0.043, -0.002, 0.019, -0.017])
```

You will not be able to easily identify which is blood pressure, which is white blood cells count and so on from the scaled data. All data elements are in the same range, this helps the algorithms perform well.

In this example since we load the dataset from sklearn, most datasets are well processed in the library, and might already be scaled and ready for use. So Line 16 and 17 are optional in this case, but this shows the best practices of data scaling.

Line 19 and 20 are to split the data into train set and test set, train set is used to train the model, test set is used to evaluate the model. Here use 80% of the data for train set and remaining for test set.

Line 22 to 25 convert the data sets to PyTorch tensors, because we will use the tensors for processing.

Line 26 to 29 move the tensors to the GPU device, if available, or CPU device. The to(device) will move a tensor to the specified device: 'cuda' for GPU, 'cpu' for CPU.

Line 30 and 31 show the size of train and test sets:

```
torch.Size([353, 10]) torch.Size([353, 1])
torch.Size([89, 10])   torch.Size([89, 1])
```

The train set has 353 data items, and test set has 89 data items.

Next, build the neural network by extending the nn.Module class, which is the base class for all neural network modules in PyTorch. It's a common practice to create a customized neural network in this way:

```
32    class LinearRegression(nn.Module):
33      def __init__(self, input_dim: int, output_dim: int)
34        super(LinearRegression, self).__init__()
35        self.fc1 = nn.Linear(input_dim, 32)
36        self.fc2 = nn.Linear(32, 16)
37        self.fc3 = nn.Linear(16, output_dim)
```

```
38          self.relu = nn.ReLU()
39      def forward(self, x):
40          x = self.relu(self.fc1(x))
41          x = self.relu(self.fc2(x))
42          x = self.fc3(x)
43          return x
```

Line 34, `super().__init__()` should be always called in the `__init__()` function of the customized class. This is to ensure the base class `nn.Module` is properly initialized.

Line 35 to 37 define the linear layers based on our neural network architecture shown in Figure 2.7.

Line 38 defines the activation function for the neural network, `nn.ReLU()` is used in this example.

The beauty of PyTorch is that we only need to define the forward process of our customized neural network, and don't need to care about things like gradient descent, or backpropagation etc., those are happened behind the scenes and PyTorch take care of them.

Therefore, Line 40 to 42 define how the layers are linked together in our neural network. `x=self.relu(self.fc1(x))` means apply ReLU function on the first linear transformation layer, which is the Input Layer to Hidden Layer 1. And then do the same thing on the second linear transformation layer.

Line 42 deals with the output, in this example it doesn't matter to apply the activation function on the output.

It's this simple to build a neural network. Then initialize the customized neural network class, and show its structure and how many learnable parameters,

```
44      model=LinearRegression(X_train.shape[1], y_train.shape[1])
45      model.to(device)
46      total_parameter=sum(p.numel()for p in model.parameters())
47      print(f"Total Parameters: {total_parameter:,}")
48      print(model)
```

Line 44 is to instantiate our `LinearRegression` class with the input size and output size, which are derived from the train dataset, as mentioned earlier input x size is 10, output y size is 1. The total learnable parameter is:

```
Total Parameters: 897
```

Line 48 prints out the structure of the neural network:

```
LinearRegression(
    (fc1): Linear(in_features=10, out_features=32, bias=True)
    (fc2): Linear(in_features=32, out_features=16, bias=True)
    (fc3): Linear(in_features=16, out_features=1, bias=True)
    (relu): ReLU()
)
```

In order to train the neural network, we need to define a Loss Function and an Optimizer.

A Loss Function, also called Cost Function, evaluates how well the model's predictions against the true value (or target value) in the output variables, it uses mathematical functions to quantifies the differences. The goal of training process is to minimize the loss, or cost, calculated by the Loss Function. There are a number of pre-defined Loss Functions, they are selected based on the type of model and the nature of the data. In this example we are dealing with regression problems, because the output of our model is the measurement of the diabetes progression which is a quantitative value. We choose the Mean Squared Error (MSE) as loss function,

$$MSE = \frac{1}{n} \sum_{i=1}^{n} (y^{(i)} - y_{pred}^{(i)})$$

Where $y^{(i)}$ is the value of the output variable in dataset, $y_{pred}^{(i)}$ is the predict value that calculated from input variables.

The Loss Function is simply defined as:

```
49    loss_fn = nn.MSELoss()
```

An Optimizer is also a required component for neural network, it is responsible for adjusting the learnable parameters in order to minimize the Loss, or Cost. A technique called Gradient descent is commonly used to achieve this. Please see the reference materials at the bottom of this book for more details of Gradient descent.

The Optimizer is simply defined as:

```
50    learning_rate = 1e-3
51    optimizer = optim.Adam(model.parameters(), lr=learning_rate)
```

The Optimizer requires a learning rate to be specified, this is needed for Gradient descent algorithm, it's a small value like `1e-3` in Line 50, which is 10^{-3}, or 0.003. Line 51 chooses `Adam` optimizer, which is pre-defined in PyTorch.

Now we have everything ready, start to train the model.

```
52    epochs = 500
53    batch_size = 64
54    for epoch in range(epochs):
55        model.train()
56        for i in range(0, len(X_train), batch_size):
57            # take a batch
58            X_batch = X_train[i:i+batch_size]
59            y_batch = y_train[i:i+batch_size]
60            # forward propagation
61            y_pred = model(X_batch)
62            loss = loss_fn(y_pred, y_batch)
63            # back propagation
64            optimizer.zero_grad()
65            loss.backward()
66            # update weights
67            optimizer.step()
68        # evaluate accuracy at end of each epoch
69        model.eval()
70        y_pred = model(X_test)
71        mse = loss_fn(y_pred, y_test)
72        mse = float(mse)
73        if epoch % 10 == 0:
74            print(f"Epoch {epoch}: Loss {mse:.8f}")
```

Line 52 and 53 specify `epochs` (iterations for training), and `batch_size`. The data will be loaded in batch, instead of one by one, for better performance in the calculation, especially efficient for GPU. So a `batch_size` is defined here, typically it is specified in the power of 2, like 16, 32, 64, 128, 256 and so on.

The main training loop is starting from Line 54, and the training mode is starting from Line 55, and evaluation mode starting from line 69.

Line 58 and 59 load the x and y data in batch, Line 61 makes a prediction using the model, Line 62 calculate the loss using the Loss Function. Line 64 and 65 do the backpropagation using the Optimizer, and Line 67 update all the learnable parameters.

The loop starting from Line 56 loads and trains the data in batch until all data is processed for an epoch, or an iteration. After one epoch is trained, Line 69 specifies the model to enter evaluation mode, in this mode the model will not do the calculations for backpropagation, not use the Optimizer and not update any parameters. It only makes predictions with test dataset, calculates the Loss and displays the results after the epoch.

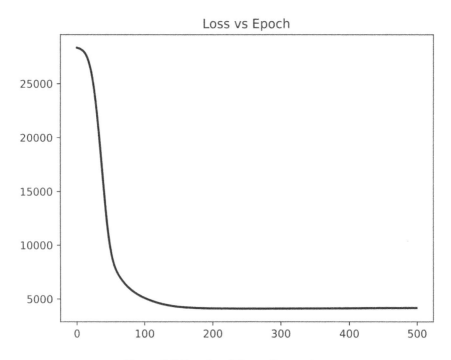

Figure 2.8 Results of Linear Regression

The results are displayed every 10 epochs in Line 73 and 74:

```
Epoch 0:   Loss 31644.39843750
Epoch 10:  Loss 31162.13476562
Epoch 20:  Loss 29006.20703125
Epoch 30:  Loss 23300.71875000
Epoch 40:  Loss 14822.46093750
...
```

After the training of 500 epochs, we can plot the history of the Loss vs Epoch as Figure 2.8.

This is a typical curve of training results of a neural network, at the beginning of the training, the Loss is very high nearly 30,000 in this example, it gradually gets down when the training proceeds, and finally it converges to a value, nearly 3,000 in this example.

We can print out the final Mean Squared Error (MSE) loss:

```
MSE: 2909.77
```

In the real-world neural network projects, the number of hidden layers and the number of nodes can be adjusted as the fine-tune process. Try to change these numbers and run the whole training and evaluation to find out a good balance of a simplified neural network and a better result.

With the model is trained property, it can be used to make predictions on new data, say there are a number of new patients with the 10 input data like blood pressure, BMI, age, etc., the data can be passed to the model to predict their progression of diabetes:

```
y_pred = model(X_new)
```

The source code is available at the Github repository.

Neural networks are a powerful technique inspired by biological neural systems, capable of learning complex, non-linear patterns through the composition of linear transformations and nonlinear activations.

2.10 Bigram and N-gram Models

A Bigram model is one of the statistical models that used in natural language processing (NLP), it's a simple model and has some limitations, thus it's superseded by the Large Language Models (LLMs). However, it's worthwhile to explain it as the basic concepts of language models. This section will implement a simple bigram model with Python.

The idea of Bigram is that when generating a sentence, a word is generated based on the previous word:

```
This -> movie
movie -> was
was -> very
very -> good
```

"movie" is generated based on "This", then "was" is generated based on "movie", and so on.

Bigram is based on the assumption that the current word is based only on the preceding word, not the earlier words.

N-gram model is based on the previous N-1 words. If N=2 then Bigram model; if N=3 then three-gram model which is based on previous 2 words; if N=4 then four-gram model, which is based on previous 3 words, and so on.

Then how the Bigram model works,

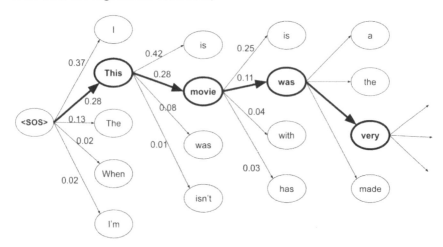

Figure 2.9 Bigram Model

As shown in above Figure 2.9, "<SOS>" (Start of Sequence) at the very left is the start token, the sentence will be generated from it. There is a number of words following the start token, each has a probability value, then the Bigram model picks up one based on the probability, in this example "This" is selected. And there is also a number of words after "This", each with a probability, again it picks up one, say "movie", and so on. The Bigram model is able to generate a sentence, one word followed by another.

In this section we use IMDB dataset to create a probability distribution for every word, then implement Bigram algorithm to generate sample sentences. The IMDB dataset contains 25,000 movie reviews, we use the words from there as our data source.

To load the IMDB dataset:

```
1   !pip install 'portalocker>=2.0.0'
2   import re
3   from torchtext.datasets import IMDB
4   train_iter = IMDB(split='train')
```

It's quite simple to load IMDB from `torchtext` package.

```
5    def tokenize(label, line):
6        line = re.sub('\s{2,}', ' ', line)
7        line = line.replace('"', '')
8        line = re.sub('\<[^)]*\>', '', line)
9        line = '<SOS> ' + line.replace('.', ' .')
10       return line.split()
11
12   words = []
13   for label, line in train_iter:
14       words += tokenize(label, line)
```

Then do some pre-processing on the data, like remove some special characters, add the start token "<sos>" before every line of text, etc. All texts in IMDB dataset are split into words and put in `words[]`, it contains about 4.6 million words.

Then create a dictionary to record what words are following a given word,

```
15   bgrams = {}
16   for i in range(len(words)-2):
17     w1 = words[i]      # the given word
```

```
18      w2 = words[i+1]    # the word after it
19      if not w1 in bgrams:
20         bgrams[w1] = {}
21      if not w2 in bgrams[w1]:
22         bgrams[w1][w2] = 1
23      else:
24         bgrams[w1][w2] += 1
```

By running the above Line 15 to 24, we have a dictionary which looks something like:

```
The words following 'This':
{'is': 3346,
 'movie': 2217,
 'film': 1165,
 'was': 612,
 'one': 197,
 ... }
```

It means the next words of "This" have 3346 "is", 2217 "movie", 1165 "film" and so on.

And calculate the probabilities of the following words:

```
25    for w in bgrams:
26       bgrams[w] = dict(sorted(bgrams[w].items(),
27                           key=lambda item: -item[1]))
28       total = sum(bgrams[w].values())
29       bgrams[w] = dict([(k, bgrams[w][k]/total) \
30                           for k in bgrams[w]])
```

After running above Line 25 to 30, we get the probabilities of each word,

```
The words following 'This':
{'is': 0.41851156973108194,
 'movie': 0.2772983114446529,
 'film': 0.14571607254534083,
 'was': 0.07654784240150093,
 'one': 0.024640400250156347,
 ... }
```

This time it means "is" has 0.418 probability to follow the word "This", and "movie" has 0.277, "film" has 0.145 and so on.

So far, we have the probability distribution of all words that follow a given word. Now we can generate sentences using Bigram algorithm:

```
31   import random
32   random.seed(8888)
33
34   def next_word(word):
35     vars = bgrams[word]
36     return random.choices(list(vars.keys()),
37             weights=vars.values())[0]
38
39   def sentence(max_word=50):
40     words = []
41     w = '<SOS>'
42     for i in range(max_word):
43       w = next_word(w)
44       if w == '.':
45         break
46       words.append(w)
47     return (' '.join(words) + '. ')
```

The function `next_word()` in Line 34 will use the probability distribution of a given word to generate its next word by random choice. `vars.keys()` in Line 36 has the list of all next words, `vars.values()` have the corresponding probability values. Line 36 and 37 randomly select one word from the lists based on the probabilities.

The function `sentence()` in Line 39 will generate a sentence from the start token <SOS> until '.' mark, or until `max_word`, by calling `next_word()` repeatedly.

Here are some generated sentences:

```
This is the movie was in their lines.
I have to a good as a movie is a movie.
This movie was very good.
This is a lot about it would love this movie, and I had a
few things and the film that the first time.
I would like a little bit of a good job is a film for the
other films of the film.
This isn't a film is a great in the best.
I have a movie.
This is a very well.
I was a lot of this film is a great deal.
```

```
As a good film.
```

Apparently, most generated sentences do not make any senses, but we are able to generate something using the Bigram model.

To recap, the Bigram model takes a word and generate the next word, the N-gram model takes N-1 word as a group and generate the next word. The latter is more complex and might require more data to build.

The source code in this section is available at the Github repository for this book.

2.11 Greedy, Random Sampling and Beam

Greedy search, Random sampling and Beam search are different algorithms used in generating the next word in the large language models.

Greedy is simple, it picks the word with the highest probability without considering anything else. For example, in Figure 2.9 in the previous section, the next words after "This" are:

Next word	Probability
is	0.42
movie	0.28
was	0.08
isn't	0.01

The Greedy simply picks the first one "is" as the next word, because it has the highest probability.

Random Sampling, on the other hand, randomly chooses a word from the probability distribution, it's not necessarily to pick the most likely one. It considers all words in the list and takes their probabilities as weights, randomly selects a word as the next.

In the example of the previous section of Bigram, we used the Random Sampling to select the next word:

```
random.choices(words, weights=probs)
```

Where `words` is the list of next words, and `probs` is the corresponding probabilities.

So, in this case it could select "`movie`" as the next word.

Top-K Random Sampling is to limit the selection in the top k items with most probabilities, say $k = 3$, it will choose from the top 3 items in the above table.

Top-P Random Sampling is to limit the selection to those words that the sum of their probability is less than or equal to a given probability. Say $p = 0.7$, the selection will be limited to the first two words, because the first one "`is`" has 0.42 probability, and the second "`movie`" has 0.28, the sum of the probabilities is 0.42+0.28=0.7.

The Greedy and Random Sampling are simple because they only consider the words in one step, without other relationships. Beam is more complicated, it keeps track of the entire search tree with multiple paths, the number of paths is specified as beam width.

For example, Figure 2.10 illustrates the idea, the search begins from the start token "<sos>" and end with the token "<EOS>", the beam width is set to 2.

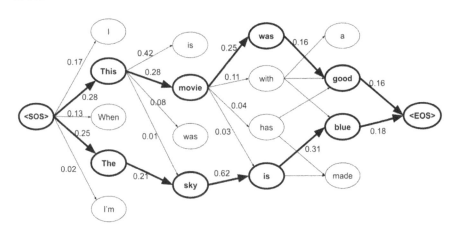

Figure 2.10 Beam Search

The Beam search algorithm keeps track of two paths, from the "<sos>" token, it takes two words with the top probabilities, "`This`" and "`The`".

And from there it keeps searching the next words with the top probabilities until the end token "<EOS>" is found, then it calculates the combined probability of each path, as shown in the below table. It turns out that the first path has a higher combined probability, then it's selected as the final result of the Beam search.

Path 1		Path 2	
<SOS>		<SOS>	
The	0.25	This	0.28
sky	0.21	movie	0.28
is	0.62	was	0.25
blue	0.31	good	0.16
<EOS>	0.18	<EOS>	0.16
Combined probability	0.0018163		0.0005018

Beam search is able to find a potential higher probability down the road, for example 0.62 in Path 1 in above table, the Greedy and Random Sampling might not find it because they only consider the next step rather than the entire path. Therefore, the Beam is an enhanced algorithm and widely used in language generation problems.

However, the Beam is complicated and could be computational expensive depends on the selection of beam width. If the beam width is set to 1, it becomes Greedy search.

Greedy:

Below is the Python implementation of Greedy search:

```
1    def greedy_search(probabilities):
2        return torch.argmax(probabilities, dim=-1)
3
4    vocab = ["h", "e", "l", "o"]  # vocabulary
5    probabilities = torch.tensor([
6        [0.4, 0.3, 0.1, 0.2],
7        [0.1, 0.7, 0.2, 0.0],
8        [0.1, 0.2, 0.5, 0.2],
9        [0.1, 0.1, 0.6, 0.2],
10       [0.2, 0.1, 0.1, 0.6] ])
```

```
11
12    output = greedy_search(probabilities)
13    generated_word = "".join([vocab[i] for i in output])
14    print(generated_word)
```

Line 1 and 2 define the `greedy_search()` function. Line 2 returns the indices of maximum probability values from the input tensor.

Line 4 specifies a vocabulary.

Line 5 to 10 define a tensor of probabilities, there are 5 rows each corresponding to an output character, and there are 4 columns, each corresponding to the index of vocabulary, e.g. the first column corresponds to "h" in vocabulary, the second for "e", and so on.

Look at the first row in Line 6, the first column has the largest probability, thus it will be selected by Greedy search, and the first character in output will be "h".

Then the second row in Line 7, the second column has the largest probability, it will be selected, then the second output will be "e". And so on.

Line 12 calls `greedy_search()` function with the probabilities tensor, and obtains the output, which looks like:

```
tensor([0, 1, 2, 2, 3])
```

Each number in the output corresponds to the index in vocabulary.

Line 13 converts the output tensor to the characters in vocabulary and join them together.

Line 14 print out the result:

```
hello
```

Random Sampling:

Below codes implement the Random Sampling:

```
1    import torch.nn.functional as F
2
3    def random_sampling(logits, top_k):
4        top_k_probs, _ = torch.topk(logits, top_k, dim=-1)
5        kth_highest_prob = top_k_probs[:, -1].unsqueeze(-1)
6        mask = logits < kth_highest_prob
7        probs = logits.masked_fill(mask, float('-inf'))
8        probabilities = F.softmax(probs, dim=-1)
9        output = torch.multinomial(probabilities, 1).squeeze(-1)
10       return output
11
12   vocab = ["h", "e", "l", "o"]  # Vocabulary
13   logits = torch.tensor([
14       [3.0, 1.0, 0.5, 0.1],
15       [0.6, 3.5, 2.5, 0.2],
16       [1.0, 0.2, 3.5, 1.5],
17       [0.3, 2.5, 4.1, 0.4],
18       [0.3, 1.0, 0.1, 4.4]
19   ])
20
21   output = random_sampling(logits, top_k=2)
22   generated_word = "".join([vocab[i] for i in output])
23   print(generated_word)
```

Line 1 import the library used in the codes. Line 3 to 10 define the random_sampling() function. The input parameters are a logits tensor and the top_k value which specifies how many top probabilities to choose from.

Line 13 to 19 specifies the input logits, which are similar to the codes for Greedy search. 5 rows for the 5 output characters, and 4 columns corresponds to indices of the vocabulary. This is the input to the random_sampling() function

Line 4 retrieves the largest top_k values of each row from the input tensor, it looks like:

```
tensor([[3.0000, 1.0000],
        [3.5000, 2.5000],
        [3.5000, 1.5000],
        [4.1000, 2.5000],
        [4.4000, 1.0000]])
```

For example, the first row has two values: 3.0 and 1.0, that is the top two values in Line 14, and the second row is the top two values in Line 15, and so on.

Line 5 finds out the last one in the top_k values, this will be a threshold to create masks.

Line 6 creates a mask based on the above threshold, the mask looks like:

```
tensor([[False, False,  True,  True],
        [ True, False, False,  True],
        [ True,  True, False, False],
        [ True, False, False,  True],
        [ True, False,  True, False]])
```

In the input logits, all values lower than the above threshold have a mask of `True`, otherwise `False`.

Line 7 fill the mask with a negative infinity −∞, which as mentioned earlier will be converted to zero by Softmax. Now it becomes:

```
tensor([[3.0000, 1.0000,   -inf,   -inf],
        [  -inf, 3.5000, 2.5000,   -inf],
        [  -inf,   -inf, 3.5000, 1.5000],
        [  -inf, 2.5000, 4.1000,   -inf],
        [  -inf, 1.0000,   -inf, 4.4000]])
```

Only the top 2 values remain in the tensor, all others become negative infinity −∞. Compare this result with the original `logits` in Line 13 to 19.

Line 8 applies Softmax on the result, then it looks like:

```
tensor([[0.8808, 0.1192, 0.0000, 0.0000],
        [0.0000, 0.7311, 0.2689, 0.0000],
        [0.0000, 0.0000, 0.8808, 0.1192],
        [0.0000, 0.1680, 0.8320, 0.0000],
        [0.0000, 0.0323, 0.0000, 0.9677]])
```

The Softmax normalizes the probabilities, meaning all values are between 0 and 1, and all values sum up to 1. And all the negative infinity −∞ become zero. Again, compare this result with the original `logits` in Line 13 to 19, only the top 2 values remain, all others become zero.

Line 9 calls `torch.multinomial()` function to randomly select one from the above result, and return the output, as below:

```
tensor([0, 1, 3, 2, 3])
```

The first value in the output is 0, which is randomly selected from the first row among 0.8808 and 0.1192, the others are ignored because they are zeros.

Similarly, the second value is 1, it's selected from the second row among 0.7311 and 0.2689.

The rest of the codes are similar to what we did for Greedy. Finally, the result is:

```
heolo
```

Every time run the code, it might generate different results, because the search method randomly picks up the available options. So, Random Sampling generates diversified outputs.

Beam:

As explained earlier, Beam is more complicated than Greedy and Random Sampling. It keeps track of the whole output sequences for k paths, and select the highest combined probabilities. In this section we do not implement it, instead demonstrate how it is used in practice.

When we use some advanced libraries, like pre-trained GPT2 model, the beam search is built-in as part of generation capabilities. The below code snippets show how it is applied:

```
1    from transformers import GPT2LMHeadModel, GPT2Tokenizer
2
3    # Load pre-trained model and tokenizer
4    model = GPT2LMHeadModel.from_pretrained('gpt2')
5    tokenizer = GPT2Tokenizer.from_pretrained('gpt2')
6    input_text = "The quick brown fox"
7    input_ids = tokenizer.encode(input_text,
8                                 return_tensors='pt')
9    attention_mask = torch.ones(input_ids.shape,
10                               dtype=torch.long)
11   # Generate sequences
```

```
12    outputs = model.generate(
13      input_ids,
14      max_length=50,
15      num_beams=5,
16      early_stopping=True,
17      attention_mask=attention_mask,
18      pad_token_id=tokenizer.eos_token_id
19    )
20    # Decode generated sequences
21    print(tokenizer.decode(outputs[0],
22                       skip_special_tokens=True))
```

Line 1 import the pre-trained GPT2 model and its tokenizer. Line 4 and 5 create the model and tokenizer from the GPT2 model.

Line 6 creates an input text, and Line 7 and 8 create input IDs from the tokenizer.

Line 9 and 10 create attention mask. Don't pay too much attention at these concepts at this moment, we will explain details in the following chapter.

Line 12 to 19 call the model to generate outputs, where Line 15 specifies the number of beams, therefore the generation will use the Beam search.

And finally, Line 21 and 22 print out the generated outputs.

In conclusion, Greedy search, Random sampling, and Beam search are all important techniques used in natural language processing (NLP) tasks like text generation, language modeling, and machine translation. Each of them has its own strengths and weaknesses, and the choice of which to use will depend on the specific task and constraints of the NLP application.

2.12 Rank of Matrices

The rank of a matrix is a concept in linear algebra that describes the dimension or the number of linearly independent rows or columns in the matrix. It's a measure that indicates the dimensions of the vector space spanned by its rows or columns, it also describes the *Linear Dependence* between its rows or columns. It's defined as the maximum number of linearly independent row vectors in the matrix, which is the same as the maximum number of linearly independent column vectors. It tells us how many dimensions of space the matrix can map vectors into without losing information.

The number of linearly independent rows is equal to the number of linearly independent columns. Either of these numbers can be used to define the rank of the matrix.

If a row in matrix is made of other rows by multiplying a scaler, then that row is dependent on other rows and not count towards the rank. If a row or column can count to the rank, it's called *linearly independent* row or column of the matrix, the rank of the matrix is the maximal number of *linearly independent* rows or columns.

Here are some key properties of the rank of a matrix:

- The rank is always a non-negative integer less than or equal to the minimum of the number of rows and columns in the matrix.
- The rank is invariant under row or column operations, such as row or column addition, scaling, or swapping.
- The rank of a matrix is equal to the number of linearly independent columns, or rows, in the matrix.
- The rank of is equal to the number of non-zero singular values of the matrix (will be introduced in the next section)

For example:

$$A = \begin{bmatrix} 3 & -1 & 2 \\ 6 & -2 & 4 \end{bmatrix}$$

The numbers in second row are made of the first row by multiplying 2. So the rank of this matrix is 1 not 2, and the number of linearly independent rows is 1.

Look at the columns of matrix A, the second column is made of first column by multiplying -1/3, and the third column is also made of first column by multiplying 2/3, so the rank is also 1 from column perspective, and the number of linearly independent columns is also 1.

Another example, look at an identity matrix I,

$$I = \begin{bmatrix} 1 & 0 & 0 & 0 \\ 0 & 1 & 0 & 0 \\ 0 & 0 & 1 & 0 \\ 0 & 0 & 0 & 1 \end{bmatrix}$$

The rank is 4, because all rows and columns are independent, and not relying on others. In another word, all rows or columns are *linearly independent.* The rank of an identity matrix is always its size, which is 4.

A matrix has full rank if its rank is equal to the smaller dimension of the matrix, i.e. the number of rows or columns whichever is less. If a matrix does not have full rank, it is called rank-deficient, which indicates that there is some redundancy in the matrix's rows or columns, as above matrix A.

The rank will be always equal or smaller than the smallest dimension of a matrix, it can not be larger than that. For example, the rank will not be larger than 3 for a 3×5 matrix. If it's 3 then it's full rank.

Why to find the rank? Normally a matrix represents the relationships between variables, the number of columns means the number of variables. The rank of the matrix tells whether there is a unique solution to solve all the variables, if the rank equals the number of variables, then there is a unique solution. If the rank is less than the number of variables, the system has either no solution or an infinite number of solutions.

The function `linalg.matrix_rank()` is used to calculate rank of a matrix.

```
1   A = torch.tensor([[3., -1., 2.],
2                     [6., -2., 4.]],
3                     dtype=torch.float32)
4   rank = torch.linalg.matrix_rank(A)
5   print('A=', A)
6   print(f"The rank of A is: {rank}")
```

The result:

```
A = tensor([[ 3., -1.,  2.],
            [ 6., -2.,  4.]])
The rank of A is: 1
```

Another example:

```
7    I = torch.eye(4)
8    rank = torch.linalg.matrix_rank(I)
9    print('I=', I)
10   print(f"The rank of I is: {rank}")
```

Line 7 creates an identity matrix, and Line 8 obtains its rank:

```
I = tensor([[1., 0., 0., 0.],
            [0., 1., 0., 0.],
            [0., 0., 1., 0.],
            [0., 0., 0., 1.]])
The rank of I is: 4
```

The rank of a matrix is a fundamental concept in linear algebra that has important applications in a wide range of fields, including machine learning, optimization, and signal processing. It will be used later in this book when we discuss about the fine-tuning of the Large Language Models.

2.13 Singular Value Decomposition (SVD)

Singular Value Decomposition (SVD) is a factorization method in linear algebra, this concept will be used later in this book for fine-tuning of Large Language Models (LLMs). We give the conclusion here without mathematical proofs.

Given a $m{\times}n$ matrix A, it can be factorized as three matrices, which is denoted as:

$$A = U \Sigma V^T$$

Where:

- A is $m{\times}n$ matrix.
- U is $m{\times}m$ orthogonal matrix, meaning $U^TU = UU^T = I_{m{\times}m}$, it's called the left-singular vectors of A.
- Σ is $m{\times}n$ diagonal matrix with non-negative real numbers on the diagonal. The values in its diagonal are called Singular values of A,

and they are normally in descending order. All other elements outside of the diagonal are zero.

- V is $n \times n$ orthogonal matrix, meaning $V^T V = VV^T = I_{n \times n}$, it's called the right-singular vectors of A.

It's illustrated as below:

$$
A_{(m \times n)} \qquad\qquad U_{(m \times m)} \qquad\qquad \Sigma_{(m \times n)} \qquad\qquad V^T_{(n \times n)}
$$

$$
\begin{bmatrix} a_{11} & a_{12} & \cdots & a_{1n} \\ a_{21} & a_{22} & \cdots & a_{2n} \\ \cdots & \cdots & \cdots & \cdots \\ a_{m1} & a_{m2} & \cdots & a_{mn} \end{bmatrix} = \begin{bmatrix} u_{11} & \cdots & u_{1m} \\ \cdots & \cdots & \cdots \\ u_{m1} & \cdots & u_{mm} \end{bmatrix} \begin{bmatrix} \sigma_1 & 0 & 0 & 0 \\ 0 & \sigma_2 & 0 & 0 \\ 0 & 0 & \sigma_r & 0 \\ 0 & 0 & 0 & 0 \end{bmatrix} \begin{bmatrix} v_{11} & \cdots & v_{1n} \\ \cdots & \cdots & \cdots \\ v_{n1} & \cdots & v_{nn} \end{bmatrix}
$$

The Singular values in Σ are associated with the magnitude of the principal axes, or directions, in the multidimensional space of A. The number of non-zero singular values of A is equal to its rank, and the number of zero singular values gives the dimension of the null space of A. This is useful for determining the dimensionality of the column space and row space of A.

There are some properties of the Singular values which are in the diagonal of Σ:

- They are always non-negative, and listed in descending order, meaning: $\sigma_1 > \sigma_2 > ... > \sigma_r$. They look something like:

  `[4.763, 1.359, 1.032, 0.855, 0.656, 0.432, 0, 0]`

- The number of non-zero singular values is equal to the rank of the matrix. Here there are r non-zero values, then the rank of this matrix is r. In above example the rank is 6. See Section 2.12 for the rank of matrix.
- There will be min(m, n) singular values for an matrix.
- The larger singular values correspond to the directions in which matrix A has the most variance, and hence, they carry the bulk of the information of the data represented by matrix A.
- Each singular value is associated with a pair of singular vectors from the orthogonal matrices U and V.

SVD is a fundamental matrix factorization technique in linear algebra with numerous properties and applications in statistics, data processing, machine learning, and more. Here we only interest in its property of **Dimensionality reduction** or **Optimal low-rank approximation**, which will be used later in this book for fine-tuning of the Large Language Models (LLMs), we want to explain the math concepts and fundamentals here.

Let's look at the example of singular values:

```
[4.763, 1.359, 1.032, 0.855, 0.656, 0.432, 0, 0]
```

There are 6 non-zero values, then the rank is 6. If we take the first 3 singular values and ignore the rests:

```
[4.763, 1.359, 1.032, 0, 0, 0, 0, 0]
```

And use these 3 singular values to re-construct the matrix using the SVD formula:

$$A' = U' \, \Sigma' \, V'^T$$

Where Σ' is the matrix with 3 singular values, its rank is lowered to 3. U' is the left 3 columns of U, and V' is right 3 columns of V.

A' is re-constructed as the **low-rank approximation** of original matrix A. And A' has the same dimensions as the original matrix A.

Then what does it mean and why we do that? By doing this we are achieving the **dimensionality reduction**. We are reducing the number of features required to represent the data (matrix A) while preserving as much variance as possible. Because we keep the top three singular values from the original, which contain most information of the original. The singular values we ignored have less information of matrix A.

The reduced rank means that the new matrix A' resides in a lower-dimensional space, even though it is presented in the same size as A. For example, a picture with 1,000 by 1,000 pixels is printed on a 5" by 5" paper, we reduce the pixels to 200 by 200 and print it on same sized paper, as the result the information is reduced but presented on the same sized paper. The important thing is the reduced picture retains the majority of features of the original one, say, there is a dog on the original picture, its low-rank approximation (size-reduced picture) is still a dog. A machine learning algorithm can identify it as a dog, but reduce the computational cost on processing the low-rank picture. This is the whole point of SVD we are talking here.

Here are the codes with PyTorch:

```
1    A = torch.rand(1000, 800)
2    rankA = torch.linalg.matrix_rank(A)
3    print("Original Matrix A:")
4    print(A)
5    print("Size of A:", A.size())
6    print("Rank of A:", rankA)
7    print("Params of A:", A.size(0)*A.size(1))
```

Line 1 is to create a tensor (matrix A) of 1,000 × 800 with random elements. Line 2 is to get its rank. The results are:

```
Size of A: [1000, 800]
Rank of A: 800
Params of A: 800000
```

Then do SVD on matrix A:

```
8    U, S, V = torch.linalg.svd(A)
```

As the result, we get U, s and v. Here s is in different format from matrix Σ, instead of a diagonal matrix, s is a vector with singular values.

The rank of the original matrix A is 800, now choose a smaller rank k=32,

```
9    k = 32
10   U_k = U[:, :k]
11   S_k = torch.diag(S[:k])
12   V_k = V[:, :k]
13   A_prime = U_k @ S_k @ V_k.T
```

Line 10 picks k columns of U, and Line 12 k columns of v.

Line 11 select top k values from s, since s is a vector rather than a matrix, use torch.diag() to create a diagonal matrix in order to re-construct the matrix with the formula.

Line 13 re-constructs the matrix A_prime, or A'. The operator @ in PyTorch is matrix multiplication which is same as torch.matmul(). The operator .T is transpose, which flips a matrix over its diagonal; or switches the row and column indices of the matrix.

A_prime is the low-rank approximation of the original A:

```
1    rankA_prime = torch.linalg.matrix_rank(A_prime)
2    print("Low-Rank Approximation A':")
```

```
3    print(A_prime)
4    print("Size of A':", A_prime.size())
5    print("Rank of A':", rankA_prime)
```

Print out its rank and size:

```
Size of A': [1000, 800]
Rank of A': 32
```

It has the same size as A, but rank is reduced to 32 from the original 800.

Singular Value Decomposition (SVD) is a powerful mathematical tool that breaks down a matrix into its constituent components—singular values and singular vectors. It's an important technique for dimensionality reduction, which retains only the top singular values and their corresponding singular vectors, this preserves the most information from the dataset.

To measure the quality of reconstruction of the dimensionality reduced Low-Rank Approximation A', it's important to compare how well the reconstructed A' performs the same tasks as A. For example, in natural language processing (NLP), this might be running a text generation task on both A' and A to compare the performance.

2.14 Conclusion

In this chapter, we've covered the basics of PyTorch and some important math concepts that are used throughout this book. We started by looking at tensors, which are a way to keep track of numbers in lists that can have many levels. They're like the building blocks for everything else we do in PyTorch.

We then looked at vectors and matrices, which are types of tensors. They're just a fancy way of talking about lines of numbers and grids of numbers, respectively. We have seen how important they are for doing math in deep learning.

We learned about the dot product, which is a simple way to combine two lists of numbers to get a single number. This is very helpful for understanding how different pieces of data relate to each other, and it's essential idea of the Transformer model we are going to introduce in next chapter.

Then, we explored Softmax function, which can take a bunch of numbers and turn them into probabilities that add up to one. Alongside it, we saw Cross Entropy, which is a way of measuring how close our model's predictions are to the true values.

We also looked at linear transformations, which are a way to move and stretch data in different directions, something that's really handy in building layers of a neural network.

Embedding was next, which is about turning things like words into numbers so that the computer can work with them more easily.

Then we came to neural networks, which are like complex networks of calculations that can learn from data. We touched on how they can recognize patterns and make predictions.

We also discussed Bigram models, which are a simple way to predict the next word in a sentence based on the previous one.

And we talked about how to pick the next word when we're generating text. We compared two ways to do this: Greedy, which always picks the most likely next word, and Random Sampling, which gives a bit of chance and can sometimes pick less likely words for variety. We also mentioned Beam which is like a smarter way to make these guesses, balancing chance with smart choices.

Finally, we discussed about the rank of matrix and the technique of singular value decomposition (SVD), which are powerful tools to process datasets, especially in terms of dimensionality reduction where we can extract the most meaningful features from high-dimensional data.

3. Transformer

Transformer model is a neural network architecture that is widely used for Large Language Models (LLMs), it becomes the fundamental of many modern natural language processing (NLP) architectures, for example OpenAI's GPT, (Generative Pretrained Transformer), Google's BERT (Bidirectional Encoder Representations from Transformers), FLAN-T5 (Fine-tuned LAnguage Net, Text-To-Text Transfer Transformer), and Bloomberg's BloombergGPT and so on. The Transformer model has become a ubiquitous and powerful tool in the field of natural language processing, powering the latest generation of large language models (LLMs).

As a neural network, the transformer model learns from mass amount of textual data, understands the context and meaning by tracking the relationships, and generates new contexts.

The transformer is an advanced machine learning architecture, it is originally proposed in the paper *Attention is All You Need*[1], *Vaswani et al.* in 2017, reference the paper at [1] in References section at the end of this book. We take this paper as the bible in this book, just implement it without asking why, because it's already approved by the success of ChatGPT and many other implementations.

The transformer architecture in most cases replaces the convolutional neural networks (CNNs) and recurrent neural networks (RNNs) in language processing, and becomes the most popular deep learning models in recent years. The transformer architecture is depicted in Figure 3.1, which includes an encoder in the left part, and a decoder in the right.

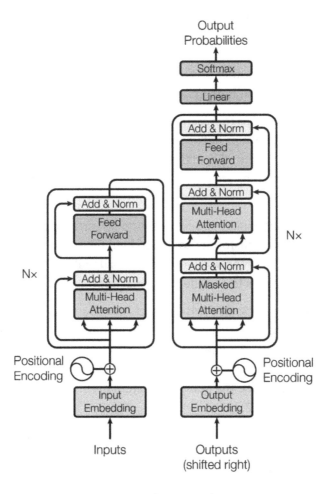

Figure 3.1 Transformer Architecture
Source from: Attention is All You Need [1], Vaswani et al, 2017.

In this chapter, we will dive into the implementation of the Transformer architecture from scratch using PyTorch. Through a step-by-step approach, we will explore the key building blocks that make up the Transformer and understand how they work together to create this powerful neural network.

The key components of the Transformer are briefly described below:

Tokenization and Embedding, in large language model, a textual sentence is called a **sequence**; and a word is called a **token**, although it does not have to be a word, it could be a character, a partial word or any special characters. Tokenization is to represent a token as a numerical value, a commonly used method is to build a vocabulary that includes all tokens (words, sub-words, or other textual units), use the index of a token in the vocabulary to represent it, this is tokenization.

Embeddings are used to represent tokens in vectors aiming at capturing the semantic relationships between tokens. In transformer models all sequences are represented in matrices with embedding, where the rows are tokens, and columns are embeddings, which was introduced in Section 2.8.

Positional Encoding, since the sequences do not provide positional information for the transformer to understand the meaning of same token at different position of the sequences, the positional encodings are added to the input sequences to provide positional information.

Attention, specifically **Scaled Dot-Product Attention**, is the heart of the Transformer, it allows the model to focus on different parts of the input sequence when generating new contexts. It calculates the attention scores by dot product operation, scales the results, and apply them to the input sequences. Dot product, the math foundation of this operation, was introduced in Section 2.3.

Multi-Head Attention, the transformer architectures use multiple heads of Attention in parallel, then the model is able to capture different aspects of relationships in the sequences.

Feedforward Networks are two linear transformations with ReLU activation function. The linear transformation was introduced in Section 2.7 and 2.9.

Layer Normalization is to normalize the neural networks in order to stabilize the training process and reduce the training time. It based on the paper of *Layer Normalization* [2], *Ba et al, 2016*, reference the paper at [2] in References section at the end of this book.

Encoder is responsible for contextualizing and understanding the input data. It's the left part of Figure 3.1 which is composed of a set sequence of layers and provides the necessary input for the model's Decoder. For example, when we do the task like questions and answers, the questions are input data and fed into the Encoder; when do the translation, the original texts are input and fed into the Encoder.

Decoder is responsible for generating the output data from the output of the Encoder as well as the previous outputs of itself as the input data. The output of the decoder will be shifted right and send back to itself as the input for next iteration. The iteration continues until a special end token is encountered. The output of decoder will be compared with the actual target in dataset and decide the differences or losses, the model will adjust the parameters to minimize the losses, like all other deep learning algorithms.

In this chapter we will deep-dive into these components to develop a solid understanding of the transformer architecture, and we will put all the pieces together to build a transformer using PyTorch, at the same time explain the paper of *Attention is All You Need*[1], *Vaswani et al, 2017*. The goal is to understand how the transformer is working behind the scenes, although our self-built transformer model might not be used in the real-world project.

We will also discuss the training process, including the choice of loss function and optimization techniques, and explore how to use the trained model for inference (or prediction).

The source codes are available at the Github repository for this book, they reference [9], [10], [11], [12] in the References section at the end of this book, they are tested and working on Google Colab environment with or without a GPU.

By the end of this chapter, you will have a deep understanding of the Transformer architecture and the ability to implement it from scratch using PyTorch. This knowledge will empower you to adapt and enhance the Transformer model for your own natural language processing projects and contribute to the ongoing advancements in the field of large language models.

Enjoy the Transformer!

3.1   Dataset and Tokenization

Preparing datasets and performing tokenization are important steps for the implementation of a Transformer model. In the previous example in Section 2.10, we built a vocabulary using the IMDB movie review dataset to demonstrate a Bigram model, this is a way to build vocabulary from scratch.

In this section we start from building a similar vocabulary from a question-answer dataset at: *https://www.kaggle.com/datasets/rtatman/ questionanswer-dataset/*. Instead of using the full dataset, we take 16 pairs of questions and answers from the dataset. The purpose of our implementation is to showcase the Transformer architecture and how it works behind the scenes, our focus is not on the data, so we only use a very small dataset in this chapter.

The dataset is defined as a python list:

```
1    question_answer = [
2      ['How often do turtles breed?',
3       'Every few years or more.'],
4      ['Where do sea turtles lay their eggs?',
5       'Holes dug into mud or sand.'],
6      ['What do beetles eat?',
7       'They often feed on plants and fungi, ...'],
8      ['What are the similarities between beetles ...?',
9       'Beetles have mouthparts similar to those ...'],
10     ...
11   ]
```

Each item in `question_answer` dataset has a question and an answer, the questions are fed into the Transformer model as the input, and the answers are expected as the output. The idea is after our Transformer model is built and trained with this dataset, it will understand the contexts and meanings of the input questions, and will learn the relationship between the input and the output, hopefully it will be able to generate the answers when questions are given as input.

Then create a vocabulary based on `question_answer`,

```
21   texts = []
22   for que_text, ans_text in question_answer:
23     text = que_text.replace('?', ' ?')
24     texts.extend(text.split())
25     text = ans_text.replace('.', ' .')
26     texts.extend(text.split())
27
28   words = sorted(list(set(texts)))
29   words = ['<PAD>', '<UNK>','<SOS>','<EOS>'] + words
```

All questions in this dataset end with "?", and all answers end with ".", separate them from the texts with a space in Line 23 and 25. And then split the texts, both questions and answers, into words in Line 24 and 26. As the result, all words as well as "?" and "." are separated as tokens. The loop from Line 22 to 26 goes through all items and eventually create a list of tokens in `texts`.

In this example, the tokens are words plus the special characters. In the real-word transformer models, different tokenization strategies are applied, some use the whole word as token, some use sub-word (partial word), some use characters, and so on.

Line 28 creates a sorted list of unique words, they are stored in `words` list. This is finally our vocabulary for the dataset.

Line 29 adds four special tokens to the beginning of the vocabulary list:

<PAD>	Padding token
<UNK>	Unknown token
<SOS>	Start of Sequence token
<EOS>	End of Sequence token

Padding token `<PAD>` is used to pad the sequences to make them the same length. The technique of padding was introduced in an example in Section 2.2. Here sequences refer to the sentences, in this case the questions and answers. In the dataset all the sequences of the questions and answers have different length, in order to process the sequences efficiently and in parallel they will be put into matrices which do not allow different length of sequences. Padding is a technique in large language model, it works like this:

```
How often do turtles breed ? <PAD> <PAD> <PAD> <PAD>
```

The length of the original sequence is 6, the padding makes the length to 10 by adding <PAD> tokens. We will find the max length of all question sequences and pad all shorter ones to the max length. And the same for the answer sequences.

The unknown token <UNK> is used to represent words that are not present in the vocabulary.

The start and end tokens <SOS> and <EOS> are used to mark the start and end of the sequences. We have already applied this concept in Section 2.10 and 2.11, when generating new sequences from the Bigram model, it starts from <SOS> token and end with <EOS> token. Both tokens are attached to the sequences for training.

By running the above codes, the vocabulary is something like below:

```
['<PAD>','<UNK>','<SOS>','<EOS>','.','?','A','At',
 'Because','Beetles','By','Can','Every','How',... ]
```

After the vocabulary is built, we will create a tokenizer which is an important component in the Transformer architecture. It's responsible for converting raw text into a format that the model can understand. The tokenizer's primary function is to take the input text and split it into a sequence of tokens, where each token represents a word, a sub-word, or a character, and so on.

The token IDs are the numerical representations of the tokens, each token is assigned a token ID by the tokenizer. The token IDs are the primary input format for the Transformer model, which is designed to process numerical sequences rather than raw texts. In the real-world models, different strategies might used to assign the IDs to tokens; in our example we simply use the token's indices in the vocabulary as the token IDs.

Create a class called `Tokenizer`, obtain the indices of the words in the vocabulary, and assign them as token IDs:

```
31    class Tokenizer():
```

```
32        def __init__(self, vocabulary):
33          self.idx2word = {index:word \
34                    for index, word in enumerate(vocabulary)}
35          self.word2idx = {word:index \
36                    for index, word in enumerate(vocabulary)}
37        def get_vocab_size(self):
38          return len(self.idx2word)
39        def encode(self, text):
40          return [self.word2idx[w] for w in text.split()]
41        def encode_word(self, char):
42          return self.word2idx[char]
43        def decode(self, encoded_text):
44          return [self.idx2word[i] for i in encoded_text]
45        def decode_text(self, encoded_text):
46          s = self.decode(encoded_text)
47          return (" ".join(s))
```

The `Tokenizer` class build two internal lookup dictionaries, one is to lookup index from a word, another one is to lookup a word from the index. The former `word2idx` is to encode the sequence by converting the tokens to IDs; the latter `idx2word` is to decode the IDs to tokens.

`get_vocab_size()` function is to obtain the size of vocabulary.

`encode()` function is to encode a sequence from tokens to IDs, and `encode_word()` is to encode a single token.

`decode()` function is to do the opposite of `encode()`, it returns a Python list of the tokens. While `decode_text()` is doing the same thing but join all tokens together and return the decoded text.

Then create an instance of the `Tokenizer` class and show the size of the vocabulary:

```
48    tokenizer = Tokenizer(words)
49    vocab_size = tokenizer.get_vocab_size()
```

The `vocab_size` is: 165, meaning there are totally 165 unique words in the vocabulary for our dataset.

For the sake of simplicity, in this example only one vocabulary is created for both the input and output sequences. Most often the input and output have separate vocabularies, especially when the input and output are in different domains, for example a translation project, the input and output are in different languages.

With the vocabulary and a tokenizer ready, we need to build a data loader with the purpose of sending the data to Transformer model in correct format, appropriate padding and batching. The batching is to group multiple input data into a single batch and then fed into the model, the purpose is to improve the efficiency and performance of the training process.

As shown in Figure 3.1, there are three sets of data:

1. Encoder input: the input data is fed into the encoder (left part of Figure 3.1) at the bottom, this is the question sequences.

2. Decoder input: the output data is fed into the decoder (right part of Figure 3.1) at the bottom, this is the answers sequences.

3. Decoder output: the output will be generated from the decoder at the top and will compare with this data set to determine the differences and calculate the loss. This is also the answers sequences.

Now make these three sets of data by `make_date()` function:

```
51    def make_data(sentences):
52      enc_inputs, dec_inputs, dec_outputs = [], [], []
53
54      for i in range(len(sentences)):
55        que_text = sentences[i][0].replace('?', ' ?')
56        ans_text_inp='<SOS> '+sentences[i][1].replace('.', ' .')
57        ans_text_out=sentences[i][1].replace('.', ' .')+' <EOS>'
58
59        enc_input = tokenizer.encode(que_text)
60        dec_input = tokenizer.encode(ans_text_inp)
61        dec_output = tokenizer.encode(ans_text_out)
62
63        enc_inputs.append(torch.LongTensor(enc_input))
64        dec_inputs.append(torch.LongTensor(dec_input))
65        dec_outputs.append(torch.LongTensor(dec_output))
66
67      return pad_sequence(enc_inputs, batch_first=True), \
68              pad_sequence(dec_inputs, batch_first=True), \
```

```
69          pad_sequence(dec_outputs, batch_first=True)
```

Line 55 prepares encoder input from question sequences. Line 56 to prepare the decoder input and Line 57 for decoder output. The start token and end token are attached to the output data.

Line 59 to 61 encode the three sequences to token IDs, and Line 63 to 65 convert the tokenized sequences to tensors. These tensors in each data set have different length, for example enc_inputs are the sequences from all questions, the length is different for each question.

Line 67 to 69 invoke pad_sequence() function, which is provided by PyTorch, to pad the sequences in the three datasets. Below is an example of how it looks like:

```
enc_inputs:
([[ 26,  37, 142, 135,  45, 142,  44,  35, 142,  80,   8],
 [ 26,  95,  36,  91,  96, 140,  34,  67,   8,   0,   0],
 [ 18, 113,  62, 153,  51,   8,   0,   0,   0,   0,   0],
 [ 18,  62, 117,  93, 144, 156, 162,  48,   8,   0,   0],
 ...
 [ 26, 104, 119, 136,  30,  85, 142, 157,   8,   0,   0]])
```

The dataset is in the form of a 2-dimensional matrix, each sequence is represented in a row, the shorter sequences are padded with 0 at the end until the max length. There are totally 16 sequences that corresponding to the 16 questions in the original dataset. Then the size of the matrix is 16 by max length.

Call the above function to obtain datasets:

```
70   enc_inputs, /
71   dec_inputs, /
72   dec_outputs = make_data(question_answer)
```

The sizes of the three datasets are:

```
enc_inputs:  ([16, 11])
dec_inputs:  ([16, 19])
dec_outputs: ([16, 19])
```

So far the data is preprocessed with token IDs, padded and batched. Now create a data loader.

PyTorch provides a utility called `torch.utils.data.DataLoader` which helps efficiently load and iterate over datasets during the training or evaluation of the models, especially for the large datasets. It can load data in batches, the batch size is specified in a parameter. It allows parallel processing because multiple batches can be processed simultaneously when GPUs are used.

The `DataLoader` can also shuffle the data by randomly arrange the data items when loading, it can prevent the model from learning the data patterns based on the order of the data.

In this example although without a large dataset, we will demonstrate how to utilize this utility. To make the datasets available for `DataLoader`, we will create a customized class that inherits from `torch.utils.data.Dataset`, and implement two methods of it. The `__len__` method returns the total length of the dataset, and `__getitem__` method returns a specific data item given an index:

```
73    class DataSet(Data.Dataset):
74        def __init__(self, enc_inputs, dec_inputs, outputs):
75            super(DataSet, self).__init__()
76            self.enc_inputs = enc_inputs
77            self.dec_inputs = dec_inputs
78            self.dec_outputs = dec_outputs
79        def __len__(self):
80            return self.enc_inputs.shape[0]
81        def __getitem__(self, idx):
82            return self.enc_inputs[idx],
83                   self.dec_inputs[idx],
84                   self.dec_outputs[idx]
```

As mentioned earlier, there are three sets of data for encoder input, decoder input and output, so each data item includes three data elements: `enc_inputs`, `dec_inputs`, and `dec_outputs`. The will be returned by `__getitem__` () function.

Then create the data loader:

```
85    batch_size = 8
```

```
86    loader = Data.DataLoader(
87                DataSet(enc_inputs, dec_inputs, dec_outputs),
88                batch_size = batch_size,
89                shuffle = True)
```

Line 86 creates the data loader.

Line 87 instantiates a `DataSet` with the datasets we created in Line 70 to 72. Line 88 specifies a batch size.

Line 89 specifies `shuffle=True`, meaning randomly shuffle the data items.

Now the dataset is ready for the Transformer model. In this section, we have laid the foundation for implementing a Transformer from scratch by focusing on preparing dataset and tokenization. We have created a small dataset in Python list with question answer pairs, built a vocabulary base on it with special tokens added. Then we created a tokenizer that can convert the raw text into numerical token IDs, and vice versa, enabling the Transformer model to work with the data.

And we preprocessed the dataset by tokenizing the questions and answers, padding the sequences to ensure a consistent length, and separating the data into encoder input, decoder input, and decoder output.

Finally, we leveraged PyTorch's Dataset and DataLoader classes to create an efficient data loading pipeline, which can handle batching, and shuffling, preparing it for use in the Transformer model.

3.2 Embedding

Embedding is a process of converting token IDs into numerical vectors that capture the semantic and syntactic relationships between tokens, it's briefly introduced in Section 2.8. In transformer architecture, see Figure 3.1, the embedding layer is the first layer at the bottom, responsible for converting the input tokens into their corresponding embedding vectors.

Based on the paper:

Similarly to other sequence transduction models, we use learned embeddings to convert the input tokens and output tokens to vectors of dimension d_{model}. The dimensionality of input and output is $d_{model} = 512$,

From Attention is All You Need[1], Vaswani et al, 2017

The dimension, or length, of the embedded vector is 512 for the Transformer model, as proposed by the paper. PyTorch has nn.Embedding() function for this purpose:

```
1    d_model = 512
2    embedding = nn.Embedding(vocab_size, d_model)
3    input = embedding(input_sequences)
4    output = embedding(output_sequences)
```

Line 1 to 4 above illustrate how the embedding is used. Line 1 specifies the length of the embedding vector, and Line 2 creates an embedding layer of the neural network with `vocab_size` and `d_model`, where `vocab_size` is the size of vocabulary. Line 3 and 4 embed the input and output sequences respectively.

As introduced in Section 2.8, the embedded data is a 2-dimensional matrix, the number of its rows is same as the length of the sequences, i.e. the length of `input_sequences`, and its number of columns is `d_model`, which is 512. The contents of the embedded data look something like:

```
tensor([[-0.3890, -0.3654,  0.4290,  ...,  -0.4368],
        [ 0.5781,  2.0202,  1.5244,  ...,   0.4218],
        [ 0.0907,  0.0958,  1.5828,  ...,  -0.5666],
        ...
        [-0.0186,  0.6410, -0.4381,  ...,  -0.2018]] )
```

Now in the Transformer model we are going to build, the data is loaded in batch, meaning `input_sequences` in Line 3 are no longer a single sequence, instead it's a 2-dimensional tensor with the size of `batch_size` by sequence length. After applying the embedding, one dimension is added to the original data block, it becomes a 3-dimentional tensor, with the size of `batch_size` by sequence length by `d_model` (512), as shown in Figure 3.2:

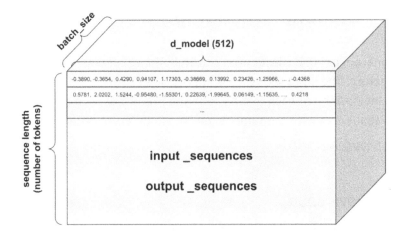

Figure 3.2 An Embedded Data Block

In summary, the dimensions of the embedded sequence are represented as a 3-dimensional tensor with the shape (`batch_size`, `seq_len`, `d_model`), where:

- `batch_size`: is the number of batches that loaded as input sequences.
- `seq_len`: is the length of the padded input sequence. It's required that all input sequences within a batch to have the same length, so the `seq_len` is typically padded to the maximum length of the sequences in the batch.
- d_model: is the size of the embedding vectors, as proposed by the paper, its value is 512. This is a hyperparameter of the model and can be adjusted based on the size of model and the size of vocabulary.

This is the basic data block for processing in the following sections in this book. All parameters in the embedding layer are learnable parameters, meaning they will be adjusted by the training process. The total number of parameters is `vocab_size` multiplied by `d_model`.

3.3 Positional Encoding

Positional encoding is a layer after the Embedding in Transformer architecture, The input sequence is not provided with any information about the position of each token within the sequence. For example, look at two sequences with the same tokens but in different order:

THIS MOVIE IS GOOD

and

IS THIS MOVIE GOOD

Both have the same words, or tokens, but have different meanings. The transformer model will not be able to differentiate them from the input embeddings. To address this, positional encoding is used to inject positional information into the input embeddings, it adds some extra information to identify the sequential order of the sequences, so that the model will be aware of the positions of the tokens. As the result, the above two sentences can be differentiated by the model.

The positional encoding happens immediately after the embedding layer in the Transformer architecture, as shown in Figure 3.3:

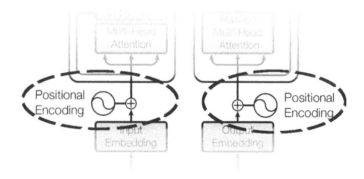

Figure 3.3 Positional Encoding
Source from: Attention is All You Need [1], Vaswani et al, 2017. Modified by author.

Based on the paper:

In order for the model to make use of the order of the sequence, we must inject some information about the relative or absolute position of the tokens in the sequence.

From Attention is All You Need[1], Vaswani et al, 2017

The paper proposed the methods for positional encoding as:

$$PE_{(pos,2i)} = \sin\left(\frac{pos}{n^{\frac{2i}{d}}}\right)$$

$$PE_{(pos,2i+1)} = \cos\left(\frac{pos}{n^{\frac{2i}{d}}}\right)$$

where:

$n = 10000$

$d = d_{model} = 512$

pos is the position of a token in sequence, $0 \leq pos \leq length/2$

i is the column indeices of the encoding vectors, $0 \leq i \leq d/2$

In the above expression, the even position of the encoding vector corresponds to sine functions, and odd positions correspond to cosine functions. The positional encoding has the same length as the embedding vector, which is d_{model} = 512. Figure 3.4 illustrates how it works on a short sequence:

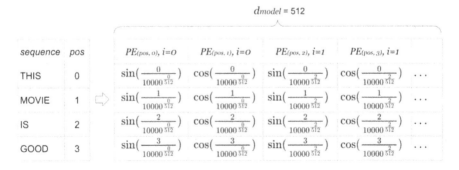

Figure 3.4 Illustration of Positional Encoding

The important thing is the positional encoding is one time parameter, it's not learnable parameter, meaning it will not be adjusted in the training process.

The `PositionalEncoding` layer is implemented as below:

```
1    class PositionalEncoding(nn.Module):
2      def __init__(self, d_model, max_len=5000, dropout=0.1):
3        super(PositionalEncoding, self).__init__()
4        self.dropout = nn.Dropout(p=dropout)
5        pe = torch.zeros(max_len, d_model)
6        position = torch.arange(0,max_len).unsqueeze(1).float()
7        div_term = torch.exp(torch.arange(0,d_model, 2).float()
8        div_term = div_term * (-math.log(10000.0) / d_model))
9        pe[:, 0::2] = torch.sin(position * div_term)
10       pe[:, 1::2] = torch.cos(position * div_term)
11       pe = pe.unsqueeze(0)
12       self.register_buffer('pe_table', pe)
13
14     def forward(self, x):
15       x = x + self.pe_table[:, :x.size(1), :]
16       return self.dropout(x)
```

The above codes implement the formula of positional encoding, and this implementation follows the convention of PyTorch neural network structures. To extend PyTorch `nn.Module` class, we should override two methods to implement our own layers, `__init__()` method to define the structure of our model and initialize the parameters, and `forward()` method to specify the forward pass. All we need to do is to define these two methods, and PyTorch provides default implementations for other methods, we don't need to override them unless there are any special requirements.

Line 1 defines the class of `PositionalEncoding()` that extends PyTorch's `nn.Module` class.

Line 2 to 12 define `__init__()` function. Line 3 is a general requirement when extending the `nn.Module`, it invokes the super (or parent) class to initialize it, this should be always called in the first statement to make sure the super class is properly initialized before our customizations.

Line 4 defines a Dropout layer, which is a technique used in neural networks to avoid Overfitting. We do not deep-dive into Overfitting and Dropout here, for more details you might want to read my another book,

Machine Learning and Deep Learning With Python[3], which is listed in [3] at References section.

To simply put, Overfitting happens when a model learns too much from the training dataset, and captures too many details from the patterns of training dataset, as the results the model does not perform well on the testing dataset, therefore fails to make accurate predictions.

Dropout is aiming to reduce the overfitting, it's introduced by the paper *Dropout: A Simple Way to Prevent Neural Networks from Overfitting*[8], *Srivastava et al, 2014.* The idea is to randomly disable, or dropout, a percentage of neuron nodes in the layers during training. In our case dropout 0.1 or 10% of the neuron nodes during the training.

Line 5 creates an all zero tensor of size `(max_len, d_model)`.

Line 6 creates a position tensor ranging from 0 to `max_len`.

Line 7 to 10 implements the formula of positional encoding, Line 9 and 10 call the `sin` and `cos` functions on the even and odd positions respectively.

Line 11 uses PyTorch's `unsqueeze()` function to add one more dimension at the position of 0, this is useful because in the future we will pass data with batch, which is in the first dimension of the data. The size of the positional encoding parameter is:

```
pe:    (1, max_len, d_model)
```

Line 12 uses PyTorch's `register_buffer` to store the positional encoding data `pe`, because the positional encoding is not learnable parameters of the Transformer model, it's one-time parameter, `register_buffer` is used to store this type of parameter. And most important thing is it can move the data to different devices together with the model, like CPUs or GPUs, if not using `register_buffer`, the parameter will not be moved together with the model.

Line 14 to 16 define the `forward()` function, the input parameter is

```
x:    (batch_size, len_seq, d_model)
```

Line 15 adds the positional encoding `pe` to the input data, the addition is based on the `len_seq` of the input data `x`, which is `x.size(1)`.

Line 16 does the dropout and returns the results.

As a quick recap of trigonometric sine and cosine functions, as shown in Figure 3.5, both are graphed as waves, which is called sinusoid. The range of both functions are from -1.0 to 1.0. There are two essential concepts: wavelength and frequency, the wavelength is the distance between two points where the wave repeats itself, in Figure 3.5 the wavelength is 2π; the frequency is the number of cycles of the wave in one second.

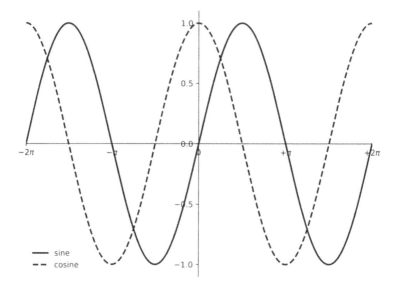

Figure 3.5 Trigonometric Sine and Cosine

Based on the above formula of positional encoding, at a given position *pos*, the wavelength λ is:

$$\lambda = \frac{2\pi n^{\frac{2i}{d}}}{pos}$$

The total dimension for every position is d_{model} = *512*, the wavelength at each dimension *i* is different, Figure 3.6 visualizes the sinusoids at dimension of 0, and 120.

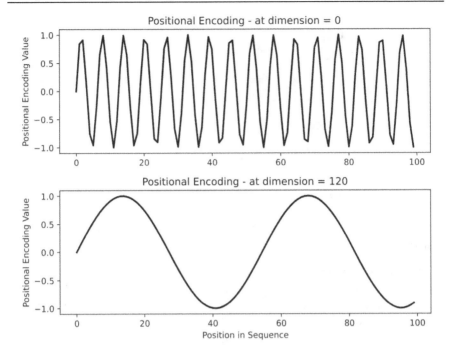

Figure 3.6 Different Wavelength at Different Dimension

The x-axis is the position of tokens in the sequence, and y-axis is the value of the positional encoding. Feel free to play with the source codes to see how the wavelengths are different at a given dimension.

Figure 3.7 shows the positional encoding from another perspective, the distribution at different location, the top one shows the 10th token, and the lower one shows the 50th token. As you can see each position has a different sinusoid, it gives a unique way of encoding each position.

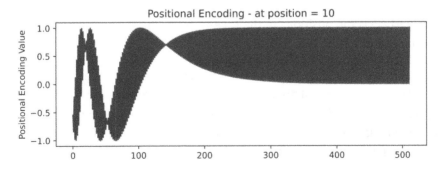

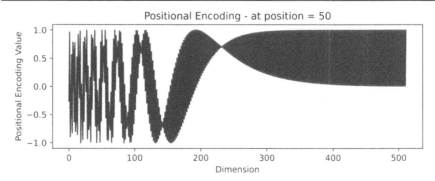

Figure 3.7 Positional Encoding at Different Position

The paper describes the reason why choose sine and cosine for this purpose:

> *The wavelengths form a geometric progression from 2π to 10000 · 2π. We chose this function because we hypothesized it would allow the model to easily learn to attend by relative positions, since for any fixed offset k, PEpos+k can be represented as a linear function of PEpos.*
>
> From Attention is All You Need[1], Vaswani et al, 2017

Figure 3.8 shows the overall positional Encoding in color intensity, where the length of sequence is 100 and dimension is 512.

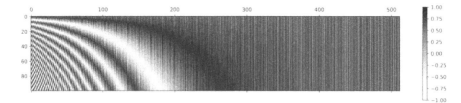

Figure 3.8 Positional Encoding Shown in Color Intensity

The vertical is the positions of the tokens, from 0 to 99; and horizontal is the dimension, from 0 to 511.

As a summary, because transformers process input sequences in a parallel, non-sequential manner, they do not inherently have a built-in understanding of the order of the tokens. Positional encoding is a technique used to incorporate the positional information of tokens in a sequence. It is an important component that allows transformers to effectively model the relationships between tokens based on their positions in the input sequence.

The sinusoid for positional encoding gives value range between -1.0 and 1.0, which is a normalized range. The wavelengths at different dimensions are different, and the distribution at different token positions are also different. Therefore, the positional encoding gives a unique way to identify each token. And finally, the values of positional encoding are not learnable, they are one-time parameters.

3.4 Layer Normalization

Layer Normalization (LayerNorm) is a popular deep neural network model widely used in natural language processing (NLP) tasks, aiming at stabilizing and accelerating the training of deep neural networks.

In Transformer architecture, there are several instances of "Add & Norm" layers, which refers to Addition and Layer Normalization, as shown in Figure 3.9:

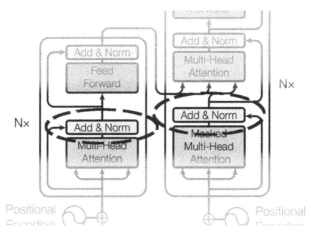

Figure 3.9 Addition and Layer Normalization Layer
Source from: Attention is All You Need [1]*, Vaswani et al, 2017. Modified by author.*

Add & Norm, or Addition and Layer Normalization, is used after the multi-head attention and feed-forward neural network layers.

The Addition refers to the operation of original input being added element-wise to the output of a layer, i.e. the input x is added to the output of Feed Forward layer:

x + FeedForward(x)

The Addition is also known as Residual connection, which helps to address the vanishing gradient problem and allows the model to learn residual mappings.

This section will focus on the Layer Normalization. To begin with the discussion, let's start with the Normalization, what is it?

A dataset often has multiple features, each might have different range of values. For example, the housing data, the number of bedrooms is a feature, its value can be 2, 3, 4 or 5; the area in square footage is another feature, its value can be 500, 1200, of 2200. The ranges of these two features are totally different, when train the model with this kind of datasets, it could take significantly longer time, because the optimization algorithms will not converge quickly when the input features are not on the same scale. The Standard Scaling introduced in Section 2.9 is one of the normalization methods.

Batch Normalization

In the large deep learning neural network projects, the dataset is loaded in batches and the training is processed also in batches. Then the method like Standard Scaling is also performed on batches. For example, the below housing dataset contains three features, the number of bedrooms, area in square feet, and the age of house, a batch includes 4 data items as below:

Bedroom	Sqft	Age
3	1,250	10
4	1,880	24
5	2,600	35
2	750	18
$\mu = 3.4$, $\sigma = 1.14$	$\mu = 1,476$ $\sigma = 764.28$	$\mu = 19.2$ $\sigma = 10.75$

The Standard Scaling will normalize the data per feature per batch, it calculates the mean μ and the standard deviation σ vertically (per feature), and then calculate the normalized values for each item as below formula:

$$X_{scaled} = \frac{X_{raw} - \mu}{\sigma}$$

The problem of Batch Normalization is the calculation is based on the batch statistics, different batches might have different patterns and different mean and standard deviation, especially in the language sequence models. This will cause inaccurate and inefficient of the training. Therefore, it comes to Layer Normalization.

Layer Normalization

Layer Normalization was proposed by the paper of *Layer Normalization* [2], *Ba et al, 2016*, reference the paper at [2] in References section at the end of this book.

In this approach, the mean μ and the standard deviation σ are calculated across the feature dimension by each data item, horizontally this time.

Bedroom	Sqft	Age	
3	1,250	10	μ = 421, σ =717.94
4	1,880	24	μ = 636, σ =1077.38
5	2,600	35	μ = 880, σ =1489.64
2	750	18	μ = 256, σ =427.16

This approach no longer depends on the batch statistics, although the housing data is not a good example for this approach, it is well suited for language sequence models.

The Layer Normalization applies to Transformer model. Here are the steps to do it, suppose there is input data:

$$x = \begin{bmatrix} x_1 & x_2 & \cdots & x_n \end{bmatrix}$$

x represents a data item, x_1, x_2, ... x_n, which are the features of the data. In the case of Transformer model, x represents an embedded token.

Calculate the mean μ and the standard deviation σ:

$$\mu \quad = \quad \frac{1}{n} \sum_{i=1}^{n} x_i$$

$$\sigma^2 \quad = \quad \frac{1}{n} \sum_{i=1}^{n} (x_i - \mu)^2$$

Then calculate the layer normalization output:

$$y = \frac{x - \mu}{\sqrt{\sigma^2 + \epsilon}} * \gamma + \beta$$

ϵ is a small constant used to prevent dividing by zero when standard deviation is near zero, its default value is 1e-5, or 10^{-5}. β and γ are learnable parameters, which are adjusted during training process to adapt and learn the appropriate scaling and shifting.

The Layer Normalization is implemented in PyTorch as following:

```
1    class LayerNorm(nn.Module):
2      def __init__(self, features, eps=1e-5):
3        super(LayerNorm, self).__init__()
4        self.eps = eps
5        self.gamma = nn.Parameter(torch.ones(features))
6        self.beta = nn.Parameter(torch.zeros(features))
7
8      def forward(self, x):
9        mean = x.mean(dim = -1, keepdim = True)
10       std = x.std(dim = -1, keepdim = True)
11       return self.gamma * (x - mean) / (std + self.eps) +
12             self.beta
```

The implementation follows PyTorch neural network conventions, only overrides two methods. In __init__() method from Line 2 to 9, the parameters of eps, gamma and beta are defined, eps is a constant and the other two are learnable parameters, and specified in nn.Parameter(). As we mentioned earlier in Section 3.3, the register_buffer is used to store non-learnable parameters, it was used to store the positional encoding parameter, here both `gamma` and `beta` are learnable parameters, they are stored in `nn.Parameter()`, PyTorch use it to store all learnable parameters.

In `forward()` function from Line 9 to 12, calculate the `mean` and `std` along the last dimension, which by our definition is the embedded vector of d_{model} = 512. The input parameter is:

```
x:    (batch_size, len_seq, d_model)
```

and the output is the same:

```
output: (batch_size, len_seq, d_model)
```

In summary, while both Batch and Layer Normalization aim to stabilize the learning process by normalizing the inputs to layers, they have different mechanisms and applications. The choice between using Batch or Layer Normalization will largely depend on the architecture of the neural network in question and the specifics of the task at hand. Transformer architecture uses Layer Normalization to improve the model's stability, convergence, and generalization.

3.5 Feed Forward

The Feed Forward layer is a simple, fully connected neural network that is applied independently to each position in the input sequence, after the self-attention mechanism in the encoder and decoder, as shown in Figure 3.10.

The purpose of Feed Forward is to add an additional layer of abstraction to the information that's been aggregated by the attention mechanism, allowing the network to further transform and combine those features before passing them on to the next layer or the output layer.

Based on the paper:

> *Each of the layers in our encoder and decoder contains a fully connected feed-forward network, which is applied to each position separately and identically. This consists of two linear transformations with a ReLU activation in between.*
>
> *From Attention is All You Need [1], Vaswani et al, 2017*

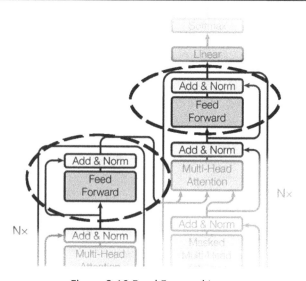

Figure 3.10 Feed Forward Layer

Source from: Attention is All You Need [1], Vaswani et al, 2017. Modified by author.

The Feed Forward layer is also called Position-wise Feedforward layer in the paper. There are three components in the Feed Forward layer, two linear transformations which introduced in Section 2.7, and a ReLU activation function which is briefly mentioned in Section 2.9.

ReLU (Rectified Linear Unit) function is defined as:

$$f(x) = \max(0, x)$$

It's a widely used activation function in neural networks. As shown in Figure 3.11, when input $x \geq 0$ the ReLU output is a straight line with slop of 1; when $x < 0$ the output is flat at 0.

ReLU function is computationally efficient because it is basically a linear function when the input values are positive, and zero when inputs are negative. And it's a non-linear function which introduces the non-linearity to the model, the non-linear transformation allows the model to learn more complex patterns and relationships.

However, it might not appropriate when the dataset includes a significant amount of negative values, because it always return zero for them, in this case other activation functions should be considered.

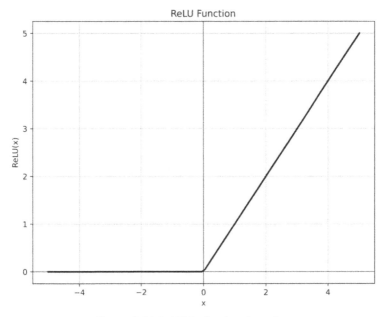

Figure 3.11 ReLU Activation Function

ReLU function is proposed for the Transformer model, based on the paper, it's defined as:

$$FFN(x) = max(0, xW_1 + b_1)W_2 + b_2$$

From Attention is All You Need [1], Vaswani et al, 2017

We can break it down to three parts, the first linear transformation is:

$$y_1 = xW_1 + b_1$$

Then apply ReLU function:

$$r = \text{ReLU}(y_1) = \max(0, y_1)$$

Finally apply the second linear transformation:

$$y_2 = rW_2 + b_2$$

Implement Feed Forward layer with PyTorch:

```
1    class FeedForward(nn.Module):
2        def __init__(self, d_ff, dropout=0.2):
3            super(FeedForward, self).__init__()
```

```
4        self.fc = nn.Sequential(
5          nn.Linear(d_model, d_ff, bias=False),
6          nn.ReLU(),
7          nn.Dropout(dropout),
8          nn.Linear(d_ff, d_model, bias=False)
9        )
10       self.ln = LayerNorm(d_model)
11
12     def forward(self, x):
13       residual = x
14       output = self.fc(x)
15       return self.ln(output + residual)
```

This is also implemented as a neural network in PyTorch, both __init__()
and forward() functions are defined here. Line 4 to 9 define a
nn.Sequential() function which is a fully connected layers that include
the first linear transformation in Line 5, ReLU activation function in Line 6,
and the second linear transformation in Line 8.

d_model in line 5 and 8 is the dimension of the embedding vector as
mentioned earlier, its value is 512. d_ff is the hidden layer of the linear
transformations, which is 2048. So the dimensions of both linear
transformations are 512 -> 2048 -> 512.

Line 7 is a Dropout layer, as mentioned earlier, it's a technique used in
neural networks to avoid Overfitting, this book will not deep-dive into it,
for more details see [3] at References section.

After ReLU function in Line 6 there are d_ff, or 2048, neuron nodes, then
Line 7 applies Dropout to disable 0.2, or 20%, of them to avoid overfitting,
the percentage can be specified in a parameter. A complex neural network
might have more Dropout layers, here we only have one.

Line 10 defines the Layer Normalization which we implemented in
previous section.

In forward() function, the input parameter is:

  x: (batch_size, len_seq, d_model)

Line 13 sets residual equals to the input x.

Line 14 executes the fully connected layers `self.fc()` on the input `x`, which is the `nn.Sequential()` network we defined in `__init__()`.

Line 15 adds the `output` to `residual`, then applies `LayerNorm` on the results, and then return the results. This implements the Add & Norm layer which is above the Feed Forward in Figure 3.10.

The output shape is:

```
output: (batch_size, len_seq, d_model)
```

The Feed Forward layer provides the model with additional capacity to learn complex, non-linear transformations of the input features. By applying a simple, fully connected neural network to each position in the input sequence independently, the Feed Forward layer complements the self-attention mechanism and contributes significantly to the transformative capacity of the model.

3.6   Scaled Dot-Product Attention

The Attention mechanism is the heart of the Transformer model, it plays an important role in capturing contextual information from input sequences. The specific type of Attention proposed in the paper is called Scaled Dot-Product Attention, which is one of the attention mechanisms, it's responsible for capturing the relationships and dependencies between different tokens in a sequence, enhancing the models to focus on relevant contextual information during the encoding and decoding processes. It's designed to efficiently calculate the attention scores between each token in the input sequences.

> *An attention function can be described as mapping a query and a set of key-value pairs to an output, where the query, keys, values, and output are all vectors. The output is computed as a weighted sum of the values, where the weight assigned to each value is computed by a compatibility function of the query with the corresponding key.*
>
> *From Attention is All You Need* [1]*, Vaswani et al, 2017*

This section we will focus on the Scaled Dot-Product Attention, it's shown in Figure 3.12.

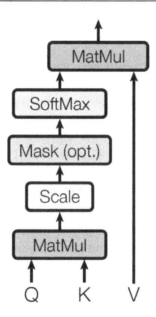

Figure 3.12 Scaled Dot-Product Attention
Source from: Attention is All You Need [1], Vaswani et al, 2017.

There are three input vectors that are derived from the input sequence,

- Query vector (Q), dimension d_k

- Key vector (K), dimension d_k

- Value vector (V), dimension d_v

The calculation proposed by the paper:

The input consists of queries and keys of dimension d_k, and values of dimension d_v. We compute the dot products of the query with all keys, divide each by $\sqrt{d_k}$, and apply a softmax function to obtain the weights on the values.

In practice, we compute the attention function on a set of queries simultaneously, packed together into a matrix Q. The keys and values are also packed together into matrices K and V.

From Attention is All You Need [1], Vaswani et al, 2017

There are several concepts and several steps involved here:

Attention Score:

The first step is to do a dot product on Q and K. The dot product is introduced in Section 2.3, `torch.matmul()` is used to calculate it for two matrices Q and K, this step is the box at the bottom of Figure 3.12, and denoted as MatMul.

The second step is to scale the dot product result by a factor of

$$\frac{1}{\sqrt{d_k}}$$

which means all elements of the dot product result are multiplied by this scaling factor. This is the second box in the bottom of Figure 3.12, and denoted as Scale.

The result is the Attention Score, defined as:

$$\frac{Q \cdot K^T}{\sqrt{d_k}}$$

Where K^T is the transpose of K. And d_k is the dimension of K.

Let's look at it in more details, Say the input sequence is:

The sky is blue

The sequence length = 4, and assume $d_{model} = d_k$ = 512. Then the matrices Q, K and V are represented the same as the input sequences as (4, 512). The calculation of the Attention Score is shown as Figure 3.13,

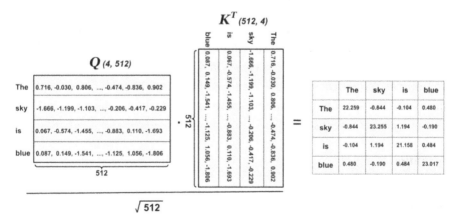

Figure 3.13 Attention Score

The size of Q is (4, 512), K is also (4, 512), the transpose of K becomes (512, 4). Then the dot product of Q and K^T is (4, 512) · (512, 4), the result is (4, 4). If you are not familiar with the dot product of matrices, see Section 2.3 for details. The result is scaled by the scaling factor, which is the square root of 512.

As the result, the Attention Score is obtained, which is a matrix of sequence length by sequence length, in this case 4 by 4, which looks like Figure 3.14:

	The	sky	is	blue
The	22.259	-0.844	-0.104	0.48
sky	-0.844	23.255	1.194	-0.19
is	-0.104	1.194	21.158	0.484
blue	0.480	-0.190	0.484	23.017

Figure 3.14 Attention Score

It indicates the relationship of each word related to other words, for example, "The" related to itself as 22.259, it relates to "sky" as -0.844, it relates to "is" as -0.104, and relates to "blue" as 0.48, and so on.

In the Attention score, the values in diagonal are much higher than others, it simply means a word has much higher relationship with itself, which makes sense. As we can see the values in diagonal is around 21 to 23, sometimes sequences might be in range of 100 to 200 or so, we should normalize the Attention Score to a same range of values which is 0 to 1. Then it comes to next step.

Attention Weights:

The purpose of Attention Weights is to apply the Softmax function on the Attention Score to obtain the normalized Attention Weights, this is the box of Softmax in Figure 3.12. It's defined as:

$$\text{softmax} \left(\frac{Q \cdot K^T}{\sqrt{d_k}} \right)$$

Softmax is introduced in Section 2.4, the purpose of Softmax is to ensure the weights are normalized to a range of 0 to 1, which makes these values interpretable as probabilities, and all scores sum up to 1.0.

As introduced in Section 2.4, Softmax tends to enhance the magnitude of the higher values of the input vectors while suppressing smaller values. Therefore, it helps the model to focus on the parts of the sequence that matter most, according to the calculated attention scores.

And also, Softmax is a differentiable function, meaning that its gradient can be calculated. This is important as backpropagation during neural network training requires gradient information to update the weights and biases.

The Attention Weight looks something like Figure 3.15:

	The	sky	is	blue	sum
The	1.000	0.000	0.000	0.000	1.000
sky	0.000	1.000	0.000	0.000	1.000
is	0.000	0.000	1.000	0.000	1.000
blue	0.000	0.000	0.000	1.000	1.000

Figure 3.15 Attention Weight (After Softmax Applied)

Because this example is too simple and there is no training process yet, the Attention Weight appears as the diagonal of 1.0 and all others 0.0. It shows the idea, the relationships between each word to other are represented in this matrix and the results are normalized.

When the input sequences are more complicated and after the training process, the elements in this matrix will be changing, they are not always 0.0 and 1.0, but the sum is always 1.0 because they are normalized. And the elements reflect the relationships between the tokens.

Scaled Dot-Product Attention

The last step is to compute the output of the Scaled Dot-Product Attention as following:

$$\text{Attention}(Q, K, V) = \text{softmax}\left(\frac{Q \cdot K^T}{\sqrt{d_k}}\right) \cdot V$$

The size of the results of Softmax function is (4, 4), the size of V is (4, 512), then the size of the final Attention is (4, 512), which looks something like Figure 3.16:

0.716, -0.030, 0.806, ..., -0.474, -0.836, 0.902
-1.666, -1.199, -1.103, ..., -0.206, -0.417, -0.229
0.067, -0.574, -1.455, ..., -0.883, 0.110, -1.693
0.087, 0.149, -1.541, ..., -1.125, 1.056, -1.806

Figure 3.16 Scaled Dot Product Attention

This means after the calculation of the Scaled Dot Product Attention, we obtain the result that is in the same size as the original input, which is in (4, 512), but the result captures the relationships between the tokens in the sequence. The relationships are added information to the original input sequences.

There are several properties of this type of attention. First it is permutation invariant, it means if swap the position of two words, for example "sky" and "blue", the values of each vector are not changed:

The	0.716, -0.030, 0.806, ..., -0.474, -0.836, 0.902
sky	-1.666, -1.199, -1.103, ..., -0.206, -0.417, -0.229
is	0.067, -0.574, -1.455, ..., -0.883, 0.110, -1.693
blue	0.087, 0.149, -1.541, ..., -1.125, 1.056, -1.806

The	0.716, -0.030, 0.806, ..., -0.474, -0.836, 0.902
blue	0.087, 0.149, -1.541, ..., -1.125, 1.056, -1.806
is	0.067, -0.574, -1.455, ..., -0.883, 0.110, -1.693
sky	-1.666, -1.199, -1.103, ..., -0.206, -0.417, -0.229

Figure 3.17 Permutation Invariant of the Attention

Of cause if not consider the Positional Encoding as introduced in Section 3.3, which is explicitly adding information for positions. This is why the Positional Encoding is important to differentiate the positions of the tokens.

The second property is the attention does not require any extra parameters, it only use the embeddings of the original sequence. Q, K and V are all derived from the original input sequence, all operations like dot product, Softmax etc. are against themselves, no other parameters involved in the calculation. Therefore this is also called "Self-Attention", because the sequence finds out the relationships by itself.

The third property is the elements along the diagonal are highest, as shown in Figure 3.15, this is because a word always has the highest relationship to itself.

This is the attention mechanism that allows the model to adjust its focus on input elements and it's an elegant solution in Transformer models, enabling it to handle long sequences effectively.

In Figure 3.12, we have covered the boxes of MatMul, Scale, SoftMax and the second MatMul. Will explain the optional Mask in next section.

Why Query (Q), Key (K) and Value (V) for Attention

The reason for using Query (Q), Key (K) and Value (V) is to enable the model to dynamically weigh the significance of different parts of the input data.

A Query is generated for each token in the sequence that the Transformer model is trying to encode or decode. It's a representation of the current word trying to find out which other parts of the sequence are relevant to it.

Imagine a reader comes to a library to find the children's books, this is the Query (Q), as shown in Figure 3.18.

In the library all books are organized in categories (the Key) and titles (the Value).

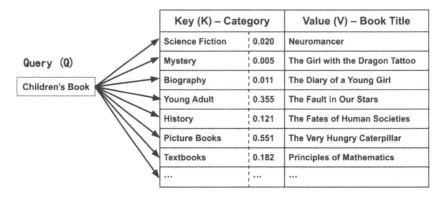

Key (K) – Category		Value (V) – Book Title
Science Fiction	0.020	Neuromancer
Mystery	0.005	The Girl with the Dragon Tattoo
Biography	0.011	The Diary of a Young Girl
Young Adult	0.355	The Fault in Our Stars
History	0.121	The Fates of Human Societies
Picture Books	0.551	The Very Hungry Caterpillar
Textbooks	0.182	Principles of Mathematics
...	...	...

Figure 3.18 Example of Query (Q), Key (K) and Value (V)

For example, in *Science Fiction* categories there is a number of titles, such as *Neuromancer*; and in *Young Adult* there is *Fault in Our Starts*, and so on. The categories are Keys (K), the corresponding titles are Values (V).

Now the Attention mechanism is to find a most relevant book titles based on the Query (Q), which in this case is the *Children's Book*. A scaled dot-product is applied on Q and K, we obtain the weighted scores in the dotted column in Figure 3.18, which means the relationships of each category with the reader's query, for example *Picture Books* has 0.551, *Young Adult* has 0.355, these two are most relevant to the query, other categories like *Mystery*, *Science Fiction*, etc. have smaller scores. The weighted scores are normalized and sum up to 1.0 with the Softmax operation.

We have found the most relevant categories in terms of weighted scores, do another dot product with the book titles (Values), we will retrieve the most relevant book titles.

This analogy will help you to better understand the attention mechanism, here the Query (Q), Key (K) and Value (V) are derived from the same input sequence, therefore this is also called Self-Attention.

Scaled Dot-Product Attention mechanism is a cornerstone of the Transformer architecture, enabling Transformers to dynamically weigh the importance of sequence elements. By allowing the model to effectively capture the relationships and dependencies between different elements in the input sequence, the attention mechanism has enabled Transformers to outperform traditional sequence-to-sequence models, particularly in tasks that require long-range understanding and contextual reasoning.

3.7 Mask

The Mask shown in Figure 3.12 also plays a crucial role in the Scaled Dot-Product Attention mechanism, ensuring the appropriate flow of information and preserving the desired properties of the attention computation.

There are two types of Masks in the Transformer model, Subsequence Mask and Padding Mask.

Subsequence Mask (Lookahead Mask)

After the attention score is calculated as Figure 3.14, the relationships between each word are obtained. The idea of the Transformer model is to predict the next word from the previous existing words, meaning when we have the first word "The", it predicts the next one which is "sky"; when we have the words "The sky", it predicts the next one "is", and so on:

The -> sky

The sky -> is

The sky is -> blue

It always makes prediction based on the previous words. So when calculate the relationships in the attention, we do not want a word to interact with any future words, for example we want the relationships of the word "is" with "The", "sky" and "is" (itself), and don't want "is" related with "blue", because "blue" is the future words which should be predicted by the model.

Therefore, a Subsequence Mask, or Lookahead Mask, is to prevent the model from "cheating" by looking at the future tokens, it is created and applied to the Attention Score, like Figure 3.19:

	The	sky	is	blue
The	22.259	mask	mask	mask
sky	-0.844	23.255	mask	mask
is	-0.104	1.194	21.158	mask
blue	0.480	-0.190	0.484	23.017

Figure 3.19 Masks on Attention Score

After a Subsequence Mask is applied, "The" only interact with itself because it's the first token without any previous ones; "sky" only interacts with "The" and "sky", which are the previous and itself; "is" interacts with "The", "sky" and "is", and so on. The masks ensure any word only interacts with its previous words, not the future ones.

The mask is an upper triangle matrix where every element above the diagonal is masked. As introduced in Section 2.2, `torch.triu()` function is used to create an upper triangle matrix:

```
1    mask = torch.triu(torch.ones(4,4), diagonal=1)
2    mask.bool()
```

`mask.bool()` function is used to convert the upper triangle matrix to boolean values, then the mask is generated as:

```
tensor([[False,  True,   True,   True],
        [False, False,   True,   True],
        [False, False, False,   True],
        [False, False, False, False]])
```

We have also introduced Softmax related basic operations in Section 2.4, to recap:

$$e^{-\infty} = 0$$

If the "mask" in Figure 3.19 is replaced with negative infinity $-\infty$, or a very large negative number like -1e9 (-10^9), it will become 0 after Softmax. This is the idea of Subsequence Mask.

Use `masked_fill_()` function to fill those True values with $-\infty$,

```
3    logits = logits.masked_fill_(mask, -float('inf'))
```

The results:

```
tensor([[22.259,    -inf,    -inf,    -inf],
        [-0.844, 23.255,    -inf,    -inf],
        [-0.104,  1.194, 21.158,    -inf],
        [ 0.480, -0.190,  0.484, 23.017]])
```

The Attention Score after masks becomes:

	The	sky	is	blue
The	22.259	-∞	-∞	-∞
sky	-0.844	23.255	-∞	-∞
is	-0.104	1.194	21.158	-∞
blue	0.480	-0.190	0.484	23.017

Figure 3.20 Attention Score with Masks Applied

After the Softmax is applied, all $-\infty$ become 0, with several rounds of training iterations, the results look something like below:

```
tensor([[1.0000, 0.0000, 0.0000, 0.0000],
        [0.1240, 0.8760, 0.0000, 0.0000],
        [0.1706, 0.1780, 0.6514, 0.0000],
        [0.2641, 0.1422, 0.1076, 0.4861]])
```

Which is shown in Figure 3.21

	The	sky	is	blue	sum
The	1.0000	0.000	0.000	0.000	1.000
sky	0.1240	0.8760	0.000	0.000	1.000
is	0.1706	0.1780	0.6514	0.000	1.000
blue	0.2641	0.1422	0.1076	0.4861	1.000

Figure 3.21 Attention Weights with Masks Applied

This means any word in the sequence only has relationships with previous words, not the future words. The future words will be predicted by the Transformer model.

Padding Mask

Another type of masks is Padding Mask, which is used to exclude irrelevant data in the padded sequences. As mentioned earlier, the amount of training data will be huge for the Transformer model, for the efficiency of computation the data is processed in batches, instead of one by one, because the computer hardware especially GPUs are designed to perform operations on multiple data points in parallel efficiently.

We have introduced the idea when preparing the batched dataset in Section 3.1.

The dataset consists of many sequences in variable lengths, they are rarely in the same length. When load multiple sequences in a batch, it's important to make them same length because PyTorch framework requires the input tensors to have a consistent shape to perform batch operations.

As an example, look at the below sequences:

The sky is blue
It's a clear day with blue sky
It is such a blue sky
The sky is brilliant beautiful blue

When preparing the dataset in Section 3.1, a special token <PAD> is added
to the end of the shorter ones, as the result all are in the same length.

The	sky	is	blue	<PAD>	<PAD>	<PAD>
It's	a	clear	day	with	blue	sky
It	is	such	a	blue	sky	<PAD>
The	sky	is	brilliant	beautiful	blue	<PAD>

Figure 3.22 Sequences with Padding

The Padding Mask will mask out the <PAD> token in the data, because it
should not be involved in calculating the Attention.

The mask is created like below:

False	False	False	False	True	True	True
False	False	False	False	False	False	False
False	False	False	False	False	False	True
False	False	False	False	False	False	True

Figure 3.23 Padding Mask

When the words are converted to tokens and the padding mask is applied,
the masked value will be filled with $-\infty$, or a very large negative number
like -1e9 (-10^9), then it becomes:

26	37	142	135	$-\infty$	$-\infty$	$-\infty$
26	95	36	91	96	140	34
18	113	62	153	51	8	$-\infty$
18	62	117	93	144	156	$-\infty$

Figure 3.24 Sequence Tokens with Padding Mask Applied

When performing the calculation of attention, the padding mask is applied
to zero out the effect of the padding tokens, effectively treating the
padding tokens as if they didn't exist.

Same as the Subsequence Mask discussed earlier, the mask is applied with
a negative infinity $-\infty$ before Softmax operation in the attention
calculation. The positions with negative infinity $-\infty$ will yield a zero when

Softmax is applied, thus ignoring the attention score on the padding positions.

The previous section introduced the Scaled Dot-Product Attention, and this section introduced the Masks. Here is the PyTorch codes to implement the Scaled Dot-Product Attention with Masks:

```
1    class ScaledDotProductAttention(nn.Module):
2      def __init__(self, dropout=0.2):
3        super(ScaledDotProductAttention, self).__init__()
4        self.dropout = nn.Dropout(p=dropout)
5
6      def forward(self, Q, K, V, mask=None):
7        attn_logits = torch.matmul(Q, K.transpose(-1, -2))
8        attn_logits = attn_logits / np.sqrt(d_k)
9        if mask is not None:
10         attn_logits = attn_logits.masked_fill_(
11                               mask, -float('inf'))
12        scores = nn.Softmax(dim=-1)(attn_logits)
13        scores = self.dropout(scores)
14        attention = torch.matmul(scores, V)
15        return attention, scores
16
17   class Mask(nn.Module):
18     def get_attn_pad_mask(self, seq_q, seq_k, pad=0):
19       batch_size, len_q = seq_q.size()
20       batch_size, len_k = seq_k.size()
21       pad_attn_mask = seq_k.data.eq(pad).unsqueeze(1)
22       return pad_attn_mask.expand(batch_size, len_q, len_k)
23
24     def get_attn_subsequence_mask(self, seq):
25       attn_shape = [seq.size(0), seq.size(1), seq.size(1)]
26       subsequence_mask = torch.triu(torch.ones(attn_shape),
27                                diagonal=1)
28       subsequence_mask.bool()
29       return subsequence_mask
```

Line 1 to 15 define a class `ScaledDotProductAttention`, Line 2 to 4 define `__init__()` method, similarly to previous ones a Dropout layer is added to reduce the overfit of the model.

Line 6 to 15 define the `forward` method that implement the algorithms of Scaled Dot-Product Attention. Line 7 performs the matrix multiplication (`matmul`) on the Q and the transpose of K matrices, Line 8 applies the scale factor. Line 9 to 11 apply masks if presented, it fills the masked data with negative infinity −∞, which is denoted as `-float('inf')` in PyThon, alternatively you can fill it with very large negative number, such as `-1e9` (-10^9).

Line 12 is to apply Softmax along the last dimension (`dim=-1`) to obtain the score, then do a Dropout on the results to reduce overfits. Finally, do another dot product with the matrix V.

Line 17 to 29 create a class for Masks, Line 18 to 22 implement the Padding Mask based on the above discussion, replacing the pad tokens with `True` by calling `data.eq(pad)`. Line 24 to 29 implement Subsequence Mask based on the discussions above. Line 26 and 27 use `torch.triu()` to create an upper triangle matrix as introduces earlier, then Line 28 to convert it to `False` and `True` values, because PyTorch needs this format for further processing. And finally return the mask.

The Sequence mask and Padding mask are necessary tools for ensuring the integrity and relevance of the attention mechanism's output. The Sequence masks, primarily used in the decoder's self-attention layers, assign a negative infinity to the future tokens, preventing the attention mechanism from attending to future tokens.

The padding mask is used to identify the padding tokens that are added to the input sequences to ensure a consistent length, ensuring that the attention mechanism focuses solely on the meaningful elements in the input.

3.8 Multi-Head Attention

Multi-head attention is a core feature of the Transformer architecture that allows the model to jointly attend to information from different representation subspaces at different positions. Instead of performing a single Scaled Dot-Product Attention, the Transformer utilizes multiple attention heads to do this in parallel, enabling it to capture different types of relationships and dependencies within the input data.

It significantly contributes to the model's self-attention ability, as shown in Figure 3.25.

The idea behind Multi-Head Attention is to break down the original attention (Scaled Dot-Product Attention) into multiple "heads", each of which can focus on different parts of the input sequence and learn distinct attention patterns. These heads are not just repetitions; they are parameterized differently and hence can pick up on a range of features or contextual meanings within the input.

After that, the output of each head is concatenated and linearly transformed to obtain the final output.

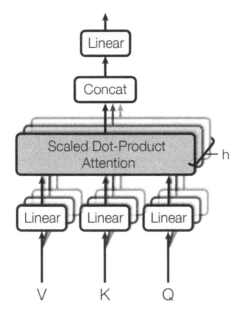

Figure 3.25 Multi-Head Attention
Source from: Attention is All You Need [1], Vaswani et al, 2017.

Based on the paper:

> *Instead of performing a single attention function with d_{model}-dimensional keys, values and queries, we found it beneficial to linearly project the queries, keys and values h times with different, learned linear projections to d_k, d_k and d_v dimensions, respectively. On each of these projected versions of queries, keys and values we then perform the attention function in parallel, yielding d_v-*

dimensional output values. These are concatenated and once again projected, resulting in the final values.

From Attention is All You Need [1], Vaswani et al, 2017

What does this mean in simpler terms? Each head is essentially processing the input information in different subspaces (or 'perspective'), and by doing so, it allows the model to capture different types of relationships in the data. For example, one head might learn to pay attention to the syntactic structure of a sentence, while another might focus more on the semantics.

To recap the previous two sections about Scaled Dot-Product Attention and Mask, which purpose is to find the amount of "attention" a token needs to pay to all other tokens in the input sequence. To calculate it, we take the dot product of the query and key matrices, and scale it down by the square root of their dimensionality, followed by a Softmax function for normalization.

Now, onto Multi-Head Attention, the purpose it is to enable the Transformer to focus on different positions and capture a variety of complex patterns. This is done by applying the attention mechanism multiple instances in parallel, which are the so-called 'heads'.

Another advantage is that because the attention is computationally expensive especially for huge amount of data and complex models like GPT, to break it down to multi-heads will help the parallel processing that can significantly improve the efficiency of computation.

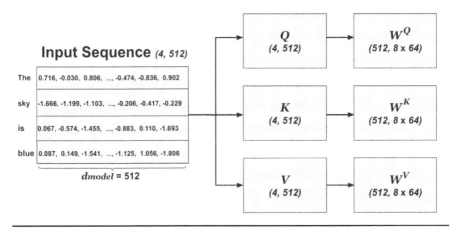

Figure 3.26 Linear Projections in Multi-Head Attention

Based on the paper, the Multi-head Attention is defined as:

$$\text{MultiHead}(Q, K, V) = \text{Concat}(head_1, head_2, \ldots, head_h)W^O$$
$$head_i = \text{Attention}(QW_i^Q, KW_i^K, VW_i^V)$$

There are several steps involved in calculating the Multi-Head Attention,

Linear Projections: The embedded input sequence is duplicated into three matrices, query Q, key K, and value V. Then linear projection layers are transforming the query Q, key K, and value V before the actual attention mechanism is applied. As the paper suggested the number of heads $h=8$, d_{model} = 512, $d_k = d_v = d_{model} / h$ = 64, then the Linear Projections are as Figure 3.26.

After the Linear Projections, the size of W^Q, W^K and W^V are $(d_{model}, h \times d_k)$ which is (512, 8×64) = (512, 512).

Then break them down to multiple heads, here the number of heads is h = 8. Each head is (d_{model}, d_k), which is (512, 64), as shown in Figure 3.27:

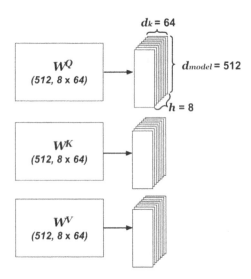

Figure 3.27 Multi Heads for W^Q, W^K and W^V

Scaled Dot-Product Attention: For each head, calculate QW^Q, KW^K and VW^V, as shown in Figure 3.28.

Then perform the Scaled Dot-Product Attention on QW^Q, KW^K and VW^V for each head independently, as described in Section 3.6.

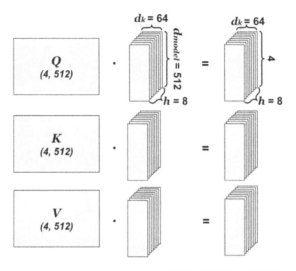

Figure 3.28 Multi Heads for QW^Q, KW^K and VW^V

The purpose of multi-head attention is to allow the model to focus on different parts of the input when generating the output. Each "head" in the multi-head attention represents a unique learned linear transformation of the input, and different heads will specialize in paying attention to different types of information.

For example, some words might have different meaning based on the contexts, such as the word "*light*", it could be a noun:

the **light** of sunshine

It could also mean something is not heavy:

it's very **light**

And it can also be a verb such as:

to **light** the fire

The different head will be able to capture these different meanings for the same word.

Multi-head attention enables the model to capture various aspects of word meaning and sentence structure. When processing a sentence, some heads might focus on individual words and their meanings, while others might recognize more complex relationships between words. This makes these models extremely effective at sophisticated natural language tasks.

Concatenation and Final Linear Projection: The individual attention outputs are concatenated, the final linear projection layer is to make sure the output is in the correct size, in this case (4, 512), as shown in Figure 3.29

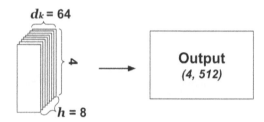

Figure 3.29 Concatenation and Final Linear Projection

As we described in Section 3.6, the output of Scaled Dot-Product Attention is the same size as the input, but captures the relationship between the tokens, or words. Now the output of Multi-Head Attention is also the same size as the input, it not only captures the relationships between tokens, but also captures different aspects of the tokens.

Here are the PyTorch implementation of Multi-Head Attention:

```
1    class MultiHeadAttention(nn.Module):
2      def __init__(self, d_model=d_model, n_heads=n_heads,
3                   d_k=d_k, d_v=d_v, dropout=0.2):
4        super(MultiHeadAttention, self).__init__()
5        self.d_model, self.n_heads = d_model, n_heads
6        self.d_k, self.d_v = d_k, d_v
7        self.W_Q = nn.Linear(d_model, self.d_k * self.n_heads)
8        self.W_K = nn.Linear(d_model, self.d_k * self.n_heads)
9        self.W_V = nn.Linear(d_model, self.d_v * self.n_heads)
10       self.fc = nn.Linear(self.n_heads * self.d_v, d_model)
11       self.ln = LayerNorm(self.d_model)
12       self.dropout = nn.Dropout(p=dropout)
13
```

```
14    def forward(self, input_Q, input_K, input_V, attn_mask):
15        n_heads, d_k, d_v = self.n_heads, self.d_k, self.d_v
16        residual, batch_size = input_Q, input_Q.size(0)
17        Q = self.W_Q(input_Q).view(batch_size, -1, n_heads, d_k)
18        Q = Q.transpose(1, 2)
19        K = self.W_K(input_K).view(batch_size, -1, n_heads, d_k)
20        K = K.transpose(1, 2)
21        V = self.W_V(input_V).view(batch_size, -1, n_heads, d_v)
22        V = V.transpose(1, 2)
23        attn_mask = attn_mask.unsqueeze(1).repeat(1,n_heads,1,1)
24        context, attn = ScaledDotProductAttention()(Q, K, V,
25                                                    attn_mask)
26        context = context.transpose(1, 2)
27                        .reshape(batch_size, -1, n_heads * d_v)
28        output = self.dropout(self.fc(context))
29        return self.ln(output + residual), attn
```

Line 2 to 12 define __init__() function, the input parameters are:

```
d_model: (=512)
n_heads: (=8)
d_k: (=64)
d_v: (=64)
dropout: (default=0.2)
```

Line 7, 8 and 9 define the linear transformation for W^Q, W^K and W^V, as illustrated in Figure 3.26.

Line 10 defines the final linear transformation layer. Line 11 defines the LayerNorm layer, and Line 12 defines the Dropout layer to reduce overfitting.

Line 14 to 29 define `forward()` function, the input parameters are:

```
input_Q: (batch_size, len_q, d_model)
input_K: (batch_size, len_k, d_model)
input_V: (batch_size, len_v, d_model)
attn_mask: (batch_size, len_seq, len_seq)
```

In the implementation, it sounds like complicated and difficult to break the sequence down to multiple heads and then concatenate them together. Thanks to PyTorch, it's as easy as reshaping the tensor to different dimensions. Say there is an input tensor **x** with size of (batch_size, len_seq, d_model), we can break it into multi-head by using tensor.view() function:

```
x.view(batch_size, -1, n_heads, d_k)
```

This will reshape x to add one dimension, because d_model=n_heads×d_k, it breaks the last dimension into two dimensions, n_head and d_k. the second parameter -1 means we don't care about that dimension, PyTorch will calculate it for us. Line 17, 19 and 21 use this technique to break them into multiple heads.

Now Q, K and V are all in the size of:

```
(batch_size, seq_len, n_heads, d_k)
```

Then we should transpose them against the 1st and 2nd dimension to become:

```
(batch_size, n_heads, seq_len, d_k)
```

This is because the Scaled Dot-Product Attention built in Section 3.6 is designed to calculate against the last two dimensions, which is (seq_len, d_k) as illustrated in Figure 3.28, and the calculation supports multiple dimensions, so this time we pass the 4-dimensional tensor, it will calculate the attention correctly. Line 18, 20 and 22 do this transpose operation.

Line 23 is to extend the attn_mask to 4-dimensional tensor, because all other matrices are in 4-dimensional. The original size of the mask is:

```
(batch_size, len_seq, len_seq)
```

Line 23 first unsqueeze it to add a dimension in the position of 1, it becomes:

```
(batch_size, 1, len_seq, len_seq)
```

Then repeat that dimension n_heads times, it becomes:

```
(batch_size, n-heads, len_seq, len_seq)
```

Line 24 and 25 send Q, K , V, and attn_mask to Scaled Dot-Product Attention layer for calculation.

After the calculation, Line 26 is to transpose the result back to the size of:

```
(batch_size, seq_len, n_heads, d_k)
```

then use same technique to reshape the tensor and merge the last two dimensions to one:

```
x.reshape(batch_size, -1, n_heads * d_k)
```

Note, `d_model` = `n_heads` × `d_k`, so we obtain the same size as the original input tensor, as the result of Line 27:

```
(batch_size, seq_len, d_model)
```

Line 28 is to apply the final linear projection layer to make sure that `n_heads` × `d_k` is linear transformed to `d_model`. In fact we have already make them happen when choosing the values of `n_heads` and `d_k`, so this step is redundant. Line 28 also do a Dropout to reduce the overfit.

Line 29 is to apply the Add & Norm layer on the Multi-Head Attention results.

To recap, the input to Multi-Head Attention layer are Q, K and V which all are duplicated from the input sequence and in the size of:

```
(batch_size, seq_len, d_model)
```

After the calculation, the output is also in the same size, but the embedded vectors in the last dimension capture the information of not only the relationships to other tokens, but also the different aspect of the same token.

This process dramatically improves the Transformer's efficiency in understanding and generating text by allowing it to focus on different parts of the input simultaneously. This makes the Transformer model remarkably useful in various Natural Language Processing (NLP) tasks, such as translation, document summarization, named entity recognition, etc.

3.9 Encoder Layer and Encoder

The Encoder is to process the input sequences, understand the context of tokens, or words, in the input sequence, and transform the understanding into high-dimensional vector representations, ready for the Decoder to process and generate the outputs. I.e., the output of the Encoder will be fed into the Decoder as input.

As shown as Figure 3.30, the Encoder is the left part of the Transformer architecture.

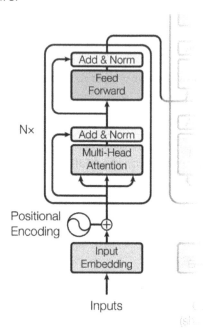

Figure 3.30 Encoder and Encoder Layer
Source from: Attention is All You Need [1], Vaswani et al, 2017. Modified by author.

Based on the paper:

The encoder is composed of a stack of N = 6 identical layers. Each layer has two sub-layers. The first is a multi-head self-attention mechanism, and the second is a simple, position wise fully connected feed-forward network. We employ a residual connection [11] around each of the two sub-layers, followed by layer normalization [1]. That is, the output of each sub-layer is LayerNorm(x + Sublayer(x)), where Sublayer(x) is the function implemented by the sub-layer itself. To facilitate these residual connections, all sub-layers in the model, as well as the embedding layers, produce outputs of dimension d_{model} = 512.

From Attention is All You Need [1], Vaswani et al, 2017

The Encoder is composed of N Encoder Layers which is highlighted in Figure 3.30, the paper suggests N=6, meaning there are 6 identical layers, each of which has two sub-layers, a Multi-Head Attention and a Feed Forward, each followed by an Add & Norm layer.

Multi-Head Attention enables the model to focus on different positions of the input sequence simultaneously. The input sequence is projected to queries (Q), keys (K) and values (V), they become the input of the Multi-Head Attention, see Section 3.8. There is an Add & Norm layer following it.

Feed-Forward consists of two linear transformations with a ReLU activation in between, see Section 3.5. It is applied position-wise, meaning separately and identically to each position. There is also an Add & Norm layer following this layer.

The inputs from the bottom go through the Input Embedding and Positional Encoding sub-layers, then feed to the N identical Encoder Layers.

Since we have already built all the building blocks, now assemble the Encoder Layer:

```
1    class EncoderLayer(nn.Module):
2      def __init__(self):
3        super(EncoderLayer, self).__init__()
4        self.enc_self_attn = MultiHeadAttention()
5        self.pos_ffn = FeedForward(d_ff)
6
7      def forward(self, enc_inputs, enc_self_attn_mask):
8        enc_outputs,attn = self.enc_self_attn(enc_inputs,
9                                              enc_inputs,
10                                             enc_inputs,
11                                      enc_self_attn_mask)
12        enc_outputs = self.pos_ffn(enc_outputs)
13        return enc_outputs, attn
```

Line 2 to 5 define __init__() function, it just simply instantiates `MultiHeadAttention` class and `FeedForward` class respectively in Line 4 and 5.

Line 7 to 13 define `forward()` function, the input parameters are:

```
enc_inputs: (batch_size, src_len, d_model)
enc_self_attn_mask: (batch_size, src_len, src_len)
```

Line 8 to 11 duplicate `enc_inputs` three times and passed to `MultiHeadAttention` as Q, K and V, also pass the attention mask `enc_self_attn_mask`.

Line 12 take output of `MultiHeadAttention`, which is the same size as `enc_inputs`, and send to `FeedForward` layer.

The Add & Norm layer is already added in both `MultiHeadAttention` and `FeedForward` classes, so no need to add it here.

The output size of this Encoder Layer is exactly same as that of the input.

The Encoder looks like Figure 3.31:

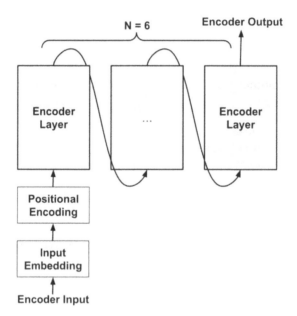

Figure 3.31 Encoder

The Encoder Input data goes through the Input Embedding, then Positional Encoding, and feeds to the first Encoder Layer, then the output feeds to the second Encoder Layer, and so on, there are totally $N = 6$ Encoder Layers. The size of Encoder Output is same as that of Encoder Input.

```
14    class Encoder(nn.Module):
15        def __init__(self):
```

```
16          super(Encoder, self).__init__()
17          self.src_emb = nn.Embedding(vocab_size, d_model)
18          self.pos_emb = PositionalEncoding(d_model, vocab_size)
19          self.layers = nn.ModuleList(
20                      [EncoderLayer() for _ in range(n_layers)])
21          self.mask = Mask()
22
23      def forward(self, enc_inputs):
24          enc_outputs = self.src_emb(enc_inputs)
25          enc_outputs = self.pos_emb(enc_outputs)
26          enc_self_attn_mask = self.mask.get_attn_pad_mask
27                              (enc_inputs, enc_inputs)
28          for layer in self.layers:
29            enc_outputs = layer(enc_outputs, enc_self_attn_mask)
30          return enc_outputs
```

Line 15 to 21 define __init__() function, Line 17 creates an Embedding layer, and Line 18 creates a PositionalEncoding. Line 19 and 20 create a model list that includes n_layers of EncoderLayer. Line 21 creates an instance of Mask class.

Line 23 to 31 define forward() function, which takes input parameter of:

```
enc_inputs: (batch_size, seq_len)
```

Line 24 does the embedding, the output size becomes:

```
(batch_size, seq_len, d_model)
```

Line 25 does the positional encoding as introduced in Section 3.3. And Line 26 and 27 obtain the attention mask based on enc_inputs as Section 3.7, the mask's size is:

```
(batch_size, src_len, src_len)
```

Then the data goes to the Encoder Layers in Line 28 and 29, the output of previous layer becomes input of next layer until all layers are iterated.

Finally Line 30 returns the output as below:

```
enc_outputs: (batch_size, seq_len, d_model)
```

In summary, the Encoder transforms the input data into a sequence of embedded vectors that hold the contextual information of each token, which the Decoder can then use to generate the desired output.

3.10 Decoder Layer and Decoder

The Decoder is responsible for generating the output data from the encoded input that it receives from the Encoder, it generates the output sequence one token at a time, using its self-attention and the attention over the Encoder's output to generate the correct output sequence. Its architecture is shown in Figure 3.32:

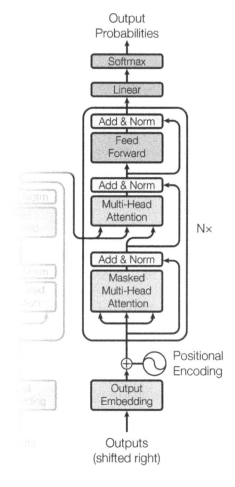

Figure 3.32 Decoder and Decoder Layers
Source from: Attention is All You Need [1], Vaswani et al, 2017. Modified by author.

The Decoder takes two types of input, the first is the output from the Encoder; the second is its own previously generated output sequences. During training, these are the target sequences but offset by one position to the right, denoted as "shifted right" in Figure 3.32.

This process is repeated for each position in the output sequence, with the outcome of each step affecting the next. The entire mechanism allows the Transformer to generate outputs that take into account both the context provided by the Encoder and the successive dependencies inherent in the output sequence.

For example, let's say there is a question and answer:

What color is the sky

The sky is blue

The question is the input to the Encoder, and the answer is the input to the Decoder at the bottom of Figure 3.32, and hopefully the Decoder can generate the same output at the top.

The first step is:

Input to Encoder: *What color is the sky*

Input to Decoder: *<SOS>*

Then the Decoder takes the result of the Encoder and the input of the Decoder, and generates a probability distribution for the next token in the sequence, and it decides to pick up the word "*The*" as next.

Output of Decoder: *The*

Next step:

Input to Encoder: *What color is the sky*

Input to Decoder: *<SOS> The*

Then the Decoder decides next word as output:

Output of Decoder: *sky*

Then next step:

Input to Encoder: *What color is the sky*

Input to Decoder: *<SOS> The sky*

Output of Decoder: *is*

And so on.

The Decoder keep generating next token until it meets the <EOS> token, or a pre-defined max length of the sequence. So the last step would be:

Input to Encoder: *What color is the sky*

Input to Decoder: *<SOS> The sky is blue*

Output of Decoder: *<EOS>*

This is why when preparing the dataset in Section 3.1, we should add the special tokens of *<SOS>* and *<EOS>* to the sequences.

As shown in Figure 3.32, same as the Encoder, the Decoder is composed of a stack of N=6 identical layers, each of them is consist of three main components:

Masked Multi-Head Attention allows the decoder to focus on different parts of the input sequences for the decoder. Unlike the one for the Encoder, the attention for the Decoder is masked to prevent the subsequent tokens from attending the calculation, see the Subsequence Mask in Section 3.7. This Masked Multi-Head Attention ensures that the predictions for a particular token can only depend on the previous outputs before it.

To recap, the Subsequence Mask is something like:

```
tensor([[False,   True,    True,    True],
        [False, False,    True,    True],
        [False, False, False,    True],
        [False, False, False, False]])
```

The upper triangle part is masked with `True`, then the attention result is something like below, also see Figure 3.21.

```
tensor([[1.0000, 0.0000, 0.0000, 0.0000],
        [0.1240, 0.8760, 0.0000, 0.0000],
        [0.1706, 0.1780, 0.6514, 0.0000],
        [0.2641, 0.1422, 0.1076, 0.4861] )
```

The masked areas are all zeros, this ensures that a token is only referencing the previous tokens in the sequence, not the future ones.

There is an Add & Norm layer following this layer.

Multi-Head Attention combines the inputs from both the Encoder and the Decoder, it allows the Decoder focus on the different parts of both inputs. This is the place that the Encoder outputs are fed into the Decoder, and the attention is calculated on both inputs. Therefore this is not self-attention any more, it's a cross-attention, the output of Encoder becomes Key (K) and Value (V), and the output of previous step of the Decoder becomes Query (Q).

This is especially useful for the task such as translation, or questions & answers. For example, the translation from Japanese to English, Japanese texts are original inputs to the Encoder, and English texts are target inputs to the Decoder, both inputs are combined here to attend the cross-attention calculation, the Key and Value are from the Encoder, the Query from the Decoder, the original Japanese texts and the target English texts are joined here for attention calculations. And then the Decoder will generate outputs of English target texts.

There is also an Add & Norm layer following this layer.

Feed-Forward is a fully connected neural network that applies linear transformations to the output of the previous Multi-Head Attention layer, a ReLU activation function is applied here. The feed-forward network is applied position-wise, meaning separately and identically to each position. There is also an Add & Norm layer following this layer.

Here is the implementation of Decoder Layer:

```
1    class DecoderLayer(nn.Module):
2      def __init__(self):
3        super(DecoderLayer, self).__init__()
4        self.dec_self_attn = MultiHeadAttention()
5        self.dec_enc_attn = MultiHeadAttention()
6        self.pos_ffn = FeedForward(d_ff)
7
8      def forward(self, dec_inputs, enc_outputs,
9                  dec_self_attn_mask, dec_enc_attn_mask):
10       dec_outputs, _ = self.dec_self_attn(dec_inputs,
```

```
11                                          dec_inputs,
12                                          dec_inputs,
13                                          dec_self_attn_mask)
14      dec_outputs, _ = self.dec_enc_attn(dec_outputs,
15                                          enc_outputs,
16                                          enc_outputs,
17                                          dec_enc_attn_mask)
18      dec_outputs = self.pos_ffn(dec_outputs)
19      # [batch_size, tgt_len, d_model]
20      return dec_outputs
```

Line 2 to 6 define the __init__() function, two Multi-Head Attention layers are defined in Line 4 and 5, and one Feed Forward layer is defined in Line 6.

Line 8 to 20 define the `forward()` function, the input parameters are:

```
dec_inputs:   (batch_size, len_target, d_model)
enc_outputs:  (batch_size, len_source, d_model)
dec_self_attn_mask: (batch_size, len_target, len_target)
dec_enc_attn_mask:  (batch_size, len_target, len_source)
```

Here `dec_inputs` is the target sequence for the input of the Decoder, `len_target` is the length.

`enc_outputs` is the outputs from the Encoder, `len_source` is the length of the source sequence.

Line 10 to 13 invoke the first Masked Multi-Head Attention, as shown in Figure 3.32, the decoder input is duplicated to three inputs to the Masked Multi-Head Attention, which are queries (Q), keys (K) and values (V), they are the input parameters of this function, and the decoder self-attention mask is also a input parameter.

Line 14 to 17 invoke the second Multi-Head Attention, the queries (Q) come from the Decoder, which is the output of the first Masked Multi-Head Attention; while the keys (K) and values (V) are coming from the outputs of the Encoder. This layer will combine both the Encoder and the Decoder to calculate the attention.

Line 18 applies the Feed Forward to the outputs, and Line 20 returns the outputs. The output parameter is:

```
dec_outputs: (batch_size, len_target, d_model)
```

The Decoder is similar to the Encoder, the inputs of decoder go through the Embedding, Positional Encoding, and then a stack of *N*=6 Decoder Layers, the output of each Decoder Layer becomes the input of the next, as shown in Figure 3.33, finally the outputs go through a Linear and then a Softmax layer.

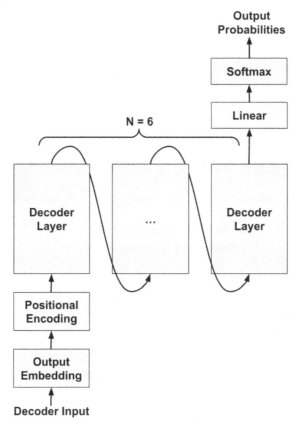

Figure 3.33 Decoder

The Output Embedding and Positional Encoding are exactly same as what we did for Encoder. The stack of Decoder Layers is also similar to that of Encoder. Here is the code for the Decoder:

```
21    class Decoder(nn.Module):
22        def __init__(self):
23            super(Decoder, self).__init__()
```

```
24          self.tgt_emb = nn.Embedding(vocab_size, d_model)
25          self.pos_emb = PositionalEncoding(d_model, vocab_size )
26          self.layers = nn.ModuleList([DecoderLayer()
27                                  for _ in range(n_layers)])
28          self.mask = Mask()
29
30      def forward(self, dec_inputs, enc_inputs, enc_outputs):
31          dec_outputs = self.tgt_emb(dec_inputs)
32          dec_outputs = self.pos_emb(dec_outputs)
33          # dec_outputs: [batch_size, tgt_len, d_model]
34
35          dec_attn_pad_mask = self.mask.get_attn_pad_mask
36                          (dec_inputs, dec_inputs)
37          dec_attn_sub_mask = self.mask.get_attn_subsequence_mask
38                          (dec_inputs)
39          dec_attn_mask = torch.gt((dec_attn_pad_mask +
40                              dec_attn_sub_mask), 0)
41          dec_enc_attn_mask = self.mask.get_attn_pad_mask
42                          (dec_inputs, enc_inputs)
43          # dec_enc_attn_mask: [batc_size, tgt_len, src_len]
44
45          for layer in self.layers:
46              dec_outputs = layer(dec_outputs,
47                                  enc_outputs,
48                                  dec_attn_mask,
49                                  dec_enc_attn_mask)
50          # dec_outputs: [batch_size, tgt_len, d_model]
51          return dec_outputs
```

Line 22 to 26 define the __init__() function, Line 24 defines the Embedding layer as nn.Embedding(), and Line 25 defines the Positional Encoding layer as PositionalEncoding() which we have implemented in Section 3.3. Line 26 and 27 define the stack of Decoder Layers in a nn.ModuleList which includes n_layers of DecoderLayer(). Line 28 instantiates a Mask() class.

Line 30 to 51 define the forward() function, the input parameters are:

```
dec_inputs:   (batch_size, len_target)
enc_inputs:   (batch_size, len_source)
enc_outputs:  (batch_size, len_source, d_model)
```

Line 31 performs the embedding on `dec_inputs`, and Line 32 for positional encoding, the output after these two steps is:

```
dec_outputs: (batch_size, len_target, d_model)
```

Line 35, 36 create padding mask, Line 37, 38 create subsequence mask on `dec_intputs`, and Line 39, 40 add them together to obtain an attention mask for decoder `dec_attn_mask`.

Then Line 41 and 42 create an attention mask for both decoder and encoder `dec_enc_attn_mask` using both `dec_inputs` and `enc_inputs`. The size of this mask is:

```
dec_enc_attn_mask: (batch_size, len_target, len_source)
```

Line 45 to 49 go through the stack of Decoder Layers, the output of a layer becomes the input the next. The other three parameters `enc_outputs`, `dec_attn_mask`, and `dec_enc_attn_mask` are same for all layers.

The output of the Decoder is:

```
dec_outputs: (batch_size, len_target, d_model)
```

The Linear and Softmax layers at the top of Figure 3.33 will be explained later, it's used in the Inference process of the Transformer.

In summary, the purpose of the Decoder is to generate output sequence from the encoded input sequence. The layers in the Decoder provide context-sensitive representations of the output sequence, informed both by the input sequence and the preceding elements of the output sequence, building up the output incrementally as it processes the sequence.

3.11 Transformer

The Transformer includes two parts, the Encoder and the Decoder, as shown in Figure 3.1 in the beginning of this chapter. Based on the paper:

Most competitive neural sequence transduction models have an encoder-decoder structure [5, 2, 35]. Here, the encoder maps an input sequence of symbol representations (x_1, ..., x_n) to a sequence of continuous representations

z = (z₁, ..., zₙ). Given z, the decoder then generates an output sequence (y₁, ...,
yₘ) of symbols one element at a time. At each step the model is auto-
regressive [10], consuming the previously generated symbols as additional
input when generating the next.
The Transformer follows this overall architecture using stacked self-attention
and point-wise, fully connected layers for both the encoder and decoder,
shown in the left and right halves of Figure 1, respectively.

From Attention is All You Need[1], Vaswani et al, 2017

We have already built the Encoder and the Decoder, now put them together to create a `Transformer` class.

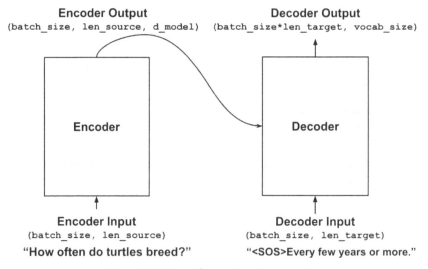

Figure 3.34 Transformer Implementation

As shown in Figure 3.34, the input sequence is sent to Encoder and its output is fed to the Decoder. The target sequence is sent to the Decoder and generate the Decoder output.

Our dataset is a number of question-answer pairs, the questions are source sequences that go to the Encoder:

"How often do turtles breed?"

Then the answers are target sequences, and sent to the Decoder, the special token is added to the beginning of the target sequences:

"<SOS>Every few years or more."

The code is as below:

```
1    class Transformer(nn.Module):
2      def __init__(self):
3        super(Transformer, self).__init__()
4        self.encoder = Encoder().to(device)
5        self.decoder = Decoder().to(device)
6        self.projection = nn.Linear(
7              d_model, vocab_size, bias=False).to(device)
8        self.softmax = nn.Softmax(dim=-1)
9      def forward(self, enc_inputs, dec_inputs):
10       enc_outputs = self.encoder(enc_inputs)
11       # enc_outputs: [batch_size, src_len, d_model]
12       dec_outputs = self.decoder(dec_inputs,
13                           enc_inputs, enc_outputs)
14       # dec_outputs: [batch_size, tgt_len, d_model]
15       dec_logits = self.projection(dec_outputs)
16       # dec_logits: [batch_size, tgt_len, vocab_size]
17       return dec_logits.view(-1, dec_logits.size(-1))
18       # outputs: [batch_size * tgt_len, vocab_size]
```

Line 2 to 8 define __init__() function, Line 4 and 5 define Encoder and Decoder respectively, to(device) specifies using GPUs or CPUs depends on the hardware availability.

Line 6 and 7 define the final Linear Transformation layer, it transforms the Decoder output from:

```
(batch_size, len_target, d_model)
```

to:

```
(batch_size, len_target, vocab_size)
```

Line 8 defines a Softmax layer, it will be used later when generating output sequences.

Line 9 to 18 define forward() function, the input parameters are:

```
enc_inputs: (batch_size, len_source)
dec_inputs: (batch_size, len_target)
```

Line 10 invokes encoder with enc_inputs as input and get the output enc_outputs. Line 12 and 13 invokes decoder with dec_inputs, enc_inputs and enc_outputs as inputs, and get the output dec_outputs.

Line 15 invokes the linear transformation to transform the `dec_outputs` to:

```
(batch_size, len_target, vocab_size)
```

Line 17 reshape the output and return the results; the output of the `Transformer` is:

```
outputs: (batch_size * len_target, vocab_size)
```

How to interpret the output of the Transformer? If the batch size is 1, meaning only one sequence input to and output from the Transformer, the output is:

```
outputs: (len_target, vocab_size)
```

Say the length of target sequence is 4, vocabulary size is 8, then the outputs look like:

```
[[ 0.67, -1.74, 14.28,   0.99,   0.57,   1.12, -4.82, -1.80],
 [-0.87,  0.26,  0.67, -3.79, -4.31, -0.20, 14.81,  0.05],
 [ 0.98,  0.09, -3.96, 13.51,   0.25, -1.95,  0.94, -3.12],
 [ 1.30, -0.08,  0.85, -6.38, 14.54,  1.74, -2.65,  1.08]]
```

Each row is corresponding to a token, or a word, of the output sequence, and each row has 8 elements that correspond to the vocabulary, the elements are probability distributions for the tokens.

After the training process each row has one element that significantly larger than others, for example in the first row the third element is 14.28, which is larger than others, it means the third in vocabulary has the largest probability to be the first token (first row) of the output, say it's "*The*".

Similarly in the second row, the second last element is the largest, say the corresponding token in the vocabulary is "*sky*". And in the following two rows, the largest elements correspond to the tokens in the vocabulary are "*is*" and "*blue*". Then we obtain the output sequence:

The sky is blue

In reality the batch size is not 1, the input data are sent in multiple sequences, then the output of the Transformer has `batch_size *` `len_target` rows, meaning all sequences in the batch are listed in the rows, the Transformer generates the output in one time. The columns are the same as above, representing the probabilities of the tokens in the vocabulary.

Now we build the Transformer model:

```
19    model = Transformer().to(device)
20    total_parameter = sum(p.numel() for p in model.parameters())
21    print(f"Parameters of the model: {total_parameter:,}")
22    print(model)
```

Line 19 instantiates the `Transformer` model, and send it to `device`, which is either CPU or GPU.

Line 20 calculate the total number of parameters of the model, and Line 21 print it out:

```
Parameters of the model: 44,324,352
```

Which means there are totally 44M learnable parameters in our model.

Line 22 print out the whole structure of the `Transformer` model:

```
Transformer(
  (encoder): Encoder(
    (src_emb): Embedding(165, 512)
    (pos_emb): PositionalEncoding(
      (dropout): Dropout(p=0.1, inplace=False))
    (layers): ModuleList(
      (0-5): 6 x EncoderLayer(
        (enc_self_attn): MultiHeadAttention(
          (W_Q):Linear(in_features=512,out_features=512,bias=False)
          (W_K):Linear(in_features=512,out_features=512,bias=False)
          (W_V):Linear(in_features=512,out_features=512,bias=False)
          (fc):Linear(in_features=512,out_features=512, bias=False)
          (ln):LayerNorm()
          (dropout): Dropout(p=0.2, inplace=False))
        (pos_ffn): FeedForward(
          (fc): Sequential(
            (0):Linear(in_feature=512,out_feature=2048, bias=False)
            (1):ReLU()
            (2):Dropout(p=0.2, inplace=False)
            (3):Linear(in_feature=2048,out_feature=512,bias=False))
          (ln): LayerNorm())))
```

```
        (mask): Mask())
    (decoder): Decoder(
      (tgt_emb): Embedding(165, 512)
      (pos_emb): PositionalEncoding(
        (dropout): Dropout(p=0.1, inplace=False))
      (layers): ModuleList(
        (0-5): 6 x DecoderLayer(
          (dec_self_attn): MultiHeadAttention(
            (W_Q):Linear(in_features=512,out_features=512,bias=False)
            (W_K):Linear(in_features=512,out_features=512,bias=False)
            (W_V):Linear(in_features=512,out_features=512,bias=False)
            (fc):Linear(in_features=512,out_features=512, bias=False)
            (ln):LayerNorm()
            (dropout): Dropout(p=0.2, inplace=False) )
          (dec_enc_attn): MultiHeadAttention(
            (W_Q):Linear(in_features=512,out_features=512,bias=False)
            (W_K):Linear(in_features=512,out_features=512,bias=False)
            (W_V):Linear(in_features=512,out_features=512,bias=False)
            (fc):Linear(in_features=512,out_features=512,bias=False)
            (ln):LayerNorm()
            (dropout): Dropout(p=0.2, inplace=False))
          (pos_ffn): FeedForward(
            (fc):Sequential(
              (0):Linear(in_features=512,out_features=2048,bias=False)
              (1): ReLU()
              (2): Dropout(p=0.2,inplace=False)
              (3):Linear(in_features=2048,out_features=512,bias=False))
            (ln):LayerNorm())))
      (mask): Mask())
    (projection):Linear(in_features=512,out_features=165,bias=False)
    (softmax): Softmax(dim=-1))
```

In summary, the Transformer architecture is a deep learning model that includes an Encoder-Decoder structure, the Encoder takes the input sequence and generates a contextualized representation, while the Decoder generates the output sequence autoregressively by attending to both the Encoder outputs and the previously generated tokens.

3.12 Training

We have built the Transformer model, the next step is to train it. There are two inputs to the model, `enc_intpus` and `dec_inputs`. The former is the source sequences, in our question-answer example, it's the questions; the latter is the target sequences, it's the answers. Both of inputs are sent in batches, therefore the parameters are:

```
enc_inputs: (batch_size, len_source)
dec_inputs: (batch_size, len_target)
```

The training process is depicted in Figure 3.35, the `enc_inputs` and `dec_inputs` are fed into the Transformer, for the Encoder and Decoder respectively. The Transformer generates the outputs, which are sent to the Cross Entropy loss function, introduced in Section 2.5, to determine how close to the true label of the target sequences, the losses are generated by the function. The whole training process is to minimize the losses, and make the outputs close enough to the target sequences.

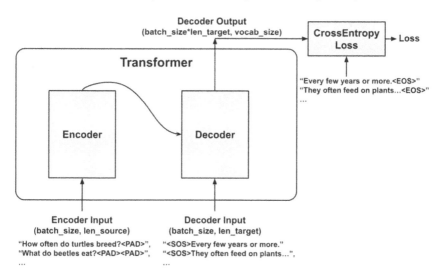

Figure 3.35 Training of the Transformer

In Section 3.1 we have prepared the dataset and the tokenization. There are three sets of data to be prepared, `enc_input, dec_input` as the input to the Transformer, `dec_output` as the true label of target sequences, that used for Cross Entropy function to compare.

For `enc_input`, we use the question texts, convert them to tokens, add padding token to the end of the shorter sequences in order to make them same length. The question texts are something like:

```
"How often do turtles breed? <PAD>...<PAD>"
"Where do sea turtles lay their eggs? <PAD>"
"What do beetles eat? <PAD>...<PAD>"
"What are the similarities between beetles ...?"
"..."
```

They are converted to below tensor:

```
enc_input:
tensor ([[ 8, 33, 18, 43, 17,  5,  0,  0,  0],
         [11, 18, 35, 43, 29, 40, 20,  5,  0],
         [10, 18, 15, 19,  5,  0,  0,  0,  0],
         [10, 14, 39, 37, 16, 15, 12, 23,  5],
         [...]])
```

As you can see the padding token is 0.

For `dec_input`, we use the answer texts, convert them to tokens, add padding token which are the same as above. As shown in Figure 3.1 -- the Transformer architecture by the paper, the data fed to the decoder should be "shifted right", it means adding a start token <sos> to the beginning of the sequence. The answer texts are something like:

```
"<SOS> Every few years or more. <PAD>...<PAD>"
"<SOS> Holes dug into mud or sand. <PAD>...<PAD>"
"<SOS> They often feed on plants and fungi. <PAD>"
"<SOS> Beetles have mouthparts similar to those ..."
"..."
```

The start of sequence token is added to every text. They are converted to:

```
dec_input:
tensor([[ 2,  7, 23, 46, 35, 29,  4,  0,  0,  0],
        [ 2,  8, 19, 27, 31, 35, 37,  4,  0,  0],
        [ 2, 10, 33, 22, 34, 36, 13, 24,  4,  0],
        [ 2,  6, 26, 30, 39, 44, 43, 32, 25,  4]
        [...])
```

The padding token is 0, and <sos> is 2. By adding a <sos> token the sequences are shifted right by one token.

For `dec_output`, it's the same as `dec_input`, the difference is instead of adding <sos> token at the beginning, add a <EOS> at the end.

```
"Every few years or more. <EOS><PAD>...<PAD>"
"Holes dug into mud or sand. <EOS><PAD>...<PAD>"
"They often feed on plants and fungi. <EOS><PAD>"
"Beetles have mouthparts similar to those ... <EOS>"
"..."
```

They are converted to:

```
dec_output:
tensor([[ 7, 23, 46, 35, 29,  4,  3,  0,  0,  0],
        [ 8, 19, 27, 31, 35, 37,  4,  3,  0,  0],
        [10, 33, 22, 34, 36, 13, 24,  4,  3,  0],
        [ 6, 26, 30, 39, 44, 43, 32, 25,  4,  3]])
```

The <EOS> token is 3, and <PAD> is 0. The idea is hoping the Transformer is learned to generate an <EOS> token at the end of output sequence, so in the future when using the model to generate sequences an <EOS> marks the end of the generation.

When training a Transformer model, same as any deep learning models, a Loss Function and an Optimizer are necessary for the learning process. The former guides the training process by providing how big the differences are from the true labels, while the latter uses this information to update the model's parameters in such a way as to reduce the differences over time. These two components provide a systematic and iterative way to learn from the data and to improve its predictions.

Here, the Cross Entropy is selected as the Loss Function, and SGD (Stochastic Gradient Descent) as the Optimizer:

```
1   learning_rate=1e-3
2   criterion = nn.CrossEntropyLoss(
3                   ignore_index=tokenizer.encode_word("<PAD>"))
4   optimizer = optim.SGD(model.parameters(),
5                   lr=learning_rate,
6                   momentum=0.99)
```

Line 2 and 3 specify the Loss Function, Line 3 specifies the <PAD> token to be ignored in the calculation, this token does not contribute to the learning process, since its purpose is to make the sequences same length for batch processing.

Line 4 to 6 specify the Optimizer, Line 5 specifies a learning rate, which is a parameter to control how much to adjust the weights of the model, the lower the value the slower the training process; the higher the value the faster the process, but might miss the optimized value. The learning rate should be fine-tuned and adjusted in a way that not too low and not too high, it should be appropriate because it affects the efficiency and outcome of the training process. For details see [13] in Reference section at the end of this book.

The training process is implemented as below:

```
7     history_loss = []
8     epochs = 100
9     for epoch in range(epochs):
10       for i, [enc_inputs, dec_inputs, dec_outputs] in
11                                    enumerate(loader):
12         enc_inputs =  enc_inputs.to(device)
13         dec_inputs =  dec_inputs.to(device)
14         dec_outputs = dec_outputs.to(device)
15         outputs = model(enc_inputs, dec_inputs)
16         loss = criterion(outputs, dec_outputs.view(-1))
17         print('Epoch:', '%d/%d' % (i+1, epoch+1),
18               'loss =', '{:.6f}'.format(loss))
19         history_loss.append(loss.item())
20
21         optimizer.zero_grad()
22         loss.backward()
23         optimizer.step()
```

Line 9 starts the loop for epochs, totally 100 epochs for this example.

Line 10 starts the loop for batches, it loads one batch at a time in this example, there are totally 16 data items, and one batch has 8 data items, there are 2 batches. Line 10 loads the three datasets from the DataLoader we built in Section 3.1.

Line 12, 13 and 14 move the three datasets to `device`, which could be CPU or GPU. The code detects the available GPUs at the beginning:

```
device = 'cuda:0' if torch.cuda.is_available() else 'cpu'
```

Line 15 invokes the Transformer model and sends `enc_inputs` and `dec_inputs` as inputs, and obtain the outputs from the model.

Line 16 invokes the Cross Entropy function with the outputs from the Transformer as the inputs, and `dec_outputs` as the true label. As mentioned earlier the size of model's output is:

```
outputs: (batch_size * len_target, vocab_size)
```

And the size of `dec_outputs` is:

```
dec_outputs: (batch_size * len_target)
```

This is the required parameters of `nn.CrossEntropyLoss()` function, it will calculate the loss of the input by comparing with the true label.

Line 17 and 18 print out the loss at each epoch, like:

```
Epoch: 1/1 loss = 5.264171
Epoch: 2/1 loss = 5.356096
Epoch: 1/2 loss = 5.259320
Epoch: 2/2 loss = 5.153419
Epoch: 1/3 loss = 5.008970
Epoch: 2/3 loss = 5.031704

. . .

Epoch: 1/100 loss = 0.033618
Epoch: 2/100 loss = 0.024889
```

Line 19 is to gather the data for visualization purpose.

Line 21, 22 and 23 are standard steps in PyTorch training loop. Line 21 zero out the gradients of all model parameters (or weights), this is necessary before the model update its weights. Line 22 tells the model to start the backpropagation, which is where the calculation of the gradients takes place. After the gradients are calculated, Line 23 tells the model to perform the updates on the parameters, or weights.

Figure 3.36 shows the curve of the losses during the training process, in the beginning the loss is large, but gradually reducing along with the iterations, finally it converges at a value near zero when the iteration approaches to 200.

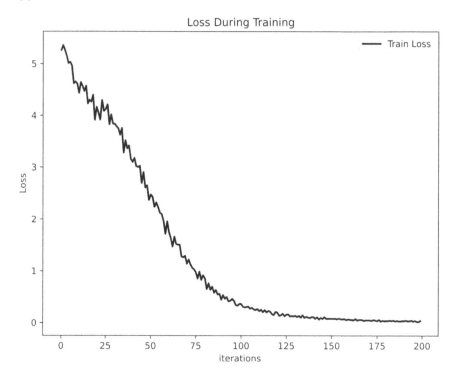

Figure 3.36 Loss During Training

Since this example does not have much data, it takes several minutes for training on CPU, and less than one minute for GPU.

3.13 Inference

Inference is the process of making predictions or generating new contents using the trained Transformer model based on the input sequences. After a model has been trained on a dataset, inference is the stage where the model uses what it has learned to interpret new, unseen data and generate outputs based on that data.

Depends on the specific requirements of the Natural Language Processing (NLP) tasks, the Transformer model is applied in different ways.

Encoder-Only: some NLP tasks can be completed by using the Encoder only, like Sentence Classification for classifying the sentiment of texts or documents into clusters and then pass through a classifier. Another example is Named Entity Recognition, which identifies the named entities within texts or documents, it requires the model to understand the context around the words in the texts.

Decoder-Only: some NLP tasks can be completed by using the Decoder only, like Text Generation, giving the model a start token or prompt, it can generate subsequent tokens one by one to produce the whole text. It works autoregressively by generating the next token based on the previous ones without requiring the Encoder inputs.

Encoder-Decoder: some tasks require both Encoder and Decoder to complete, like Machine Translation, the source language texts are sent to the Encoder as inputs, the Decoder will output the target language texts. Another example is Question and Answers, the Encoder processes the question texts, and the Decoder generates the answers. One more example is Text Summarization, the Encoder processes the original texts, while the Decoder generates the shorter texts to summarize it.

In this example, we use Encoder-Decoder mode to perform inference.

As shown in Figure 3.37, the questions are input to the Encoder, since Inference is about the new and unseen data inputs, the questions are slightly different from what we provided for training. For example, the question is:

Beetles eat what?

Where in the training dataset the similar one is:

What do beetles eat?

After the Encoder processes the input data, its output is sent to the Decoder. And a start token <sos> is sent to Decoder as input. Then it generates the output of the next token after <sos>, which is *"They"*.

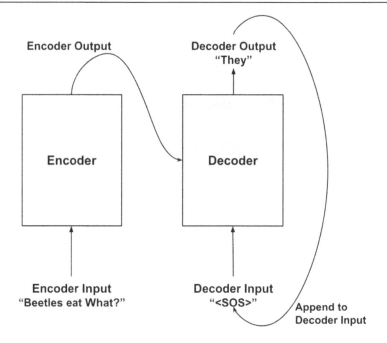

Figure 3.37 Inference

Then the output is concatenated to the end of the Decoder input, which becomes: "<sos> They", it's sent to the Decoder again, the Decoder generates the next token as "*often*". This process repeats again and again, each time generate one token, until the <EOS> token is generated by the Decoder, or the max number of tokens is generated.

Finally, the Decoder generates:

They often feed on plants and fungi, break down animal and plant debris, and eat other invertebrates. <EOS>

How do the Decoder search for the next token from the outputs? As mentioned earlier the output of the Decoder is

```
outputs: (batch_size * len_target, vocab_size)
```

If the `vocab_size` is 8, an output token looks something like:

```
[[ 0.67, -1.74, 14.28,  0.99,  0.57,  1.12, -4.82, -1.80]]
```

The columns are probability distributions of the token, and the index of the column is the tokens in the vocabulary, for example, the first column corresponds to the first word in the vocabulary, the second column is the second word, and so on.

Section 2.11 introduced the decoding algorithms of Greedy search, Beam search and Random Sampling. To recap, Gready search simply selects the highest probability from the list, in the above case, it selects the third column which probability is 14.28.

Random Sampling is to randomly select one from the top k probabilities, in the above case, let's say k = 3, meaning select one from the top 3 probabilities, then what we do is to keep the top 3 probabilities and mask out others, like below:

```
[[ 0.00,   0.00,  14.28,   0.99,   0.00,   1.12,   0.00,   0.00]]
```

Then, randomly choose one from the top 3, and the 3 probabilities become the weight for the choice. In this case the top 1 is significantly larger than the others, so it's most likely to be selected. If k = 1, it becomes Greedy because only the highest probability is selected.

Beam search is complicated, instead of selecting the most probable tokens at each step, it keeps track of multiple possible sequences, and choose the one with highest combined probabilities, see Section 2.11 for details.

In this section we implement the Greedy and Random Sampling algorithms:

```
1    def Greedy(logits):
2        return torch.argmax(logits, dim=-1, keepdim=False)
3
4    def RandomSampling(logits, k=5):
5        top_k_probs, _ = torch.topk(logits, k, dim=-1)
6        kth_highest_prob = top_k_probs[:, -1].unsqueeze(-1)
7        mask = logits < kth_highest_prob
8        probs = logits.masked_fill(mask, 0)
9        return torch.multinomial(probs).squeeze(-1)
```

Line 1 and 2 implements Greedy algorithm, it calls `torch.argmax()` to return the indices of the highest probabilities from the input tensor `logits`.

Line 4 to 9 implements Random Sampling, Line 5 finds out the top k probabilities from the tensor.

Line 6 finds out the probability value of the last one, which is the threshold for creating mask; Line 7 creates a mask basked on the threshold.

Line 8 applies the mask to the probabilities, and Line 9 calls the `torch.multinomial()` to get indices based on the top k probabilities, and return the results.

`torch.multinomial()` is a function used for sampling from a probability distribution, it draws samples from the distributions considering their weights. For example, the below tensor,

```
[[ 0.00,   0.00, 0.79,   0.08,   0.00,   0.13,   0.00,   0.00]]
```

Only three non-zero values in the tensor, which are the top three, others are masked out because they are lower than the threshold. The function will choose one from the three non-zero ones considering the weights, 0.79 is most likely selected because it has the largest weight, while 0.08 and 0.13 could also be selected but less likely because they have smaller weights. The function returns the index of the chosen value. This is how the Random Sampling works.

Below codes implement the Inference:

```
11    def Inference(model, enc_input, start_token, end_token,
12                      max_len=32, topk=None):
13        enc_outputs = model.encoder(enc_input)
14        dec_input = torch.zeros(1, 0).type_as(enc_input.data)
15        next_token = start_token
16        cnt = 0
17        while next_token != end_token and cnt < max_len:
18           dec_input = torch.cat(
19                       [dec_input.to(device),
20                       torch.tensor([[next_token]],
21                              dtype=enc_input.dtype).to(device)], -1)
22          dec_outputs = model.decoder(dec_input,
23                                      enc_input,
24                                      enc_outputs)
25          projected = model.projection(dec_outputs)
26          projected = model.softmax(projected)
```

```
27        if topk == None:
28            prob = Greedy(projected.squeeze(0))
29        else:
30            prob = RandomSampling(projected.squeeze(0), topk)
31        next_word = prob.data[-1]
32        next_token = next_word
33        cnt += 1
34    return prob
```

Line 11 to 34 define the `Inference()` function, its input parameters are:

`model`: the Transformer model.

`enc_input`: the input to the Encoder, or the question texts.

`start_token`: <SOS> token.

`end_token`: <EOS> token.

`max_len`: if the outputs do not have <EOS> token, this is the max length to generate the outputs.

`topk`: specify k for Random Sampling algorithm, if not specified, default to Greedy.

Line 13 passes `enc_input` to the Encoder to obtain the output `enc_outputs`.

Line 14 creates a tensor for the Decoder input, this is a zero tensor, which datatype is specified the same as `enc_input`.

Line 17 starts a while loop, the loop continues until the `next_token` is <EOS> or the count of output tokens reaches `max_len`, whichever comes first.

Line 18 to 21 concatenates `dec_input` to `next_token` which datatype is specified the same as `enc_input`.

`next_token` is initialized to <SOS> in Line 15, so the first `dec_input` is <SOS>, it's sent to the Decoder to generate outputs, the `next_token` is the last one in the Decoder's outputs, it's then concatenated to the `dec_input` in the next loop and sent to the Decoder again, and generate `next_token` again, this process is repeated until the loop ends.

Line 22 to 24 call the Decoder with the input parameters, and obtain the Decoder's outputs.

Line 25 calls the model's `projection()` function which is defined in `Transformer` class, it's a linear transformation to convert the size of Decoder's output from:

```
(batch_size, len_target, d_model)
```

to:

```
(batch_size, len_target, vocab_size)
```

The last dimension of the Decoder's output tensor is `d_model` (which is 512), the linear transformation converts it to `vocab_size`, which means the index of the last dimension corresponds to the tokens in the vocabulary. This is important because eventually we should pick up the corresponding token from the vocabulary.

Line 26 performs the Softmax on the `projected` outputs, this layer is also defined in `Transformer` class. The Softmax is performed on the last dimension which is the one of `vocab_size`. The idea is the Softmax normalizes the probability distributions, meaning all elements are in the range between 0 and 1, the sum of all the probabilities is equal to 1. This helps the next step of using either Greedy or Random Sampling algorithms to choose the most likely one.

Line 25 and 26 implement the Linear and Softmax boxes at the top in Figure 3.32, the output of this step is something like:

```
[[ 0.00,   0.00,   0.79,   0.08,   0.00,   0.13,   0.00,   0.00]]
```

If using Random Sampling, it randomly chooses from the top k probabilities considering their weights, in this case it randomly chooses one from 0.79, 0.08 and 0.13 considering the weights when $k = 3$, so the results could be one from index #2, #3 or #5 of the vocabulary (the index starting from 0).

Line 27 and 28 calls `Greedy` if `topk` is not specified. And Line 29 and 30 calls `RandomSampling` when `topk` is specified.

`Greedy` or `RandomSampling` returns a list of indices of the token in the vocabulary, the last one in the list is the newly generated token. For example, the first loop, it generates:

```
([17])
```

Second loop, it generates:

```
([17, 64])
```

And then the following loops:

```
([17, 64, 88])
([17, 64, 88, 110])
([17, 64, 88, 115, 115])
([17, 64, 88, 110, 115, 130])
([17, 64, 88, 110, 115,  88, 4])
([17, 64, 88, 110, 115, 130, 4, 3])
```

Every loop it generates a new token at the last. Line 31 takes the last one and Line 32 sets it to `next_token`, and then back to the loop and repeat from Line 18. If the `next_token` is <EOS>, or the number of generated tokens reaches `max_len`, stop the loop.

Line 34 returns the result.

The below codes use `Inference()` to generate answers from a list of questions:

```
1    evaluation = [
2        ['What animal larger than elephant?', ''],
3        ['What years do turtles breed?',  ''],
4        ['Where turtles lay eggs?', ''],
5        ['How do otters keep warm?', ''],
6        ['...']]
7    evl_enc_inputs, _, _ = make_data(evaluation)
8    evl_loader = Data.DataLoader(DataSet([evl_enc_inputs]), 8 )
9    [evl_enc_inputs] = next(iter(evl_loader))
10
11   for i in range(len(evl_enc_inputs)):
12       predict = Inference(model,
13                       evl_enc_inputs[i].view(1, -1).to(device),
14                       start_token=tokenizer.encode_word("<SOS>"),
15                       end_token=tokenizer.encode_word("<EOS>"),
16                       topk=5)
17       q = evl_enc_inputs[i].tolist()
18       q = [x for x in q if x != tokenizer.encode_word("<PAD>")]
19       question = tokenizer.decode_text(q)
20       answer = tokenizer.decode_text(predict.tolist())
21       question = question.replace(" ?", "?")
```

```
22      answer = answer.replace(" .", ".").replace("<EOS>", "")
23      print(question, '->', answer)
```

Line 1 to 6 create some evaluation questions, they are similar but not the same as the original questions created in Section 3.1.

Line 7 to 9 use the questions list to create data loader for batch loads.

Line 11 to 23 loop through these questions to generate answers.

Line 12 to 16 calls `Inference()` function with required parameters, the model, the input to encoder, start and end token etc.

Line 17 converts the question (tokenized sequence) from tensor to list. And Line 18 removes the padding token <PAD>.

Line 19 uses `tokenizer` to decode the question sequence, now it becomes texts, this is for printing purpose.

Line 20 uses `tokenizer` to decode the answers generated by `Inference()` function, now it is texts, also for printing purpose.

Line 21 and 22 is to remove some spaces before "." and "?". When a token is decoded to word, a space is added before it, same for "." and "?", in normal English language, there are no space before them, this is why we want to remove these spaces, for printing purpose.

The answer text comes with <EOS> at the end, remove it as well.

Line 23 print out the results, questions with answers, which looks like:

```
Where turtles lay eggs? -> Holes dug into mud or sand.
What years do turtles breed? -> Every few years or more.
How do otters keep warm? -> A layer of air trapped in their
fur.
. . .
```

The source codes are available in the Github repository, try to play with the codes, you might want to change the evaluation questions, and see how Greedy and Random Sampling works.

The Greedy might be stable, meaning every time generate pretty much same results, because its behavior is predictable and can be easily replicated. On the other hand, Random Sampling might be diversified to some degree, because it makes choices randomly from a set of available options. Since our dataset is quite small, it might not make much sense in the generated answers when they are diversified. But when the Transformer model is trained with a huge amount of data, the Random Sampling might be a better strategy.

In this section, we didn't implement Beam algorithm due to its complexity. It is often used during the inference process for the Transformer to find the most probable sequence of outputs. Beam search, as an optimization of the standard breadth-first search algorithm, takes advantage of the Transformer model's ability to evaluate the probability of a token given a context. The algorithm is especially important when deploying these models because it greatly increases the likelihood of producing a contextually appropriate output as compared to simpler algorithms like Greedy. In a real-word Large Language Model project, always consider Beam algorithm together with others, it might be the better one.

3.14 Conclusion

As we wrap up this chapter of the Transformer model, a type of Large Language Models (LLMs), we've come a long way from the beginning, and walked through the process of building a Transformer model from scratch using PyTorch.

We started off by diving into the basics of how the Transformer works, looked at the self-attention mechanisms, as well as the layers that help the model focus on different parts of the data, and how these layers fit together, they are including Embedding, Positional Encoding, Layer Normalization, Fully Connected Feed Forward, Scaled Dot-Product Attention and Multi-Head Attention, Masks, Encoder and Decoder. We pieced together the model bit by bit, making sure we understood each part and how it contributed to the whole picture.

After putting together the model, we trained it using a small collection of the questions-answers dataset. This gave us a peek into the model's learning process. It was like teaching a new language to children, gradually expanding their understanding and comprehension. We also leveraged the power of GPUs and batching data to expand the parallel processing capabilities, which makes the training process not just possible, but practical.

We have used the Data Loader to group and load data in batches, and feed the Transformer model with manageable chunks of data at a time, enabling it to learn from multiple examples simultaneously and make better use of the GPU's resources.

Then we moved on to the Inference phase and see it in action, understand the input questions and come up with its own answers. We saw how the Transformer, using everything it learned during training, could take on tasks such as questions & answers, machine translation or summarizing stories.

We used the techniques of Greedy and Random Sampling to select the appropriate tokens from the outputs. We have introduced, although not implemented, the Beam search which essentially helps the model make smarter choices when it's creating new text.

While building a Transformer model from scratch can be a valuable learning experience, it's important to note that in real-world projects, there are many pre-built models and libraries available that can be used as a starting point. These pre-built models have been extensively tested, optimized, and fine-tuned for a variety of tasks, and can save significant time and effort compared to building everything from scratch.

By understanding the underlying principles of the Transformer architecture through this chapter, which lays a solid foundation that is invaluable for both academic understanding and practical application, you'll be better equipped to make informed decisions about using pre-built models or building your own, depending on the requirements of your project.

4. Pre-Training

P re-training an LLM, is akin to a student studying broadly to get smarter before specializing in one subject, or a child absorbing the vast knowledge of language through observation and learning. A Transformer model needs to learn a lot about language before it gets really good at something specific, say machine translation. Pre-training is a phase of discovery where the model draws patterns and meanings from a massive corpus of text data.

Having put together our own Transformer model from scratch in the last chapter, we have acquired the fundamental knowledge of the inner workings of it. In this chapter, we will take a deep dive into the process of pre-training a Transformer model from scratch, using a machine translation task as our example.

We'll show you how to set up the model for the pre-training and feed it lots of data. Don't worry, we have some easy-to-follow hands-on code examples for this chapter that will help you through every step: how to prepare the dataset, build vocabulary, leverage GPU acceleration, monitor the training progress, save checkpoints for future use, and finally make inference from the model.

Our first task is machine translation, where pre-training the Transformer model to understand English and translate it into German. We'll start by preparing a dataset for this complex task. This dataset is a collection of English-German sentence pairs that our model will learn from. We'll use PyTorch's `torch.nn.Transformer()` as a ready-to-use module, treating it like a black box for our model. We have already learned how to build the Transformer model from scratch in the last chapter and understood how each building block work behind the scenes. We won't build it from scratch this time but will learn how to prepare and feed in data to get the best results out of this powerful neural network model.

Through the hands-on practice in this chapter, we will explain how to:

- Load and preprocess the Multi30k dataset, including tokenization and handling of padding.
- Prepare the data in batches using PyTorch's `DataLoader`, ensuring efficient training.
- Pre-train the PyTorch `nn.Transformer` model on the machine translation task.
- Perform inference with the pre-trained model.

Giving the fact that pre-training a LLM normally needs a huge set of data on a complex model, and requires extensive computational resources, in this chapter's example, the dataset size and model complexity have been carefully chosen to ensure the example can be run effectively on limited computational resources, e.g. a single GPU on Google Colab environment.

Pre-training is step 3b in the life cycle of LLM in Figure 1.2.

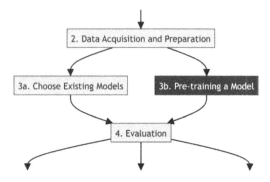

Beyond the practical exercises, it's important to situate our work within the big picture of natural language processing (NLP). Thus, we will introduce some of the most prominent pre-trained LLMs, such as GPT, BERT, and FLAN-T5, that dominate the field. Given the computationally intensive nature of pre-training models, we will also discuss computational resources.

Furthermore, we will explore the prompt engineering and in-context learning, which are important techniques for effectively utilizing pre-trained models in various applications.

Finally, we will briefly introduce the Pipelines feature provided by the HuggingFace library, which simplifies the deployment and usage of pre-trained models for a wide range of natural language processing tasks.

By the end of this chapter, you will have a comprehensive understanding of the pre-training process for Transformer models, as well as the broader landscape of pre-trained LLMs and their practical applications.

4.1 Machine Translation

Machine translation is an application of Artificial Intelligence that automatically translates text from one language to another. The Transformer model revolutionized the field with its high-quality translations and efficient training processes. Unlike the traditional sequence-to-sequence models which relied heavily on Recurrent Neural Networks (RNNs), the Transformer model uses self-attention mechanisms to process input and output data in parallel, speeding up translation without sacrificing accuracy.

The Transformer model has the potential to deliver high-quality and accurate translations with a properly sized dataset for training. The more training data available, the more adept the model will be at capturing the semantic contexts of the texts.

The pre-training of a Transformer model is a resource-intensive task that generally involves large datasets and significant computational power. It is normally performed on a huge corpora of text data, the Transformer model itself is also high complexity, even the model we built in last chapter has 44 million of learnable parameters. Some well-known models like GPT or BERT contain millions or billions of parameters. With such complexity model and huge amount of data, the pre-training runs for long time on multiple GPUs, in most cases it runs for days or even weeks. These factors make pre-training a resource-heavy endeavor, which is why often only well-funded organizations or research groups undertake such projects.

With this consideration in mind, the example of this book will demonstrate the pre-training of Transformer with a scaled-down approach, instead of the multi-million-word datasets. It's a smaller dataset that captures the essence of the pre-training tasks. This way, the core idea of pre-training, allowing a Transformer model to learn the general structure and patterns of a language, is preserved without the prohibitive computational cost.

The pre-training example in this chapter can be run on any cloud-based Python environment with a single GPU, normally available in the free tier plan, such as Google Colab, Kaggle, or Amazon SageMaker Studio Lab, etc.

To begin our journey into machine translation, a high-quality dataset is important. For our purposes, we will be using the Multi30k dataset, which is a collection of 30,000 parallel English and German sentences.

Multi30k Dataset is used for this pre-training purpose, it's a multilingual collection of images and their corresponding descriptions, which was originally designed for automatic image captioning. The dataset provides both English and German descriptions for 30,000 images, it's a valuable resource for the tasks like image captioning and machine translation. We will use the English and German sentences for machine translation purpose in this example.

The sentences in Multi30k dataset are not direct translation of one another but are independently constructed sentences that describe the images in a natural and descriptive way. The original paper is *Multi30K: Multilingual English-German Image Descriptions* [14], *Elliott et al, 2016*. See [14] in the References section at the end of this book.

As an example, a pair of sentence looks like:

English: *People are fixing the roof of a house.*

German: *Leute Reparieren das Dach eines Hauses.*

English will be used as the source language of this example, and German will be as the target.

nn.Transformer() Class is a built-in Transformer architecture within PyTorch framework, it encapsulates the essence of the original Transformer with encoder and decoder layers. As shown in Figure 4.1.

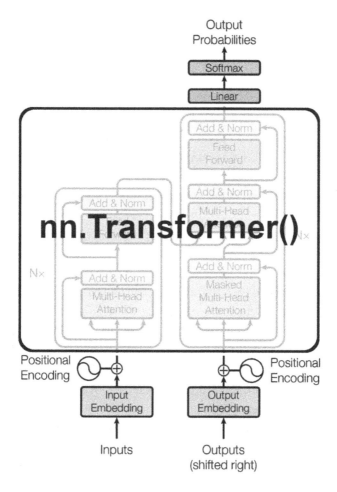

Figure 4.1 nn.Transformer() model
Source from: Attention is All You Need [1], Vaswani et al, 2017. Modified by author

This chapter we will use this `nn.Transformer()` as the Transformer model, the process of pre-training involves teaching the model to understand and translate the source language (in our case, English) into the target language (German), using the Multi30k dataset.

Here is a high-level overview of the steps of pre-training:

1. **Load Multi30k dataset, Tokenization and Embedding**: Load the dataset into the memory, each sentence in the dataset needs to be broken into tokens (by words or sub-words), which are then converted into numerical vectors. These are known as embeddings, which represent the semantic meanings of the tokens. As introduced in the last chapter, the dimension of the embedded vector is `d_model`, which is 512 by the paper. However in this example we use 256 instead, as mentioned earlier we want to balance the computational resources in order to run it on a cloud based single GPU environment. Because the dataset has 30,000 pair of sentences, we want to control the size of learnable parameters of the Transformer model, so that it can be running within one hour in most cloud-based environments.

2. **Encoder Learning:** The encoder part of the Transformer model processes the input sentences, using self-attention to weigh the importance of each word in relation to others in the sentence. The English sentences are the source, they will be fed into the Encoder, which is the Inputs at the bottom-left of Figure 4.1.

3. **Decoder Learning:** The decoder part of the Transformer model processes the target, the German sentences are fed into the decoder at the bottom-right of Figure 4.1. The decoder predicts the output tokens sequentially, relying on self-attention and the output from the encoder to produce the translation.

4. **Optimization:** Throughout pre-training, an optimization process minimizes the difference between the model's output and the correct translation. This usually is performed by a loss function such as Cross-Entropy Loss and an Optimizer like Adam (Adaptive Moment Estimation) or SGD (Stochastic Gradient Descent). A learning rate is often employed by the Optimizer to adjust the

learning speed during training, this ensures better model convergence and stability.

Through these steps, nn.Transformer() model gains the ability to grasp sentence structure and semantic meaning for both English and German, and ready for the machine translation task.

4.2   Dataset and Tokenization

The preparation of dataset is step 2 in the life cycle of LLM in Figure 1.2:

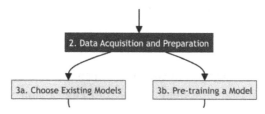

Load Multi30k Dataset

A convenient way to load Multi30k is from Hugging Face ecosystem, which is a company that widely recognized for its work in the domain of artificial intelligence (AI), particularly in natural language processing (NLP). They have created and maintain a variety of tools and resources that are used by researchers, developers, and companies around the world to facilitate and streamline the development of NLP-related tasks and applications.

One of the tools is datasets library, which gives access to a vast collection of datasets that are used for training and benchmarking machine learning models. We will load our dataset from there:

```
1    !pip install datasets
2    from datasets import load_dataset
3    dataset = load_dataset("bentrevett/multi30k")
```

Line 1 is to install datasets library, Line 2 to import it. Line 3 is to load the Multi30k dataset from the Hugging Face ecosystem, that's it. The dataset is now in the memory.

Then, print out the loaded dataset,

```
4    print(dataset)
```

It shows:

```
DatasetDict({
    train: Dataset({
        features: ['en', 'de'],
        num_rows: 29000     })
    validation: Dataset({
        features: ['en', 'de'],
        num_rows: 1014     })
    test: Dataset({
        features: ['en', 'de'],
        num_rows: 1000     })
})
```

There are three sub-sets inside `dataset`, which are `train`, `validation` and `test`, each of them has fields of `'en'` for English and `'de'` for German; `train` has 29,000 pairs of sentences, `validation` has 1,014, and `test` has 1,000.

Print out some data,

```
5    print(dataset['train']['en'][0])
6    print(dataset['train']['de'][0])
```

It looks like:

```
Two young, White males are outside near many bushes.
Zwei junge weiße Männer sind im Freien in der Nähe vieler
Büsche.
```

Build Vocabulary and Tokenization

Based on the English and German data loaded from the dataset, we need to build the vocabulary for each. In the last chapter for simplicity reasons, we built one vocabulary for both the source and the target, that was because of the questions and answers task, both are in the same language, and share the same vocabulary. Normally in complex natural language processing tasks, two vocabularies are created one for the source, one for the target. Especially in the case of machine translation, the source and the target are not in same language, they usually can not share a common vocabulary.

In the last chapter we used Python `split()` function to separate the words from the sentences, which means the space between two words is deemed as a delimiter to separate the words, and those words are used to build the vocabulary. This is for simplicity reason, but not a good way to do the job, it's not accurate when dealing with complex natural language tasks. For example, *"don't"*, or *"you're"* should be separated as *"do not"*, or *"you are"*, German and other languages have the similar cases, the `split()` function is not able to do this.

SpaCy will be used for this purpose, it's an open-source software library for advanced Natural Language Processing (NLP) in Python, designed for practical, real-world tasks and applications, and it's particularly known for its speed and efficiency. It supports 75+ languages, and provides pre-trained machine learning models that can be used for language processing.

The `en_core_web_sm` and `de_core_news_sm` are two such pre-trained models for tokenization purpose, the former is for English and the latter for German. Basically they are small language model trained on written news and web texts such as blogs, news and comments, etc. featuring vocabulary, syntax, entities and words. Tokenization is the process of breaking up a piece of text into individual tokens (usually words or sub-words). Both English and German have language-specific rules for tokenization, the SpaCy models are specialized of doing this kind of tasks. Despite their small size, they are fairly accurate in tokenizing texts. Their names are ending with _sm, indicating a small model, which are lightweight and less resource-intensive, so they are faster for applications that do not require high computational resources.

```
11    !pip install spacy
12    !python -m spacy download en_core_web_sm
13    !python -m spacy download de_core_news_sm
14
15    spacy_en = spacy.load("en_core_web_sm")
16    spacy_de = spacy.load("de_core_news_sm")
```

Line 11 instals SpaCy library, and Line 12 and 13 instal the English and German models. Line 15 and 16 load both models.

```
17   def tokenize_en(text):
18       return [tok.text for tok in spacy_en.tokenizer(text)]
19   def tokenize_de(text):
20       return [tok.text for tok in spacy_de.tokenizer(text)]
```

Then use their `tokenizer()` function to separate the words from the sentences. Line 17 and 18 process English and Line 19 and 20 for German. For example, the English sentence is:

```
Two young, White males are outside near many bushes.
```

is converted to:

```
['Two', 'young', ',', 'White', 'males', 'are', 'outside',
'near', 'many', 'bushes', '.']
```

While the German sentence:

```
Zwei junge weiße Männer sind im Freien in der Nähe vieler
Büsche.
```

is converted to:

```
['Zwei', 'junge', 'weiße', 'Männer', 'sind', 'im', 'Freien',
'in', 'der', 'Nähe', 'vieler', 'Büsche', '.']
```

Now the sentences are separated to the individual words, we are able to build vocabularies for English and German.

```
21   def build_vocab(texts, tokenizer):
22       vocabs = []
23       for text in texts:
24           vocabs.extend(tokenizer(text))
25       return sorted(list(set(vocabs)))
```

`build_vocab()` function puts all words in a list, remove duplicated words, and return a sorted unique list of words, which is the vocabulary.

Same as what we did in the last chapter, create four special tokens: padding token, start of sentence token, end of sentence token and unknow token:

```
26   PAD_TOKEN = "<PAD>"   # Padding token
27   SOS_TOKEN = "<SOS>"   # Start-of-sentence token
```

```
28    EOS_TOKEN = "<EOS>"   # End-of-sentence token
29    UNK_TOKEN = "<UNK>"   # Unknown token
```

When creating the vocabularies, these special tokens are added to the beginning of the list:

```
31    en_vocab = [PAD_TOKEN, SOS_TOKEN, EOS_TOKEN, UNK_TOKEN] + \
32              build_vocab(dataset['train']['en'] + \
33                    dataset['validation']['en'] + \
34                    dataset['test']['en'], tokenize_en)
35    de_vocab = [PAD_TOKEN, SOS_TOKEN, EOS_TOKEN, UNK_TOKEN] + \
36              build_vocab(dataset['train']['de'] + \
37                    dataset['validation']['de'] + \
38                    dataset['test']['de'], tokenize_de)
```

Line 31 to 34 build English vocabulary, the four special tokens are placed in the beginning in Line 31, the dataset includes `train`, `validation` and `test` sub-sets, add them together in the vocabulary. The `train` and `validation` sets will be used in the training process, and `test` will be used in the inference process later.

Now we have created two vocabularies, one for the source which is English, another one for the target German. Obtain the size of them:

```
39    SRC_VOCAB_SIZE = len(en_vocab)
40    TRG_VOCAB_SIZE = len(de_vocab)
```

```
EN vocab: 11158
DE vocab: 19953
```

It means English has totally 11,158 tokens (words or sub-words) in the vocabulary, while German has 19,953.

This is fairly small size of the data, compared with normal pre-training of the Transformer model. As mentioned earlier we want to keep the size in a manageable level, both the sizes of data and the parameters of the model, in order to run the code on a single GPU cloud environment, while we can demonstrate the essence of the pre-training process.

At this point the vocabularies look like:

English:

```
['<PAD>', '<SOS>', '<EOS>', '<UNK>', ' ', '!', '"', '126',
'13', ..., 'Actors', 'Acura', 'Adidas', 'Adobe', ...]
```

German:

```
['<PAD>', '<SOS>', '<EOS>', '<UNK>', ' ', '!',
 '21-Tüten', 'A', 'A&M', "A's", 'AMC-Gebäude', 'ARRIVO',
 'ATM-Maschine', 'Abbildung', 'Abdeckung', 'Abdeckungen',
 ...]
```

Then create a `VocabTokenizer` class, which converts a token to a number based on its position, or index, in the vocabulary, and vice versa.

```
41    class VocabTokenizer(nn.Module):
42      def __init__(self, vocabulary):
43        super().__init__()
44        self.vocab_size = len(vocabulary)
45        self.idx2word = {index:word for index, word in
46                                    enumerate(vocabulary)}
47        self.word2idx = {word:index for index, word in
48                                    enumerate(vocabulary)}
49      def encode(self, text):
50        return [self.word2idx[w] for w in text]
51      def decode(self, token):
52        return [self.idx2word[i] for i in token]
53      def __call__(self, text, encode=True):
54        if encode:
55          return self.encode(text)
56        else:
57          return self.decode(text)
```

Line 42 to 48 define the `__init__()` function, it retrieves the size of vocabulary, and creates two dictionaries, `self.word2idx` is used to lookup the index for a token; `self.idx2word` to lookup the opposite way, from an index to a token. They are basically used to convert the tokens to and from the corresponding numerical values (token IDs), and prepare for the Embedding layer.

Line 49 and 50 do the `encode()`, which convert tokens to token IDs, or the indices in the vocabulary; Line 51 and 52 do the `decode()`, which convert the token IDs back to the tokens.

Line 53 to 57 override the `__call__()` function of the class, basically this is a internal function of `nn.Module` class, it allows a PyToch object to be called as a function. For example when we implement `nn.Model` class in

earlier sections, we only implement its __init__() and forward()
function, don't need to care about others. Then it is called like this:

```
mymodule = MyModule()
output = mymodule(input)
```

Here, mymodule is an object, and call it in the same way of calling a
function, meaning we don't need to call mymodule.forward(input),
because __call__() function takes care of everything, it's by default
calling forward().

We implement __call__() here to invoke encode() and/or decode() in
the same way.

Then instantiate the class:

```
58    vocab_tokenizers = {
59        'en': VocabTokenizer(en_vocab),
60        'de': VocabTokenizer(de_vocab)  }
```

It is used as this way, when encoding English tokens to IDs:

```
vocab_tokenizers['en'](english_tokens)
```

when decode the IDs to tokens:

```
vocab_tokenizers['en'](english_outputs, False)
```

We are doing this is because we want to pass vocab_tokenizers as
parameters to other classes/functions.

4.3 Load Data in Batch

When training a Transformer model, or any machine learning models, it's
essential to load the data in batch, meaning to load multiple data items
simultaneously for processing. There are several reasons for that:

Sometimes the datasets for pre-training can be very large, often too large
to fit entirely into memory, and result with out-of-memory errors when
attempting to load them in full. Loading them in batches can ensure that
only a portion of data is in the memory at a given time.

In most cases the training operation in machine learning are parallelizable with the power of GPUs, even CPUs can process multiple data points simultaneously. The data in batches allows it to leverage these hardware capabilities to perform efficiently, as they can process many data items at once, rather than one at a time.

Training with batches allows the model to update its weights in bulk, which leads to faster convergence, compared with updating the weights for one data item at a time.

The size of the batch is not a one-size-fits-all number, it can depend on a variety of factors. The size is often adjusted based on the performance of the model considering the balance of computational efficiency and the model accuracy. Typically, the batch size is the power of 2, such as 8, 16, 32, 64, ..., and practically speaking 32, 64 or 128 are often good starting point, then adjust the number based on the results. However the organization with significant hardware resources might choose much larger number as the batch size.

In this example we set the batch size to 128:

```
1    batch_size = 128
```

In order to prepare the data for pre-training, we create a class that extend `torch.utils.data.Dataset`, and implement three key methods of it. The purpose is to provide a mechanism for loading and processing data in batch, specific to our loaded Multi30k dataset. By extending this class, we can easily integrate our data into the PyTorch ecosystem and make use of features such as data loading, batching, shuffling, and so on.

The three key methods to implement are __init__(), which is used to set things up and initialization; __len__(), which is to retrieve the total number of the data items; __getitem__(idx), which is to retrieve the idx-th item of the data.

```
1    class En2De_Dataset(Dataset):
2        def __init__(self, raw_dataset,
3                             src_tokenizer,
4                             tgt_tokenizer,
5                             vocab_transforms):
6            self.raw_dataset = raw_dataset
```

```
7          self.src_tokenizer = src_tokenizer
8          self.tgt_tokenizer = tgt_tokenizer
9          self.vocab_transforms = vocab_transforms
10     def __len__(self):
11         return len(self.raw_dataset)
12     def __getitem__(self, idx):
13         src = self.src_tokenizer(self.raw_dataset[idx]["en"])
14         src = self.vocab_transforms["en"](src)
15         tgt = self.tgt_tokenizer(self.raw_dataset[idx]["de"])
16         tgt_in = self.vocab_transforms["de"]([SOS_TOKEN] + tgt)
17         tgt_out = self.vocab_transforms["de"](tgt + [EOS_TOKEN])
18         return src, tgt_in, tgt_out
```

Line 2 to 9 define the __init__() function, it receives the raw dataset, both tokenizers, and a vocab_transforms that created above.

Line 10 and 11 define __len__() function which just simple return the length of raw_dataset.

Line 12 to 18 define __getitem__(idx) function, it returns a single data item at the specified idx location. The required input data to the Transformer model is generated here. The English text is the source and obtained from:

```
self.raw_dataset[idx]["en"]
```

It's retrieved by Line 13, for example:

```
A guy works on a building.
```

Line 14 encodes the tokens to IDs, which is:

```
tensor([106, 5569, 11068, 7282, 1947, 2999, 20])
```

These token IDs are the indices of the words in the vocabulary.

Similarly Line 15 obtains the corresponding target German text, for example:

```
Ein Typ arbeitet an einem Gebäude.
```

Line 16 encodes it with German tokens, and add a sos_TOKEN to the beginning,

```
tensor([1, 2586, 11652, 13269, 13094, 14531, 3857, 23])
```

Similarly Line 17 add an EOS_TOKEN at the end:

```
tensor([2586, 11652, 13269, 13094, 14531, 3857, 23, 2])
```

Line 18 returns three tensors, src, tgt_in, tgt_out. The requirements for Transformer input data are exactly same as what we did in the last chapter, the source is the input to the Encoder of the Transformer; the tgt_in is the target input, which is fed to the Decoder as input, it's right-shifted with the first one as sos_TOKEN; the tgt_out is the true data which is used to compare with the Decoder output in the Loss function, it has an EOS_TOKEN at the end. We did exactly the same thing as that in the last chapter.

Since the data is loaded in batch, the sentences, or sequences, in a batch might have different lengths, we have to pad them to the same length for further processing, create a function to do it,

```
21    def padding(batch):
22        src = [torch.tensor(item[0]) for item in batch]
23        tgt_in = [torch.tensor(item[1]) for item in batch]
24        tgt_out = [torch.tensor(item[2]) for item in batch]
25        return pad_sequence(src, True, padding_value=0), \
26                  pad_sequence(tgt_in, True, padding_value=0), \
27                  pad_sequence(tgt_out, True, padding_value=0)
```

Basically, it will add padding tokens to the end of shorter sequences, and make the batch has the same length as the longest one. This is also the same as that in the last chapter.

Then invoke the above class and prepare the data:

```
31    train_data = En2De_Dataset(dataset['train'],
32                  tokenize_en, tokenize_de, vocab_tokenizers)
33    val_data = En2De_Dataset(dataset['validation'],
34                  tokenize_en, tokenize_de, vocab_tokenizers)
35    train_loader = DataLoader(train_data, batch_size=batch_size,
36                  collate_fn=padding, shuffle=True)
37    val_loader = DataLoader(val_data, batch_size=batch_size,
38                  collate_fn=padding, shuffle=False)
```

Line 31 and 32 instantiate En2De_Dataset class for the train set, and Line 33 and 34 do the same for the validation set.

Line 35 and 36 call `DataLoader` to obtain the batched train data, and Line 37 and 38 the same for the batched validation set. The `DataLoader` is a PyTorch class that abstracts the complexity of fetching batches of data from a `Dataset`. `shuffle=True` means randomly shuffling the data every iteration to reduce model overfitting. `collate_fn` specify a function to handle a batch, in this example, we specify `padding()` as `collate_fn`, which will add padding tokens to the batch.

After a batch is loaded by `train_loader`, a sample batch has:

Source data size: `torch.Size([128, 24])`

Target_in size: `torch.Size([128, 29])`

Target_out size: `torch.Size([128, 29])`

The sizes are different from batch to batch, but it ensures that all sequences in a batch are in the same size.

4.4   Pre-Training nn.Transformer Model

After gaining the foundational understanding by building a Transformer model from scratch in the last chapter, we will be leveraging the pre-built classes from PyTorch's `nn.Transformer` which can greatly simplify the implementation process. This module is a flexible and efficient implementation of the standard Transformer architecture, and we will explore how to incorporate it into a deep learning workflow.

Since this is an implementation of the Transformer architecture, it's also based on the paper of *Attention is All You Need*[1], *Vaswani et al.* in 2017, which introduced the idea of the attention mechanisms, replacing the traditional recurrence and convolutional layers for sequence processing tasks.

As shown in Figure 4.1, the `nn.Transformer` covers both the Encoder and Decoder, however we need to implement the Positional Encoding, Embedding, and create masks. PyTorch has built-in Embedding module, but not Positional Encoding in the current version at the time of this writing. We will reuse the one in the last chapter.

Now, create the customized Transformer model:

```
1    class TransformerModel(nn.Module):
2      def __init__(self, src_vocab_size, tgt_vocab_size,
3                   d_model, nhead, num_encoder_layers,
4                   num_decoder_layers, dim_feedforward,
5                   dropout=DROPOUT, max_length=MAX_LENGTH):
6        super(TransformerModel, self).__init__()
7        self.src_embed = nn.Embedding(src_vocab_size, d_model)
8        self.tgt_embed = nn.Embedding(tgt_vocab_size, d_model)
9        self.pos_enc = PositionalEncoding(d_model, max_length)
10       self.transformer = nn.Transformer(
11           d_model=d_model,
12           nhead=nhead,
13           num_encoder_layers=num_encoder_layers,
14           num_decoder_layers=num_decoder_layers,
15           dim_feedforward=dim_feedforward,
16           dropout=dropout,
17           batch_first=True,
18       )
19       self.output_layer = nn.Linear(d_model, tgt_vocab_size)
20     def forward(self, src, tgt, src_mask, tgt_mask,
21                 src_padding_mask, tgt_padding_mask,
22                 memory_padding_mask):
23       src_emb = self.src_embed(src)
24       src_emb = self.pos_enc(src_emb)
25       tgt_emb = self.tgt_embed(tgt)
26       tgt_emb = self.pos_enc(tgt_emb)
27       output = self.transformer(
28         src_emb, tgt_emb,
29         src_mask, tgt_mask,
30         src_key_padding_mask=src_padding_mask,
31         tgt_key_padding_mask=tgt_padding_mask,
32         memory_key_padding_mask=memory_padding_mask)
33       return self.output_layer(output)
34     def encoder(self, src, src_mask):
35       input = self.src_embed(src)
36       input = self.pos_enc(input)
37       return self.transformer.encoder(input, src_mask)
38     def decoder(self, tgt, memory, tgt_mask):
39       input = self.tgt_embed(tgt)
40       input = self.pos_enc(input)
41       return self.transformer.decoder(input, memory, tgt_mask)
```

The input parameters are:

`src_vocab_size`: size of source vocabulary

`tgt_vocab_size`: size of target vocabulary

`d_model`: dimension of embedded vector

`nhead`: number of heads for the Multi-Head Attention

`num_encoder_layers`: number of the Encoder layers

`num_decoder_layers`: number of the Decoder layers

`dim_feedforward`: dimension of the Position-Wise Feed-Forward layer

`dropout`: dropout rate

`max_length`: max length of the sequences

Line 7 and 8 initialize the Embedding layer for the source and target respectively using `nn.Embedding()` which is PyTorch built-in class. Line 9 initializes the Positional Encoding layer, there is no built-in class for this at the current version of PyTorch, we re-use the codes defined in Section 3.3.

Line 10 to 18 initialize the `nn.Transformer()` class, and pass the required parameters. Line 17 `batch_first=True` means the sizes of input and output are `[batch_size, seq_len, d_model]`, the datasets we prepared are in this size.

Line 19 defines the final output layer which is a linear transformation from d_model to target vocab size.

Line 20 to 33 define the `forward()` function, the input parameters are:

`src`: the batched source sequence, in size `[batch_size, seq_len]`

`tgt`: the batched target sequence, in size `[batch_size, seq_len]`

`src_mask`: the mask for source sequence

`tgt_mask`: the mask for target sequence

`src_padding_mask`: the padding mask for source sequence

`tgt_padding_mask`: the padding mask for target sequence

`memory_padding_mask`: the mask for the Encoder output

Line 23 to 26 apply the Embedding and Positional Encoding layers on the input for source and target respectively.

Line 27 to 32 invoke the Transformer with required parameters. This is the black-box in Figure 4.1 that hides details of everything inside the Transformer architecture.

Line 34 to 37 explicitly invoke the Encoder with the Embedding and Positional Encoding; and similarly Line 38 to 41 do with the Decoder. This is used in the Inference phase only, because the source sequence is fed to the Encoder once, it's output which is `memory` in Line 38 is fed to the Decoder, which is called iteratively, and the output is generated one by one until `<EOS>`, or `max_length`.

Then define some constant variables that will be using in the model:

```
42    D_MODEL = 256
43    NHEAD = 4
44    NENC_LAYER = 3
45    NDEC_LAYER = 3
46    FFN_DIM = 256
47    DROPOUT = 0.25
48    MAX_LENGTH = 256
```

The paper recommends that `d_model` is 512, which is the dimension of the embedded vector; the number of heads of multi-head attention is 8; the number of Encoder/Decoder layers are 6 and 6 respectively; the position-wise Feed-Forward dimension is 2048. In our example as mentioned earlier, we want to manage the size of not only the dataset but also the model size, in order to run it without highly equipped hardware. Therefore we choose the half of what the paper recommended, that is `D_MODEL=256`, number of heads `NHEAD=4`, number of Encoder/Decoder layers `NENC_LAYER=3` and `NDEC_LAYER=3`, position-wise Feed-Forward dimension `FFN_DIM=256`.

Also define a dropout rate of 0.25, which is typically used in the neural network layers to reduce the overfitting during training. The max length of sequence is defined as `MAX_LENGTH=256`. This number should be bigger than the max length of the sentences in the dataset.

Now instantiate the model:

```
51    device = 'cuda:0' if torch.cuda.is_available() else 'cpu'
52    model = TransformerModel(
```

```
53        src_vocab_size = SRC_VOCAB_SIZE,
54        tgt_vocab_size = TRG_VOCAB_SIZE,
55        d_model = D_MODEL,
56        nhead = NHEAD,
57        num_encoder_layers = NENC_LAYER,
58        num_decoder_layers = NDEC_LAYER,
59        dim_feedforward = FFN_DIM,
60    ).to(device)
61
62    total_parameter = sum(p.numel() for p in model.parameters())
63    print(f"Parameters of the model: {total_parameter:,}")
```

Line 51 check if a GPU is available. And Line 52 to 60 create the model and send to the `device`, either CPU or GPU.

Line 62 and 63 obtain the total parameters of the model and print it out:

```
Parameters of the model: 16,259,057
```

It means this model has 16M parameters.

We also need to create masks for the input data:

```
64    def create_mask(src, tgt, pad_idx=PAD_IDX):
65        src_seq_len = src.shape[1]
66        tgt_seq_len = tgt.shape[1]
67        src_mask = torch.zeros((src_seq_len, src_seq_len),
68                        device=device).type(torch.bool)
69        tgt_mask = model.transformer.
70                    generate_square_subsequent_mask(tgt_seq_len)
71        src_padding_mask = (src == pad_idx)
72        tgt_padding_mask = (tgt == pad_idx)
73        return src_mask, tgt_mask, \
74                src_padding_mask, tgt_padding_mask
```

This function creates all required masks for the data. Line 67 and 68 create source mask which is a square matrix with size of source sequence length.

Line 69 and 70 creates subsequence mask by calling `nn.Transformer`'s `generate_square_subsequent_mask()` function, it creates the mask as described in Section 3.7, the mask looks like:

```
tensor([[0., -inf, -inf, -inf, -inf, -inf],
        [0.,   0., -inf, -inf, -inf, -inf],
        [0.,   0.,   0., -inf, -inf, -inf],
```

```
          [0.,    0.,    0.,    0.,  -inf,  -inf],
          [0.,    0.,    0.,    0.,    0.,  -inf],
          [0.,    0.,    0.,    0.,    0.,    0.]])
```

This is required by the Self-Attention mechanism, reference the previous chapter for how it works.

Line 71 and 72 create padding masks for the source and the target respectively. Basically, it masks out the <PAD> token from the input data, see in Section 3.7 for details.

We also need to create a loss function and an optimizer:

```
75    criterion = nn.CrossEntropyLoss(ignore_index=PAD_IDX)
76    optimizer = optim.Adam(model.parameters(),
77                           lr=learning_rate,
78                           betas=(0.9, 0.98),
79                           eps=1e-9)
```

The loss function is CrossEntropy, and optimizer is Adam. Line 75 set `ignore_index=PAD_IDX`, meaning the padding value will not be used to calculate the loss. For more details, please reference:

https://pytorch.org/docs/stable/generated/torch.nn.CrossEntropyLoss.html

https://pytorch.org/docs/stable/generated/torch.optim.Adam.html

Then the training process:

```
81    for epoch in range(epochs):
82      model.train()
83      train_batches = len(train_loader)
84      train_losses = 0
85      for i, [src, tgt_in, tgt_out] in enumerate(train_loader):
86        src = src.to(device)
87        tgt_in = tgt_in.to(device)
88        tgt_out = tgt_out.to(device)
89        src_mask, tgt_mask, \
90        src_pad_mask, tgt_pad_mask = create_mask(src, tgt_in)
91        tgt_mask = tgt_mask.to(device)
92        optimizer.zero_grad()
93        logits = model(src, tgt_in, src_mask, tgt_mask,
94                       src_pad_mask, tgt_pad_mask, src_pad_mask)
95        logits = logits.reshape(-1, logits.size(-1))
96        train_loss = criterion(logits, tgt_out.view(-1))
```

```
97          train_losses += train_loss.item()
98          train_loss.backward()
99          optimizer.step()
```

Line 81 begins the training loop.

Line 82 sets the model in train mode, meaning it will update the model weights based on the loss and gradient.

Line 85 starts the loop of loading batches from `train_loader`. The data is loaded to `src`, `tgt_in` and `tgt_out`.

Line 86 to 88 and 91 move the data to `device`, either CPU or GPU.

Line 89 and 90 create all required masks.

Line 93 and 94 invokes the model with require input data and masks, and get the output `logits`, its size is `[batch_size, seq_len, vocab_size]`.

Line 95 changes its size to `[batch_size*seq_len, vocab_size]`.

Line 96 calculates the loss with CrossEntropy function, it compares the model's output `logits` with the `tgt_out`, its size is re-shaped to `[batch_size*seq_len]`.

Line 92, 98 and 99 are standard PyTorch steps to instruct the model to update its weights based on the calculated loss and the gradients.

Within each epoch loop, after the training process, we also do the validation against the validation subset:

```
100     model.eval()
101     val_batches = len(val_loader)
102     val_losses = 0
103     with torch.no_grad():
104        for i, [val_src, val_tgt_in, val_tgt_out] in
105                               enumerate(val_loader):
106          val_src = val_src.to(device)
107          val_tgt_in = val_tgt_in.to(device)
108          val_tgt_out = val_tgt_out.to(device)
109          src_mask, tgt_mask, \
110          src_pad_mask, tgt_pad_mask = \
111                    create_mask(val_src, val_tgt_in)
112          tgt_mask = tgt_mask.to(device)
113          output = model(val_src, val_tgt_in, src_mask,
```

```
114                          tgt_mask, src_pad_mask, tgt_pad_mask,
115                          src_pad_mask)
116         output = output.reshape(-1, output.size(-1))
117         val_loss = criterion(output, val_tgt_out.view(-1))
118         val_losses += val_loss.item()
119    print('Epoch %d' % (epoch+1),
120         'Train loss = {:.6f};'.format(train_losses),
121         'Validation loss = {:.6f}'.format(val_losses)
```

Line 100 set the model to evaluation mode, it instructs the model only produce the output without updating its weights, the dropout is disabled, meaning the dropout neurons will participate in the calculation. Normally the Dropout only affect training phase not the evaluation.

Line 103 instructs the model to disable the gradients, which will reduce memory usage and speed up computations, because the back-propagation is disabled.

The evaluation phase is basically same as training phase, load the batch data from validation set and retrieve the source, target_in and target_out, create the masks, move them to device, either CPU or GPU, send everything to the model as inputs, and obtain the output. And then calculate the loss using the CrossEntropy function.

At the end, print out the train loss and evaluation loss, the result looks like:

```
Epoch 1 Train loss = 4.964918; Validation loss = 4.130655
Epoch 2 Train loss = 3.875258; Validation loss = 3.604441
Epoch 3 Train loss = 3.436359; Validation loss = 3.297237
Epoch 4 Train loss = 3.113854; Validation loss = 3.056929
. . .
Epoch 99 Train loss = 0.647833; Validation loss = 2.372330
Epoch 100 Train loss = 0.648825; Validation loss = 2.373083
```

It takes about half an hour for 100 epochs on Google Colab environment with a T4 GPU.

After the training save the model:

```
122    MODEL_PATH = 'outputs/en2de_checkpoint_100epochs.pth'
123    torch.save(model, MODEL_PATH)
```

At a later time, we can load the saved model for inference, or to continue the training,

```
124    model = torch.load(MODEL_PATH)
```

The curves for train loss and validation loss are shown in Figure 4.2:

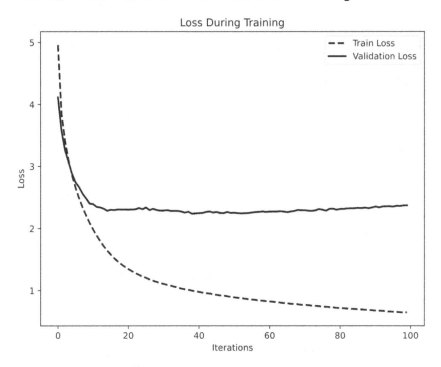

Figure 4.2 Training for English to German Machine Translation

Typically, pre-training transformer models requires access to massive datasets spanning a wide range of topics and domains in order for the model to develop broad and general knowledge. However, in this particular example, we used a more constrained dataset focused specifically on machine translation, by keeping the scope narrow, we presented an approach that can be run without the need for extensive hardware, while illustrating the core concepts of pre-training the Transformer model.

4.5 Inference

We have completed the pre-training on the Transformer model with the built-in `nn.Transformer` class on the Multi30k dataset, which contains pairs of English and German sentences, it's time to use the model to perform the Inference - translating new English sentences into German. This process involves several steps: preparing the test set as the input data, using the model to generate predictions, and then converting those predictions back into human-readable text.

The model is pre-trained on the train set, and the inference will be performed on the test set. Because the test set has different sentences, so the model treats the test set as new data.

The process is the same as illustrated in Figure 3.37, remember when we created the Transformer model the Encoder and Decoder are explicitly created as separate methods, then can be invoked separately. When the model generates an output sequence, the Encoder will be called once with the source (the English sequence) as input, the Decoder will be called iteratively and produce the output token one at a time.

Specifically, the English sentence:

```
A guy works on a building.
```

is passed to the Encoder, and generate an output `memory`. Then <sos> token is passed to the Decoder as input, at the same time `memory` is also fed into the Decoder as input, it produces the output as:

```
<SOS> Ein
```

The next iteration sends the above output to the Decoder as input, and `memory` is also an input, the Decoder produces the output as:

```
<SOS> Ein Typ
```

And so on, the following iterations will produce:

```
<SOS> Ein Typ arbeitet
<SOS> Ein Typ arbeitet an
<SOS> Ein Typ arbeitet an einem
<SOS> Ein Typ arbeitet an einem Gebäude
```

```
<SOS> Ein Typ arbeitet an einem Gebäude.
<SOS> Ein Typ arbeitet an einem Gebäude.<EOS>
```

The iteration stops when `<EOS>` is produced, or `max_len` of tokens are produced.

Same as the last chapter, the Greedy, Random Sampling and Beam algorithms can be used when producing the output tokens. And we introduced the Greedy and the Random Sampling in the last chapter, see Section 3.13. Now for the sake of simplicity, we use Greedy only, here is the `translate()` function that performs inference on the model:

```
1    def translate(model, src, max_len=MAX_LENGTH,
2                       start_symbol=SOS_IDX, end_symbol=EOS_IDX):
3        model.eval()
4        src = src.to(device)
5        src_l = src.shape[1]
6        src_mask = torch.zeros((src_l, src_l)).type(torch.bool)
7        src_mask = src_mask.to(device)
8        memory = model.encoder(src, src_mask)
9        memory = memory.to(device)
10       tgt = torch.ones(1,1).fill_(start_symbol)
11                         .type(torch.long).to(device)
12       for i in range(max_len-1):
13           _, tgt_mask, _, _ = create_mask(src, tgt)
14           tgt_mask = tgt_mask.to(device)
15           out = model.decoder(tgt, memory, tgt_mask)
16           prob = model.output_layer(out[:, -1])
17           next_word = torch.argmax(prob.squeeze(0), dim=-1)
18           tgt = torch.cat([tgt, torch.ones(1,1).type_as(src.data)
19                          .fill_(next_word)], dim=1)
20           if next_word == end_symbol:
21               break
22       return tgt
```

The `translate()` function receives the following parameters:

`model`: the pre-trained Transformer model.

`src`: the source sequence (English).

`max_len`: the max length of tokens to produce, default MAX_LENGTH.

`start_symbol`: start token, default SOS_IDX.

`end_symbol`: end token, default EOS_IDX.

Line 3 sets the model to evaluation mode, Line 4 move `src` to `device`, either CPU or GPU.

Line 5 to 7 create `src_mask` based on the `src`, move it to `device`.

Line 8 and 9 call the Encoder to obtain the output `memory` and move it to `device`.

Line 10 and 11 create `tgt`, the initial input data for the Decoder, which is `start_symbol`, or <sos> token, only. Set its datatype to `torch.long`, and move it to `device`.

Line 12 starts the iteration for producing the output tokens, it stops when reaches `max_len`.

Line 13 obtains the target mask, Line 14 moves it to the `device`.

Line 15 calls the Decoder with target input `tgt`, Encoder output `memory`, and the target mask `tgt_mask`, and obtain the output `out` from the Decoder.

Line 16 calls the `model`'s `output_layer()` function to perform the linear transformation on the Decoder output, it converts the dimension from `d_model` to the target vocab length, the output is `prob`, which is the probabilities of the token.

Line 17 performs the Greedy search, it takes the max probability value from `prob` and obtains the `next_word`.

Line 18 and 19 concatenates the `next_word` to the end of `tgt`, which becomes the new input to the Decoder for next iteration.

Line 20 and 21 checks if the `next_word` is <EOS> token, if yes then break the loop.

Line 22 returns `tgt` as output of the translation, which is something like:

```
tensor([[1, 2586, 11652, 13269, 13094, 14531, 3857, 23, 2]])
```

The numbers are the token IDs of the words in the target vocabulary, the <sos>, which value is 1, is at the beginning, and <EOS>, value of 2, is at the end.

Finally, do the translation with the `test` sub-set.

```
31   test_data = En2De_Dataset(dataset['test'],
32                             tokenize_en,
33                             tokenize_de,
34                             vocab_tokenizers)
35   test_loader = DataLoader(test_data, batch_size=1,
36                            collate_fn=padding,
37                            shuffle=False)
38   test_iterator = iter(test_loader)
39   for i in range(10):
40     source, target, _ = next(test_iterator)
41     target = target[:, 1:]
42     output = translate(model, source)
43     en = list(source.view(-1).cpu().numpy())
44     de = list(target.view(-1).cpu().numpy())
45     pred = list(output.view(-1).cpu().numpy())
46     pred = [x for x in pred if x not in [SOS_IDX, EOS_IDX]]
47     print("English:",
48           " ".join(vocab_tokenizers["en"](en, encode=False)))
49     print("German: ",
50           " ".join(vocab_tokenizers["de"](de, encode=False)))
51     print("Predict:",
52           " ".join(vocab_tokenizers["de"](pred,encode=False)))
```

Line 31 to 34 build a dataset from the test sub-set. And Line 35 to 37 create a DataLoader based on it. The `batch_size` is set to 1, every time it picks one data item, which is an English-German pair.

Line 38 create an `iterator` from the data loader, it randomly picks up a batch of data, in this case batch size is 1, it picks up one data item.

Line 39 starts a loop of 10, we will generate ten translations.

Line 40 picks up an English-German pair.

Line 42 sends the source, which is English, for translation, and obtains the result.

Line 43 to 45 convert source, target and translation output to Python lists. And Line 46 removes the start and end tokens.

Line 47 to 52 print out the results, like below:

```
English: People are fixing the roof of a house .
German:  Leute Reparieren das Dach eines Hauses .
```

```
Predict: Leute reparieren das Dach eines Hauses .


English: A guy works on a building .
German:  Ein Typ arbeitet an einem Gebäude .
Predict: Ein Typ arbeitet an einem Gebäude .


English: A group of people standing in front of an igloo .
German:  Eine Gruppe von Menschen steht vor einem Iglu .
Predict: Eine Gruppe von Leuten steht vor einem Iglu .

 . . .
```

In the above results, English and German are from the original test sub-set, Predict is produced from our pre-trained Transformer model. From the results we can see the predicted outputs are very close, if not same, to the original German sentences, which means the model is properly trained for this task.

This section outlines the general steps involved in inference with a pre-trained model on a sequence translation task. As a summary, Training and Inference are two distinct phases in the lifecycle of a Transformer model. Training is to learn from the dataset, the model is updating its weights based on the loss, or the difference between the model's predictions and the actual targets in the backpropagation process. And the output is produced one time, compared with one by one in the inference phase, this is achieved by the Subsequence Masks, which prevent the model from "cheating" by seeing future tokens in the target sequences.

On the other hand, the Inference is to make predictions using the pre-trained model on the new data. The model is set in evaluation mode, which is an immutable state, meaning the model will not update the weights, the dropout is disabled, there are no backpropagation processes. The model produces the output iteratively, meaning produces tokens one by one. The masks still apply to the data as the Training phase. The Inference consumes less computational resources compared with Training phase.

The source code for the English-German translation is available at the Github repository and named En2De_Translation.ipynb. There is another one En2Fr_Translation.ipynb for your reference, it translates

English to French, everything is similar to the German one, however it demonstrates how to load the dataset from a csv file. The dataset is much larger, the trainset has 158K language pairs, compared with 29K in English-German one, therefore it will take longer time in training phase, nearly 3 hours on a single T4 GPU.

4.6 Popular Large Language Models

Large Language Models (LLMs) have revolutionized the field of generative Artificial Intelligence (AI) and Natural Language Processing (NLP) with their ability to understand and produce human-like texts. These models range from tens of millions to hundreds of billions of parameters. The paper *A Survey of Large Language Models* [15], *https://doi.org/10.48550/arXiv.2303.18223* gives an overview of the existing pre-trained LLMs that available today.

In the realm of academic research, one indicator of emerging interest and advancement is the volume of scholarly publications on a topic. In recent years, there has been a remarkable surge in the number of papers submitted to arXiv mentioning "Large Language Model" in their titles or abstracts. Figure 4.3 shows the cumulative numbers of papers published on arXiv that include the word "Language Model":

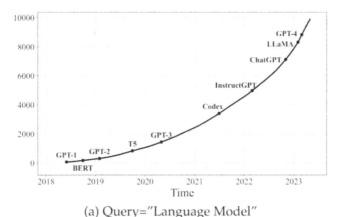

(a) Query="Language Model"

Figure 4.3 Number of papers on arXiv with "Language Model"
Source from: A Survey of Large Language Models [15],
https://doi.org/10.48550/arXiv.2303.18223

And Figure 4.4 shows the same with the word "Large Language Model".

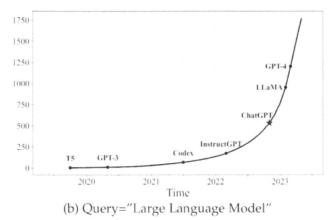

(b) Query="Large Language Model"

Figure 4.4 Number of papers on arXiv with "Large Language Model"
Source from: A Survey of Large Language Models [15],
https://doi.org/10.48550/arXiv.2303.18223

This indicates that lots of researchers are diving into this area and finding new stuff to say and share about it. This is a hot topic that's grabbing a lot of attention in the science world. And there are many pre-trained models are developed and available to public as of today. Figure 4.5 shows a timeline of existing Large Language Models with the size larger than 10B in recent years:

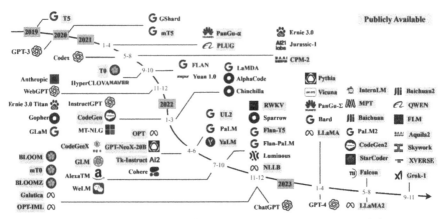

Figure 4.5 An Overview of the Existing Large Language Models
Source from: A Survey of Large Language Models [15],
https://doi.org/10.48550/arXiv.2303.18223

Below is an overview of some of the most notable models, most of them are available as open-source.

GPT (Generative Pre-trained Transformer):

- Developed by OpenAI, it started with GPT and has evolved through GPT-2, GPT-3 and GPT-4 with the latter being one of the most powerful language models available.
- It is known for its high-quality text generation and has generated buzz across multiple industries for its applications.

GPT-2:

- A predecessor to GPT-3, this large transformer-based language model has 1.5 billion parameters.
- Despite its smaller size compared to GPT-3, it still showcases remarkable text generation capabilities.

GPT-3:

- With 175 billion parameters, GPT-3 is one of the most advanced AI language models available.
- It is not open-source, but its API is available to the public through OpenAI's paid services.

BERT (Bidirectional Encoder Representations from Transformers):

- Developed by Google AI, it revolutionized the understanding of context in language models by training on a large corpus in a bidirectional manner.
- The model has several variations, including RoBERTa (optimized BERT with more data and training time), and ALBERT (a lite version for optimized memory usage).

RoBERTa (Robustly optimized BERT approach)

- Developed by Facebook AI, an optimized version of BERT.
- It is pre-trained on an even larger corpus of text and for longer than BERT, resulting in improved performance across many benchmarks.

T5 (Text-to-Text Transfer Transformer) by Google AI:

- T5 reframes all NLP tasks into a text-to-text framework, making it a versatile solution for a wide spectrum of language processing tasks.
- It can be used for translation, summarization, question answering, and more.

FLAN-T5 (Fine-tuned LAnguage Net, Text-To-Text Transfer Transformer):

- Released together with paper *Scaling Instruction-Finetuned Language Models*[16], https://doi.org/10.48550/arXiv.2210.11416, published by Google researchers.
- Flan-T5 is an encoder-decoder model pre-trained on a variety of language tasks.
- Trained on supervised and unsupervised datasets with the goal of learning mappings between sequences of text, i.e., text-to-text.

XLNet by Google:

- An extension of BERT, XLNet leverages permutation-based training to overcome some of the limitations in BERT's training strategy.
- It is available in large configurations and demonstrates strong performance on various NLP tasks.

BLOOM by the BigScience:

- Over 1,000 AI researchers worked together to make a multilingual large language model bigger than GPT-3 and free to use.
- 176B parameters, 59 languages
- The focus is on ethical considerations and multilingual capabilities.

DistilBERT:

- A smaller, faster, lighter, and cheaper version of BERT, this model retains 95% of BERT's performance with 40% fewer parameters.
- It is distilled knowledge from BERT and is more suitable for use-cases where computational resources are limited.

ERNIE (Enhanced Representation through kNowledge Integration):

- Developed by the Baidu research team, ERNIE is a series of powerful models, especially in Chinese tasks, including ERNIE1.0, ERNIE2.0, ERNIE3.0, ERNIE-Gram, ERNIE-health, etc.
- It is a language understanding model that integrates lexical, syntactic, and semantic knowledge.

These pre-trained LLMs have greatly simplified many complex tasks across NLP by providing a strong starting point for fine-tuning on specific tasks and datasets. Most in the above list are publicly available as open-source, while many of them are not completely open-source due to their large size and computational requirements, like GPT-3, their capabilities can often be accessed via APIs or through shared interfaces.

The open-source models like BERT, GPT, FLAN-T5, and their derivatives provide powerful tools for academic research and practical applications, and their open nature facilitates collaboration and innovation in the NLP community, leading to continuous improvements and the training of even more specialized models.

Figure 4.6 shows the parameter size and where the data is collected for some most popular models.

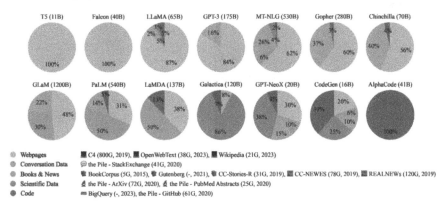

Figure 4.6 Parameter Size and Data Collection for Existing LLMs
Source from: A Survey of Large Language Models [15],
https://doi.org/10.48550/arXiv.2303.18223

Some models focus purely on the data from webpages, some are balanced from webpages, books and news as well as scientific data, and some focus more on the codes. By carefully reviewing the datasets for these pre-trained LLMs, you will be able to choose one that best fit your specific needs, aligns with your requirements and goals.

All these pre-trained LLMs follow the same Transformer architecture of Figure 3.1. However, just like all the students are in the same school, but they learned different majors with different focus and strengths. The LLMs split off into three distinct branches: encoder-only, decoder-only, and encoder-decoder models.

Encoder-only models:

The Encoder-only models, as its name suggested, only utilize the left part of Figure 3.1, the Encoder. They like the friend who's really good at listening and analyzing what you're saying but doesn't say much back. They read text and get what's going on, which makes them awesome for tasks like sorting your emails, finding info (like a searcher), or figuring out if a review is thumb-up or thumb-down.

As shown in Figure 4.7:

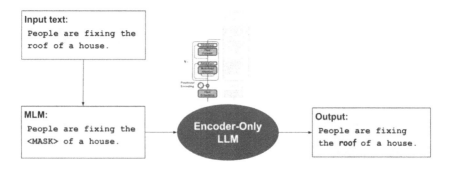

Figure 4.7 Encoder-only LLM Pre-training

They are pre-trained using a variety of tasks that require the model to understand and analyze input text deeply. It utilizes a technique called Masked Language Modeling (MLM), for example the original text is:

People are fixing the roof of a house.

The texts (or tokens) are randomly masked, like this:

People are fixing the <MASK> of a house.

The objective of the pre-training is to predict the masked tokens in order to reconstruct the original text. The models try to guess missing parts of the input texts, figuring out language patterns and context along the way.

Another technique used for pre-training is called Next Sentence Prediction (NSP), the models read two sentences and decide if the second one follows the first in a logical way.

During pre-training, the model goes through tons of text, like websites, books, articles, and so on, practicing MLM and NSP tasks over and over. By exposing the model to a diverse set of information and asking it to predict masked words and the relation between sentences, it gets pretty good at understanding language – like the grammar, the nuances, and the way ideas are connected.

Use cases:

- Sentiment analysis
- Named entity recognition
- Text classification

Sample models:

- BERT
- DistilBERT
- RoBERTa

Decoder-only models:

The Decoder-only model is only the right part of Figure 3.1. Unlike the Encode-only ones, they love speaking. Give them a start, and they'll take it and run with it, spinning out stories or completing your sentences. They're useful for creative writing aids or when you need to draft a bunch of texts. GPT is a good example of this type of models.

The Decoder-only also called Causal Language Modeling, the model looks at a sequence of words and then predicts what word comes next, one step at a time. Say if the input sequence is:

People ...

The model might say *"are"* following the previous words, based on what commonly follows in that sentence, as shown in Figure 4.8:

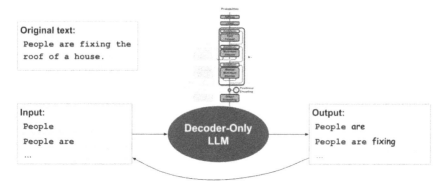

Figure 4.8 Decoder-only LLM Pre-training

Then the output *"People are"* is send back to the input of LLM, this time the model might guess the next word as *"fixing"*. This process is going back and forth iteratively until it reaches a given max length of word or meets the special end token.

The model learns from vast amount of data, from novels and news articles to websites, as they read, they constantly guess what words come next. They are trained not only to guess the next word, but also to understand the meaning of the texts. Eventually the Decoder-only models become storytellers, and ready to compose texts that feels natural.

Use cases:

- Text generation

Sample models:

- GPT family
- BLOOM

Encoder-decoder models:

The Encoder-decoder models use both parts of Figure 3.1, the Encoder as well as Decoder. They've acquired the skills in both understanding and producing texts.

This type of models is the combination of Encoder and Decoder, the former reads the texts and outputs the embedded representation that the Decoder understands, as we explained in the last chapter. The latter uses that output together with its input texts to produce new story.

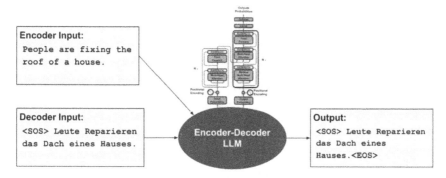

Figure 4.9 Encoder-Decoder LLM Pre-training

Our previous examples are Encoder-decoder model, the example in Chapter 3 was dealing with question answering task, the one in Chapter 4 is for translation task. As shown in Figure 4.9, the source texts are sent to the Encoder and the right-shifted target texts are sent to the Decoder, the LLM understands the information from the Encoder, together with the input from the Decode, it produces the output texts.

The Encoder-Decoder models become adept at a broad range of tasks, from translation and summarization to question-answering and text completion, enabling them to not only understand but also generate human-like text.

Use case:

- Translation
- Text summarization
- Question answering

Example models:

- T5
- FLAN-T5
- BART

Choosing existing models is step 3a in the life cycle of LLM in Figure 1.2.

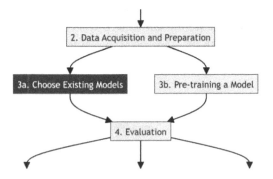

In summary, the choice between Encoder-only, Decoder-only, and Encoder-Decoder models is determined by the specific requirements of the tasks, which are the needs for understanding the texts, generating the texts, or both. Each model architecture brings unique advantages to the table and can be selected based on the specific objectives of the language processing goals.

4.7 Computational Resources

Most of the LLMs are huge, both the number of parameters and the amount of dataset, and it requires tons of memory to store the data and to perform the pre-training. Sometimes the below error message pops up:

`CUDA out of memory.`

It typically indicates that the Graphics Processing Unit (GPU), which uses CUDA (Compute Unified Device Architecture) as its computing platform, has run out of memory during a computation, often when running the LLMs, sometime even loading the dataset.

In this section, let's do the estimation to understand what computational resources are needed for the LLMs.

How much memory is needed to store a LLM with 1 billion parameters:

1 parameter (32-bit float datatype) = 4 byte

1 billion parameter = 4 x 10^9 = 4GB

This means to store the weights of a LLM of 1B params needs 4GB of RAM. This is only to store the model, the additional memory is needed to train the model.

	Bytes per param
Model weights	4
Adam optimizer	8
Gradients	4
Activations and others	8
Total	**24**

The GPU memory needed to train a LLM with 1B params:

$24 \times 10^9 = 24GB$

This is only 1B model, some LLMs have 100B or even 500B params:

100B params need $100 \times 24 \times 10^9 = 2,400GB$

500B params need $500 \times 24 \times 10^9 = 12,000GB$

This is a huge amount of memory, when the model's size gets larger, it needs to be split cross multiple GPUs for training, ranging from several hundreds to thousands of GPUs.

A memory optimization strategy is called Quantization, with the goal of reducing the precision of the numbers used to represent the model's weights. This is done to decrease the model's memory footprint and, as a result, the computational resources required for both training and inference.

Normally the neural networks use **FP32** (32-bit single-precision floating-point format) as the standard datatype for the weights, as shown in Figure 4.10:

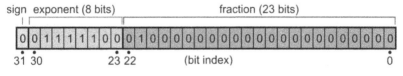

Figure 4.10 FP32 Data Format

The FP32 includes:

1 bit for sign

8 bits for exponent

23 bits for fraction

The range of FP32 is 1.175494×10^{-38} to 3.402823×10^{38}.

This datatype is not only used for weights, but also for gradients, optimizer, activations and so on. It is supported in PyTorch as `torch.float` and TensorFlos as `tf.float32`.

FP32 takes 4 bytes, the objective of Quantization is to reduce the memory by using other types of data instead.

FP16 is half-precision floating-point datatype, as Figure 4.11:

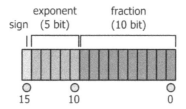

Figure 4.11 FP16 Data Format

The FP16 has:

1 bit for sign

5 bits for exponent

10 bits for fraction

Its range is from 5.96046×10^{-8} to 65504. In deep neural network training process, it seems the reduced precision is not critical to the calculation, the benefit is faster and reduced requirement for memory. And both PyTorch and TensorFLow support this datatype. It was not well supported by old GPUs but gets supported by most recent GPUs.

Therefore, FP16 is one of the candidates to replace FP32 in terms of Quantization for not only the training phase but also the inference phase.

BFLOAT16, or **BF16** is another 16-bit, or 2 byte, format developed by Google Brain, called Brain Floating Point Format. It becomes popular choice for deep neural networks, many LLMs are trained using BLOAT16. It's a hybrid between half-precision floating-point (FP16) and single-precision floating-point (FP32), as Figure 4.12

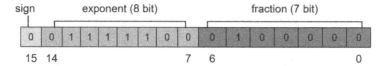

Figure 4.12 BF16 Data Format
Source from bfloat16 floating-point format. In Wikipedia.
https://en.wikipedia.org/wiki/Bfloat16_floating-point_format

The BFLOAT16 has:

1 bit for sign

8 bits for exponent

7 bits for fraction

Its range is from 1.18×10^{-38} to 3.39×10^{38}, it's often described as truncated version of FP32, it uses the same 8-bit to represent exponent and truncates the fraction part from 23-bit to 7 bit. As the result it has the same range as FP32, with reduced precision. PyTorch supports it as `torch.bfloat16`, and TensorFlow as `tf.bfloat16`.

BFLOAT16 is a good candidate to replace FP32 in terms of Quantization, because it's half the size of FP32 that significantly save the memory for LLMs, and many deep learning neural networks don't require the full precision of FP32, they can still achieve the high performance with reduced precision.

In most cases the data range is more important than high precision in deep learning neural networks, BFLOAT16 provides the same data range as FP32, so it's compatible with FP32 and requires minimal software changes to replace it. While FP16 provides reduced data range, additional scaling factors might need if use FP16 to replace FP32.

If FP32 can be successfully replaced by the 16-bit datatype, either BFLOAT16 or FP16, the memory required for a 1B params LLM could reduce from 24GB to 12GB, that's a significant memory saving. However, the pre-training with the lower-precision datatype might lead to increased instability in the training phase or a reduced accuracy if not managed correctly. Some considerations in the training strategies might include techniques such as mixed-precision training, where FP32 is used for certain parts of the training process that need higher-precision calculations; and BFLOAT16 is used for the other parts of the training.

As a quantitative analysis on the computational resources, the term of FLOP/s (Floating Point Operations Per Second) is a standard measure of computer performance, especially in the field of calculations that make heavy use of floating-point calculations such as pre-training of LLMs.

Here are the scales of it:

A kiloflop/s = 10^3 FLOP/s

A megaFLOP/s = 10^6 FLOP/s

A gigaFLOP/s = 10^9 FLOP/s

A teraFLOP/s = 10^{12} FLOP/s

A petaFLOP/s = 10^{15} FLOP/s

An exaFLOP/s = 10^{18} FLOP/s

The modern GPUs can reach teraFLOP/s or petaFLOP/s scale, and the pre-training of the popular LLMs is also in this scale.

A petaFLOP/s-day is a unit for the amount of computation, which is the operation of a full day, or 24 hours, at a petaFLOP/s. There are 86,400 seconds in a full day, therefore:

petaFLOP/s-day = 86,400 petaFLOP/s = 8.64×10^{-19} FLOP/s

Figure 4.13 depicts the computation of pre-training in petaFLOP/s-days for the well-known LLMs, such as BERT, RoBERTa, T5, and GPT-3. The T5-3B model (3B params), the bar in the middle of Figure 4.13, needs 100 petaFLOP/s-days; while the bar at the very right is GPT-3 (175B parame), it needs 3640 petaFLOP/s-days.

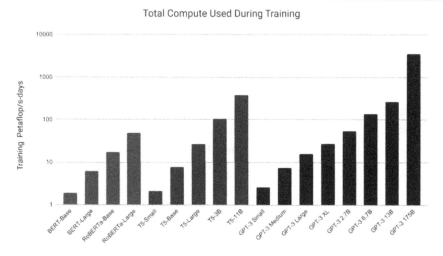

Figure 4.13 Computational Resources for Pre-training on BERT, T5 and GPT-3
Source from: Language Models are Few-Shot Learners[17], Brown et al. 2020,
https://arxiv.org/abs/2005.14165, modified by Author.

Figure 4.14 denotes the total tokens, params and computation resources for these models.

Model	Total train compute (PF-days)	Total train compute (flops)	Params (M)	Training tokens (billions)	Flops per param per token	Mult for bwd pass	Fwd-pass flops per active param per token	Frac of params active for each token
T5-Small	2.08E+00	1.80E+20	60	1,000	3	3	1	0.5
T5-Base	7.64E+00	6.60E+20	220	1,000	3	3	1	0.5
T5-Large	2.67E+01	2.31E+21	770	1,000	3	3	1	0.5
T5-3B	1.04E+02	9.00E+21	3,000	1,000	3	3	1	0.5
T5-11B	3.82E+02	3.30E+22	11,000	1,000	3	3	1	0.5
BERT-Base	1.89E+00	1.64E+20	109	250	6	3	2	1.0
BERT-Large	6.16E+00	5.33E+20	355	250	6	3	2	1.0
RoBERTa-Base	1.74E+01	1.50E+21	125	2,000	6	3	2	1.0
RoBERTa-Large	4.93E+01	4.26E+21	355	2,000	6	3	2	1.0
GPT-3 Small	2.60E+00	2.25E+20	125	300	6	3	2	1.0
GPT-3 Medium	7.42E+00	6.41E+20	356	300	6	3	2	1.0
GPT-3 Large	1.58E+01	1.37E+21	760	300	6	3	2	1.0
GPT-3 XL	2.75E+01	2.38E+21	1,320	300	6	3	2	1.0
GPT-3 2.7B	5.52E+01	4.77E+21	2,650	300	6	3	2	1.0
GPT-3 6.7B	1.39E+02	1.20E+22	6,660	300	6	3	2	1.0
GPT-3 13B	2.68E+02	2.31E+22	12,850	300	6	3	2	1.0
GPT-3 175B	3.64E+03	3.14E+23	174,600	300	6	3	2	1.0

Figure 4.14 Computational Resources for Pre-training on BERT, T5 and GPT-3
Source from: Language Models are Few-Shot Learners [17], Brown et al. 2020,
https://arxiv.org/abs/2005.14165

For the computing power of GPUs, Nvidia A100 with 80GB memory has 312 teraFLOP/s on BFLOAT16 or FP16 datatype, and 156 teraFLOP/s on TF32 datatype. Which means three A100/80GB GPUs running at full efficiency on 16-bit datatype for one full day can reach about a petaFLOP/s-day.

Nvidia V100 with 32GB memory has 16.4 teraFLOP/s on single-precision floating-point.

Based on these GPU specs, and the required computation from Figure 4.14, you can estimate how many GPUs running how many days to perform the pre-training for different LLMs in different param sizes.

It's difficult to run such big models within one GPU, based on the paper of *Efficient Large-Scale Language Model Training on GPU Clusters Using Megatron-LM* [18], *2021, https://arxiv.org/abs/2104.04473*, the GPT-3 with 175B params would require about 288 years with a single Nvidia V100 GPU. Therefore, the pre-training for LLMs is usually performed in a distributed computing environment with multiple GPUs.

Based on the same paper, it takes 34 days to train the same model with 1024 A100 GPUs, the model has 300 billion tokens; it takes 84 days to train a 1 trillion params LLM with 450 billion tokens with 3072 A100 GPUs.

Below table lists the parameter size, data (corpus) size, and training cost for some of the most popular LLMs.

Name	Number of parameters	Corpus size	Training cost (petaFLOP-day)
GPT-1	117 million		
BERT	340 million	3.3 billion words	9
XLNet	~340 million	33 billion words	
GPT-2	1.5 billion	40GB (~10 billion tokens)	
GPT-3	175 billion	300 billion tokens	3640
GPT-Neo	2.7 billion	825 GiB	
GPT-J	6 billion	825 GiB	200
Megatron-Turing NLG	530 billion	338.6 billion tokens	
Ernie 3.0 Titan	260 billion	4 Tb	
Claude	52 billion	400 billion tokens	
GLaM	1.2 trillion	1.6 trillion tokens	5600
Gopher	280 billion	300 billion tokens	5833

LaMDA	137 billion	1.56T words, 168 billion tokens	4110
GPT-NeoX	20 billion	825 GiB	740
Chinchilla	70 billion	1.4 trillion tokens	6805
PaLM	540 billion	768 billion tokens	29250
OPT (Open Pretrained Transformer)	175 billion	180 billion tokens	310
YaLM 100B	100 billion	1.7TB	
Minerva	540 billion	38.5B tokens from webpages filtered for mathematical content and from papers submitted to the arXiv preprint server	
BLOOM	175 billion	350 billion tokens (1.6TB)	
Galactica	120 billion	106 billion tokens	
AlexaTM	20 billion	1.3 trillion	
LLaMA	65 billion	1.4 trillion	6300
Cerebras-GPT	13 billion		270
Falcon	40 billion	1 trillion tokens	2800
BloombergGPT	50 billion	363 billion tokens on Bloomberg's data sources, plus 345 billion tokens from general purpose datasets	
PanGu-Σ	1.085 trillion	329 billion tokens	
OpenAssistant	17 billion	1.5 trillion tokens	
PaLM 2	340 billion	3.6 trillion tokens	85000
Llama 2	70 billion	2 trillion tokens	
Falcon 180B	180 billion	3.5 trillion tokens	
Mixtral 8x7B	46.7B		
Phi-2	2.7B	1.4T tokens	
Eagle 7B	7.52B	1.1T tokens	
Gemma	2B and 7B	6T tokens	

Source from: https://en.wikipedia.org/wiki/Large_language_model.
Modified by author.

Hopefully this section can give a general idea of how much efforts to pre-train the LLMs.

4.8 Prompt Engineering and In-context Learning (ICL)

As some terminologies, the process of LLMs to produce texts is known as *Inference*; the input text that you feed into the model is called *Prompt*; the container that hold the prompt is called the *Context*, which could be a context window that appears as the user interfaces that the users can input text into, it could also be a block of memory that developers use to feed to LLMs programmatically.

In-Context Learning (ICL) is a method that creates input examples directly into the prompt of an LLM, which produces the outputs in the Inference. This approach enables pre-trained LLMs to deal with new tasks by leveraging the context provided, rather than undergoing specific fine-tuning of the model's parameters.

Prompt Engineering is the process of refining prompts that input to the LLMs to produce textual outputs, it's a technique that the engineers use when refining LLMs with specific prompts.

Prompt Engineering is step 5a in the life cycle of LLM in Figure 1.2:

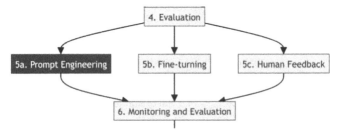

Zero-shot learning (ZSL):

In Zero-shot learning, the engineers or users provides a prompt without any examples, and the LLM will figure out the meanings of the prompt and produce the output based on what it has been trained.

As shown in Figure 4.15, the prompt is created by providing a customer review, and instruct the LLM to classify it as Positive, Negative or Neutral.

The LLM receives no examples of the desired task from the prompt, it must rely entirely on its pre-trained understanding to infer what is being asked and how to respond. In this example, hopefully the LLM can generate Positive as the output.

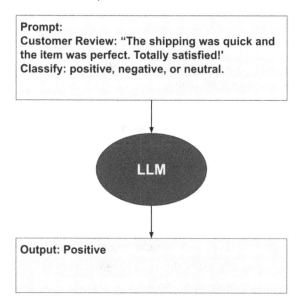

Figure 4.15 Zero-shot learning

Let's send it to ChatGPT-3.5 and see what happen.

You:

Customer Review: "The shipping was quick and the item was perfect. Totally satisfied!'.
Classification: positive, negative, or neutral.

ChatGPT:
Classification: Positive

It successfully classifies it as Positive.

In Zero-shot Learning, the LLM may be given a description of a task or a direct question, it has to generate an appropriate response without any specific prior context, or examples, that directly relates to the task.

One-shot learning (OSL):

One-shot learning is basically same as Zero-shot, we give LLM model one example of the task to help it understand what we're referring to, this example serves as context and the model should generalize from it and complete the task with new inputs.

For example,

> *You:*
>
> *Customer Review: "The restaurant was terrible, and the service was even worse. Not going back there again."*
>
> *Classification: Negative.*
>
> *Customer Review: "The new update is almost useless, the new features seem not relevant to our business flow."*
>
> *Please classify this review as positive, negative, or neutral.*
>
> *ChatGPT:*
>
> *Classification: Negative*

In this case we give the LLM an example of a customer review which is classified as Negative. We want the LLM to learn from the example, then give it another customer review and let it to classify. This time it gives the output of Negative with a reason.

Few-shot learning (FSL):

Since ChatGPT is well-established LLM, in most of cases it gives the outputs that in line with what we expected. However, if a specific LLM does not produce the desired output, we might need to give it more examples to learn.

This comes Few-shot learning, where the LLM is provided with a few examples (more than one but usually not many) that describe the task, the model uses these examples to understand the pattern of the task and applies what it has learned to new inputs.

> *You:*
>
> *Customer Review 1: "I love this new movie, one of the best movies I've seen, definitely worth watching again!"*
>
> *Classification: Positive.*

Customer Review 2: "The movie was a total waste of time and money, absolutely boring."

Classification: Negative.

Customer Review 3: "It's an average restaurant, the food is okay, but nothing special."

Classification: Neutral.

Please classify the following review: "This restaurant was clean in general, but it took a while to get my foods served."

Please classify this review as positive, negative, or neutral.

ChatGPT:

Classification: Neutral

Here we give ChatGPT three examples of customer reviews with the corresponding classification, it learns from what we provided. Then give it a new customer review and let it to give us an output.

Sometimes 2 or 3 examples might not enough to make the LLM performs well, we can provide some more examples. However, if more than 5 or 6 examples can not make it performs well, maybe the prompt engineering is not appropriate to train the model, in this case might think to use Fine-tuning, which will be introduced in the next chapter.

In the above examples, maybe Positive, Negative and Neutral are generic categories for classification, you might want to try some specialized classes, e.g. A for positive, B for negative and C for Neutral, and see how ChatGPT learn from your Few-shot prompts.

Zero-shot, One-shot and Few-shot learning on LLMs are considered to be In-Context Learning (ICL), which is the capability of the LLMs to learn from the context provided in the prompt without any gradient updates on the weights. This means that instead of training the model with a large dataset and then using it for inference, the model uses the information contained within a given prompt to decide how to respond appropriately.

The ICL is particularly powerful because it allows the model to adapt to a wide variety of tasks without any explicit re-training or fine-tuning. We just simply provide examples in the prompts, which could be zero, one, or a few examples, we can effectively guide the LLM to understand the task and generate the relevant responses.

The ICL is just like human to learn things, when children are provided with several samples of dog, they are able to tell dogs without further explicit instructions.

The key to ICL is how to craft the prompt, a well-designed prompt can lead to significantly better performance on the task, which doesn't have to be explicitly covered during the model's pre-training. To create the prompt is considered as a bit of an art mixed with engineering, in most of cases you might need to try several times to get a good prompt.

ChatGPT provides a web user interfaces, so we have the context window to put the prompt in. If an LLM does not come with a user interface, we can interact with the model programmatically, the next section will introduce how to do it.

4.9   Prompt Engineering on FLAN-T5

In this section we will use FLAN-T5, an open-source LLM available for commercial use, as the pre-trained model to conduct the prompt engineering. FLAN-T5 is briefly mentioned in the previous section, it's a combination of two things: FLAN (Finetuned LAnguage Net) and T5 (Text-To-Text Transfer Transformer), which is developed and published by Google, as the paper *Scaling Instruction-Finetuned Language Models*[16], https://doi.org/10.48550/arXiv.2210.11416.

T5 is trained by converting everything into a text-to-text format, which means it treats every task like a translation problem. So, whether it's summarizing, classifying, answering questions, etc., it all becomes a matter of translating text from one form to another.

FLAN-T5 is an improved version of T5, an encoder-decoder model pre-trained on a variety of language tasks with both supervised and unsupervised datasets. It's good at understanding and generating language across a wide spectrum of tasks.

Figure 4.16, sourcing from the paper, shows an overview of FLAN-T5, which is fine-tuned using carefully crafted prompts across various language models on 1.8K tasks phrased as instructions.

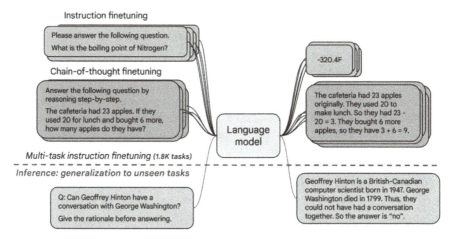

Figure 4.16 FLAN-T5 Model
Source from: Scaling Instruction-Finetuned Language Models [16],
https://arxiv.org/abs/ 2210.11416v5

FLAN-T5 model is pre-trained based on prompting, therefore it shows improved performance on in-context learning tasks compared to its T5 predecessor, which means it can better understand and perform tasks as zero-shot, one-shot and few-shot learning.

FLAN-T5 is available from HuggingFace libraries at, *https://huggingface.co/docs/transformers/model_doc/flan-t5*

It has several variants:

- FLAN-T5 small (77M params)
- FLAN-T5 base (248M params)
- FLAN-T5 large (783M params)
- FLAN-T5 XL (2.85B params)
- FLAN-T5 XXL (11.3B params)

We are going to use FLAN-T5 large version. First install the required packages:

```
1    !pip install transformers
```

```
2    !pip install sentencepiece
3    !pip install accelerate
```

Then import the model:

```
4     from transformers import T5Tokenizer,
5                        T5ForConditionalGeneration
6     def load_model(model_name):
7       tokenizer = T5Tokenizer.from_pretrained(model_name)
8       model = T5ForConditionalGeneration
9                     .from_pretrained(model_name)
10      return tokenizer, model
11    tokenizer, model = load_model('google/flan-t5-large')
```

In the Hugging Face `transformers` library, loading a model includes two main components: the tokenizer and the actual model class. `T5Tokenizer` is to load the tokenizer of FLAN-T5, which is responsible for preprocessing text for the model. As explained earlier tokenization is the process of translating the original text into token IDs which are the numerical representations that can be processed by the model. The tokens can represent words, sub-words, or characters, different models have different rules for tokenization, therefore it's important to retrieve their corresponding tokenizer. Line 7 is to load the tokenizer from the specific model given by `model_name`.

In Section 4.2 we built our tokenizer from scratch, in the real-world LLM projects it's common practice to load the tokenizer together with the pre-trained model, it is specialized to handle tasks for the model, such as splitting the input text into tokens, adding special tokens (like padding tokens, start and end of sequence tokens), converting tokens to their corresponding IDs and building attention masks, and so on.

`T5ForConditionalGeneration` in Line 8 retrieves the transformer model specified by `model_name`, and load its pre-trained weights. It is ready to process the inputs, and produce the outputs.

Line 10 returns both `tokenizer` and `model`.

Line 11 invokes `load_model()` to load `google/flan-t5-large` model.

Then, create a function to generate outputs with the model:

```
12    def generate_output(tokenizer, model, input_text,
```

```
13                            max_length=200):
14      input_ids = tokenizer(input_text,
15                            return_tensors="pt").input_ids
16      outputs = model.generate(input_ids, max_length=max_length)
17      response = tokenizer.decode(outputs[0],
18                            skip_special_tokens=True)
19      return response
```

`generate_output()` function produces outputs from the input texts. Its input parameters are:

`tokenizer:` tokenizer of the specified model.

`model:` the specified model.

`input_text:` the input texts.

`max_length:` the max length of the produced output, default 200 here.

Line 14 and 15 retrieves the token IDs from the tokenizer on the input text, where `return_tensors="pt"` means the output is in the format of PyTorch tensors, the `input_ids` are the numerical IDs (or token IDs) that generated by the tokenizer on the input text.

For example, the input text "*How are you doing?*" will be tokenized as:

```
input_ids = tensor([[571, 33, 25, 692, 58, 1]])
```

Line 15 obtains the output from the model's `generate()` function, the `input_ids` is fed into the function, together with a `max_length`. The output is something like:

```
tensor([[0, 27, 31, 51, 1399, 5, 1]])
```

Line 17 and 18 uses the `tokenizer` to decode the produced output to the human-readable texts, something like:

I'm fine, thanks.

In Line 18 `skip_special_tokens=True` specifies to remove the special tokens from the `outputs`. If not remove them, we get the response with special tokens:

<pad> I'm fine, thanks.</s>

Line 19 returns the `response.`

If curious about how big the model is, we can print out the total number of the parameters of the model, this is optional:

```
20    total_parameter = sum(p.numel() for p in model.parameters())
21    print(f"Parameters of the model: {total_parameter:,}")
```

```
Parameters of the model: 783,150,080
```

For Zero-shot learning, we craft the prompt as the input text, send to FLAN-T5 model, and obtain the output. Here we use the same prompt as the one we sent to ChatGPT:

```
22    prompt = f"""
23    Customer Review: 'The shipping was quick and the item was
24    perfect. Totally satisfied!'.
25    Classification: Positive, Negative, or Neutral.
26    """
27    output = generate_output(tokenizer, model, prompt)
28    print(output)
```

The result is the same as ChatGPT:

```
Positive
```

For One-shot learning:

```
29    prompt = f"""
30    Customer Review: 'The restaurant was terrible, and the
31    service was even worse. Not going back there again.'
32    Classification: Negative.
33
34    Customer Review: 'The new update is almost useless, the new
35    features seem not relevant to our business flow.'
36    Classification: Positive, Negative, or Neutral.
37    """
38    output = generate_output(tokenizer, model, prompt)
39    print(output)
```

The result is also the same as ChatGPT:

```
Negative
```

For Few-shot learning:

```
41    prompt = f"""
42
```

```
43    Customer Review 1: 'I love this new movie, one of the best
44    movies I've seen, definitely worth watching again!'
45    Classification: Positive.
46    Customer Review 2: "The movie was a total waste of time and
47    money, absolutely boring."
48    Classification: Negative.
49    Customer Review 3: "It's an average restaurant, the food is
50    okay, but nothing special."
51    Classification: Neutral.
52
53    Please classify the following review: 'This restaurant was
54    clean in general, but it took a while to get my foods
55    served.'
56    Classification: Positive, Negative, or Neutral.
57    """
58    output = generate_output(tokenizer, model, prompt)
      print(output)
```

We get the result:

```
Negative
```

The result is different from ChatGPT which was Neutral, but it makes sense to classify it as Negative.

This is the idea of In-context Learning and Prompt Engineering, which is considered as a bit of an art mixed with engineering, you will need to craft the prompts that can guide an LLM to give desired outcomes. In most of cases you might need to try several times to get a good prompt. The effectiveness of LLMs in producing accurate and relevant outputs is not solely a result of their pre-training and datasets but also relies heavily on the artful crafting of prompts that guide the models.

In-context Learning (ICL) enables the LLMs to learn the specific task from examples within the prompt in the context, effectively leveraging prior experiences acquired from its training data. This form of learning demonstrates the adaptability of language models and their capability to infer context without explicit pre-training for specific tasks.

Prompt Engineering is a skill as much as a technical practice, which means creatively designing prompts that exploit the LLMs inherent capabilities. This process often requires iterating prompts, analyzing the model's responses, refining input for clarity and direction, and sometimes subtly adjusting the model towards desired outputs.

As the conclusion, while AI has made significant advances in the field of language processing, the human roles remain critical in deriving the desired outputs from the LLMs. Effective communication with these models requires a deep understanding of how they interpret and generate outcomes.

With In-context Learning and Prompt Engineering, through careful prompt design and iterative refinement, we can guide LLMs to generate highly relevant and tailored outputs for our specific needs. We not only explore the full potential of these models, but also chat with AI feels as easy and natural as talking to a friend.

However, as we have discussed above, prompt engineering also comes with challenges and limitations. Crafting effective prompts requires skill and domain knowledge, and the outputs of LLMs can be unpredictable or biased. Carefully considering prompt context and other factors is important to obtaining reliable and useful results.

4.10 Pipelines

The concept of pipelines is offered by the HuggingFace library, which provides a powerful and user-friendly interface for working with state-of-the-art language models and NLP tasks. It simplifies the process of using models for different Natural Language Processing (NLP) tasks.

Pipelines are essentially pre-packaged routines that handle all the necessary steps from data preprocessing to the application of a model and post-processing of its output. In the HuggingFace's transformer library, a pipeline wraps several processes:

1. Preprocessing: Text data needs to be formatted in a way that the model can understand, which includes tokenization and encoding into token IDs. Pipelines handle these steps automatically.
2. Model Inference: After preprocessing, data is fed into an LLM to generate predictions. Depending on the task, this could be a single

model or a cluster of models. The pipeline invokes the appropriate model(s) with the correct parameters.

3. Post-processing: The raw output from the model often needs to be decoded into a more human-readable format. For example, extraction of the predicted class labels in classification tasks, or generating human-readable text from token IDs in generation tasks.

4. Task-specific components: For tasks like question-answering, text summarization, text generation, sentiment analysis, etc., pipelines may include additional components specific to these tasks to fine-tune performance. HuggingFace provides a wide range of ready-to-use pipelines for common tasks such as:

- `sentiment-analysis`: Determines if the input text is positive or negative.
- `question-answering`: Extracts an answer from a text given a question.
- `text-generation`: Produces text following a given prompt.
- `translation_xx_to_yy`: Translates text from language xx to language yy, e.g., `translation_en_to_fr`.
- `summarization`: Creates a summary of a given text.
- `and so on`

It's simple and straightforward to use it, for example we do a translation from English to French task:

```
1    from transformers import pipeline
2    # Load the translation pipeline
3    translator = pipeline("translation_en_to_fr")
```

Line 1 is to import `pipeline` library from `transformers` package.

Line 3 is to load the pipeline for `translation_en_to_fr`.

```
4    # Input text to translate
5    text = "Will you help me with my homework?"
6    # Translate the text
7    translation = translator(text)[0]["translation_text"]
8    print(f"English: {text}")
9    print(f"Frenchn: {translation}")
```

Line 7 is to perform the task. The results are:

```
English: Will you help me with my homework?
Frenchn: Avez-vous de l'aide pour mes devoirs?
```

As you can see, we don't need things like loading the model, tokenizing the input text, decoding the output, etc. The pipeline takes care of everything.

HuggingFace translation pipeline supports many language pairs out of the box, and you can easily switch to a different language pair by specifying the appropriate task name (e.g., `"translation_fr_to_en"` for French to English translation). Similarly, you can create pipelines for `question-answering`, `text-generation`, and more.

Let's look at another example of Sentiment analysis, it's a process of using LLMs to analyze and determine the emotional tone or sentiment conveyed in a piece of text, the goal is to classify the sentiment as positive, negative, or neutral.

```
11    # sentiment_pipeline = pipeline("sentiment-analysis")
12    sentiment_pipeline = pipeline(
13                         model="cardiffnlp/twitter-roberta-
14                         base-sentiment-latest ")
```

The pipeline can be created with the task name, `sentiment-analysis` as Line 11. Alternatively, a model name can be specified when invoking `pipeline()`, as Line 13 and 14, in this example we use `cardiffnlp/twitter-roberta-base-sentiment-latest` model to perform the task.

Give it a customer review to analyze:

```
21    prompt1 = f"""
22    Customer Review: 'The shipping was quick and the item was
23    perfect. Totally satisfied!'.
24    """
25    sentiment_pipeline(prompt1)
```

It comes with a label of `positive` and a score of `0.98`.

```
[{'label': 'positive', 'score': 0.9825846552848816}]
```

Then two more customer reviews:

```
26    prompt2 = f"""
```

```
27   Customer Review: 'The restaurant was terrible, and the
28   service was even worse. Not going back there again.'
29   """
30   sentiment_pipeline(prompt2)
```

[{'label': 'negative', 'score': 0.9405812621116638}]

```
31   prompt3 = f"""
32   Customer Review: 'This restaurant was clean in general, but
33   it took a while to get my foods served.'
34   """
35   sentiment_pipeline(prompt3)
```

[{'label': 'neutral', 'score': 0.5042181015014648}]

In addition to specifying a model name, you can customize the pipeline by passing various parameters to control the behavior of the models, such as setting the maximum output length, number of beams, or configuring other task-specific settings, reference the documentations in HuggingFace's website, *https://huggingface.co/docs/transformers/ pipeline_tutorial*

4.11 Conclusion

This chapter has provided comprehensive insights into the processes of pre-training LLMs (Large Language Models), offering both foundational knowledge and practical guidance.

We embarked on this journey with a hands-on example of pre-training using PyTorch's `nn.transformer()` module on the Multi30k dataset, including loading the dataset, preparing the data with tokenization, building a DataLoader to effectively retrieve the data in batches, setting up the main training loop and performing the inference. This practice effectively bridges the gap between theoretical understanding and practical application.

Given the fact that the pre-training of LLMs typically demands substantial computational power, we have carefully crafted the code examples to be executable within the confines of a single GPU environment. To ensure practicality, we have moderated the scale of both the model and the dataset, enabling the execution of these examples without extensive hardware requirements. This approach is intended solely to demonstrate the concept of pre-training the LLMs, where typically a vast amount of data is used.

Building on the foundation of pre-training, we also explored the landscape of established language models such as GPT, BERT, FLAN-T5, and so on, unraveling their structural complexities and diverse applications. This overview provided context to the state-of-the-art technologies that shape the field of Natural Language Processing (NLP).

The chapter also discussed the challenges of computational resources which remains a critical bottleneck in the development and scaling of the LLMs.

We explored the approach of Prompt Engineering and In-Context learning, the simple yet important strategy that empower LLMs to align more closely with specific tasks and domains. We showcased these techniques not only as theoretical concepts but also through tangible, programmatically driven examples.

Overall, this chapter armed you with a solid understanding of pre-training transformer models, an overview of existing and prominent pre-trained LLMs, and techniques for optimizing model performance through prompt engineering, equipping you with the knowledge and skills to navigate the rapidly evolving field of natural language processing (NLP).

5. Fine-Tuning

F ine-tuning the large language models (LLMs) has emerged as a powerful technique for adapting these general-purpose models to perform specific downstream tasks in the specific domains with impressive performance, just like a medical student going through residency to become a doctor. This chapter explores various approaches and methodologies that can be employed to tailor these models to your organization's unique requirements.

We begin with introducing the concept of Transfer learning which forms the foundation of fine-tuning. Transfer learning allows us to leverage the knowledge and patterns learned by a pre-trained model on a vast corpus of data and adapt it to a new task or domain with relatively small amounts of task-specific data. This approach has proven remarkably effective, enabling rapid model customization while leveraging the powerful capabilities inherent from the original pre-trained LLMs.

Next, we walk through a hands-on example of fine-tuning the FLAN-T5 model on Tweetsum dataset, providing a practical demonstration of the fine-tuning process. This is a task that illustrates both the theory and practice of fine-tuning that behind transfer learning. This will solidify your understanding of the steps involved and equip you with the skills necessary to fine-tune LLMs for your own applications.

Full fine-tuning of an LLM is typically a resource-intensive process, as it updates the parameters of the entire model to fit a specific dataset. This can require considerable computational power, usually clusters of GPUs to handle the calculations and data throughput. Considering this, we have crafted our practical example to be as accessible as possible, carefully optimizing it to work within the constraints of a single GPU environment.

Building upon this foundation, we explore Parameter-Efficient Fine-Tuning (PEFT) techniques, which aim to reduce the computational and memory requirements of fine-tuning while maintaining performance. We dive into methods such as LoRA (Low-Rank Adaptation), Adapters, and Prompt Tuning, each offering unique advantages and trade-offs. A detailed examination of LoRA, complete with code examples, will provide you with a deeper understanding of this efficient fine-tuning approach.

Evaluating the performance and capabilities of pre-trained or fine-tuned LLMs is a crucial step in understanding their strengths, limitations, and areas for improvement. This chapter also explores various evaluation techniques and benchmarks specifically designed to assess the quality and effectiveness of LLMs across different tasks and domains.

This chapter introduces two widely adopted evaluation metrics: ROUGE (Recall-Oriented Understudy for Gisting Evaluation) and BLEU (Bilingual Evaluation Understudy). The former is commonly used to evaluate the quality of text summaries generated by LLMs, the later is employed to assess the quality of machine translation outputs. Accompanying code examples will provide you with a hands-on understanding of how to implement and interpret these evaluation metrics.

Furthermore, we briefly discuss several well-known benchmarks that serve as comprehensive evaluation frameworks for LLMs. These include GLUE (General Language Understanding Evaluation) and its counterpart, SuperGLUE, which assess language understanding and reasoning capabilities across a diverse set of tasks. Additionally, we introduce SQuAD (Stanford Question Answering Dataset) and HELM (Holistic Evaluation of Language Models), which focus on question answering and holistic language model evaluation, respectively.

Subsequently, we move to the realm of reinforcement learning, a powerful paradigm for fine-tuning LLMs. Specifically, we explore into Reinforcement Learning from Human Feedback (RLHF), a methodology that leverages human preferences and feedback to iteratively refine and improve the behavior of LLMs. Then we introduce TRLX, a framework designed to facilitate the implementation of RLHF, providing a structured approach to incorporating human feedback into the fine-tuning process.

Throughout this chapter, the goal is to seamlessly integrate theoretical knowledge with practical guidance, covering key concepts, novel techniques, and the cutting edge of fine-tuning LLMs. By blending conceptual insights and hands-on techniques, this chapter will equip you with the necessary tools and strategies to effectively fine-tune LLMs for the specific use cases.

5.1 Fine-Tuning

In the previous sections, we understood the strength of In-context Learning and Prompt Engineering, however there are still some limitations and challenges.

Zero-shot learning is to perform a task without having seen any examples in the prompt context, the drawbacks is the lack of domain specificity. The models may default to generalized knowledge, missing nuances of domain-specific language or concepts. This results in responses that can be too broad or mismatched to specialized requirements.

One/few-shot learning attempts to mitigate this by providing one or a few examples to the model. This fine-tuning technique helps the model better grasp the task's context. However, the model may still struggle with consistency and the depth of understanding necessary for complex or highly specialized tasks. The limited examples may not capture enough variation to guide the model towards robust performance, leading to unpredictable quality in the responses.

The examples provided as one/few-short learning in the prompt might take too much space in the context window that reduces the rooms for providing other useful information.

A smaller LLM might not be able to perform well, or even fail, on the specified tasks.

Fortunately, there is an effective solution called **Fine-tuning** to address the above challenges, it's a concerted approach to customizing LLMs for specific domains. Through fine-tuning, LLMs are effectively taught the intricacies of a targeted domain, improving the model's predictive capabilities and coherence on relevant subjects.

As shown in Figure 5.1, at first a LLM is pre-trained with the large corpus of data, we can pre-train it from scratch by ourselves, or select a pre-trained one from the popular LLMs introduced in the previous chapter. The next step is to fine-tune it with domain-specific data, this is a very important step for improving the model's ability to perform specific tasks, such as text summarization, question answering, machine translation for specific area, etc.

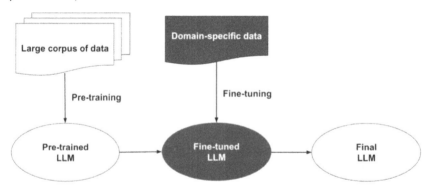

Figure 5.1 Fine-tuning

This technique is called **Transfer Learning**, taking a pre-trained LLM and continuing the training process on a smaller and more specific dataset to adapt the model to a particular task or domain. Transfer learning is pivotal in developing sizable LLMs like GPT and BERT, this strategy is to repurpose the model to a different yet related task. The idea behind Transfer learning is that the knowledge a model acquired in pre-training can be applied to facilitate the resolution of a different problem.

Fine-tuning is a supervised learning process, the LLMs are using datasets with labeled examples to update their weights. An example of the labeled data is a pair of prompt and label:

Prompt:

Customer Review: 'The restaurant was terrible, and the service was even worse. Not going back there again.'

Label:

Classification: Negative

Another example for machine translation in the medical area:

Prompt:

Translate English to German: 'People with diabetes have to constantly check their blood sugar levels.'

Label:

Menschen mit Diabetes müssen ihren Blutzuckerspiegel ständig kontrollieren.

Whether to conduct fine-tuning on the LLM depends on the evaluation of the pre-trained model, if it perfectly satisfies the goal and meets all the requirements, the fine-tuning might not be necessary. If you pre-train the model with your dataset, most likely the LLM will satisfy your goals, because the dataset is collected based on your requirements and goals. However, if choose a pre-trained model you might need to carefully evaluate it, although it is trained with large corpus of data, it might not contain enough details in your specific domain, and a fine-tuning is typically necessary.

Fine-tuning is step 5b in the life cycle of LLM in Figure 1.2:

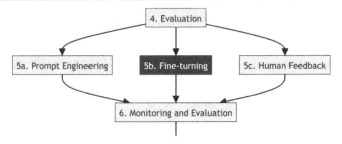

In the example for this section, we use the `TweetSum` dataset which is described and available at:

https://github.com/sarahaman/CIS6930_TweetSum_Summarization

It's a text summarization dataset, including three csv files:

- tweetsum_train.csv, 869 records for training
- tweetsum_valid.csv, 108 records for validation
- tweetsum_test.csv, 110 records for testing

Import the libraries and load the data:

```
1    import torch
2    from datasets import load_dataset, Dataset, load_metric
3    from transformers import T5Tokenizer
4    from transformers import T5ForConditionalGeneration
5    from transformers import TrainingArguments
6    from transformers import Trainer
7    device = 'cuda:0' if torch.cuda.is_available() else 'cpu'
8
9    tweetsum = load_dataset('csv',
10        data_files={'train': 'datasets/tweetsum_train.csv',
11                    'validation': datasets/tweetsum_valid.csv',
12                    'test': 'datasets/tweetsum_test.csv'})
13   print(tweetsum)
```

Line 9 uses `load_dataset()` function from `datasets` library to load the three csv files, this is a very convenience function to load different type of data sources. It can load dataset from HuggingFace hub, from local machine in csv, or json format, from Github repository, etc. Here the three csv files are downloaded from the above Github link, and loaded by this function.

The data is loaded to `tweetsum` in Line 13, which looks like:

```
DatasetDict({
    train: Dataset({
        features: ['inputs', 'summaries'],
        num_rows: 869
    })
    validation: Dataset({
        features: ['inputs', 'summaries'],
        num_rows: 108
    })
    test: Dataset({
        features: ['inputs', 'summaries'],
        num_rows: 110
    })
})
```

It's a Python dictionary with `train`, `validation` and `test`. Each record has two features, `'inputs'` and `'summaries'`, which will be the prompt and label for our fine-tuning.

Then load FLAN-T5 Small model:

```
21    def load_model(model_name):
22      tokenizer = T5Tokenizer.from_pretrained(model_name)
23      model=T5ForConditionalGeneration
24                          .from_pretrained(model_name)
25      return tokenizer, model
26    tokenizer, model = load_model('google/flan-t5-small')
27    total_parameter = sum(p.numel() for p in model.parameters())
28    print(f"Parameters of the model: {total_parameter:,}")
```

This is the same as what we did earlier when doing the zero-shot Prompt Engineering, the difference is this time we load `flan-t5-small` model, and its total parameter is:

```
Parameters of the model: 76,961,152
```

As an evaluation of the model, we want to examinate whether the model can perform well on the dataset. Suppose the dataset is collected based on our requirements, we want to understand how the model performs on it.

Do a zero-shot inference with the test subset:

```
31    indices = torch.randint(0, tweetsum['test'].num_rows, (5,))
32    for idx in indices:
33        i = idx.item()
34        prompt = "Summarize: " + tweetsum['test'][i]['inputs']
35        output = generate_output(tokenizer, model, prompt)
36        print("Prompt:", prompt)
37        print("Target:", tweetsum['test'][i]['summaries'])
38        print("Predict:", output)
39        print()
```

Line 31 is to generate 5 random indices. And Line 32 to 39 print out 5 random records of input prompt, the target label, and the model's predicted output, one of them is something like:

Prompt:

*Summarize: AmericanAir I need to change my last name to my married name on my AAdvantage acct. Help.
 Our specialists are available to help. Give them a call at 8008828880. ...*

Target:

The customer is asking to change their name. The agent asked the customer to call them at 800-882-8880 for further assistance.

Predict:

AmericanAir

Apparently, the model generated output does not capture the correct summary. This is just a preliminary evaluation on the selected pre-trained model, it's important to perform a full evaluation to ensure it aligns with the organization's specific requirements and goals. This process can be quite complex and resource-intensive though. It is step 4 in the life cycle of LLM in Figure 1.2:

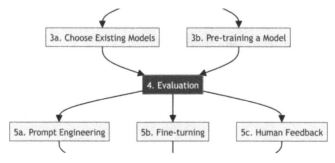

The evaluation process leverages the methods of not only human assessment, but also benchmark metrics like BLEU, ROUGE, etc. which will be introduced later.

Next, tokenize the dataset and prepare for the fine-tuning:

```
41    def tokenize_function(example):
42        prompt = ["Summarize: " + s for s in example['inputs']]
43        example['input_ids'] = tokenizer(prompt,
44                                    padding="max_length",
45                                    truncation=True,
46                                    return_tensors="pt").input_ids
47        example['labels'] = tokenizer(example['summaries'],
48                                    padding="max_length",
49                                    truncation=True,
50                                    return_tensors="pt").input_ids
51        return example
52    tokenized_datasets = tweetsum.map(tokenize_function,
53                                    batched=True)
```

Line 52 and 53 use the datasets' `map()` function to do the tokenization, the purpose of `map()` is to speed up the data processing, it allows to apply a processing function to each example in a dataset either individually or in batches.

The tokenization is performed inside the processing function defined in Line 41 to 51, `tokenize_function(example)`. The `map()` invokes it with `example` parameter, Line 42 create the `prompt` based on its `'inputs'` column.

Then Line 43 to 46 call `tokenizer` to tokenize the prompt, the `tokenizer` is the one that was loaded from the FLAN-T5 Small model. It creates an `'input_ids'` column in `example`.

Similarly Line 47 to 50 create a `'labels'` column by tokenizing `'summaries'` in the dataset.

This step creates two more columns: `['input_ids', 'labels']` which are the tokenized prompt and true label that will be using for fine-tuning.

Optionally, we can use `.filter()` to reduce the number of data in the dataset. Because in Google Colab environment with single GPU, it often gives *"CUDA out of memory"* error due to the size of the dataset and the model, in this case we want to reduce the dataset to make it work on the environment.

```
54    tokenized_datasets = tokenized_datasets.filter(
55                    lambda example, index: index%4==0,
56                    with_indices=True )
57    print(tokenized_datasets)
```

Line 54 to 56 pickup those recodes with `index%4==0`, which means take one record from every four, or a quarter of the original data. If `index%3==0`, that will take one record from every three; `index%10==10`, one record from every ten, and so on.

Line 57 prints out the structure of `tokenized_datasets`:

```
DatasetDict({
    train: Dataset({
        features: ['inputs', 'summaries', 'input_ids', 'labels'],
        num_rows: 218
    })
    validation: Dataset({
        features: ['inputs', 'summaries', 'input_ids', 'labels'],
        num_rows: 27
    })
    test: Dataset({
        features: ['inputs', 'summaries', 'input_ids', 'labels'],
        num_rows: 28
    })
})
```

It shows the features (columns) and the size of the `train`, `validation` and `test` subsets:

`inputs`: the original input texts from the dataset.

`summaries`: the original summary texts from the dataset.

`input_ids`: tokenized inputs.

`labels`: tokenized summaries.

The amount of data is a quarter of the original dataset, as explained earlier, we want it to run on a single GPU environment. In real-world projects, the dataset should be prepared in line with the organization's requirements and goals, the fine-tuning process typically needs extensive computational resources depends on the amount of data and the size of the model.

Here is the fine-tuning:

```
61    batch_size = 8
62    epochs = 80
63    training_args = TrainingArguments(
64        evaluation_strategy = "epoch",
65        learning_rate=2e-5,
66        per_device_train_batch_size=batch_size,
67        per_device_eval_batch_size=batch_size,
68        weight_decay=0.01,
69        logging_steps=1,
60        num_train_epochs=epochs,
71        output_dir = 'outputs' )
72    trainer = Trainer(
73        model=model,
74        args=training_args,
75        train_dataset=tokenized_datasets['train'],
76        eval_dataset=tokenized_datasets['validation'])
77    trainer.train()
```

Line 61 and 62 specify the `batch_size` and `epochs`. A bigger `batch_size` might cause *"CUDA out of memory"* error, if that happens just try a smaller size.

Line 63 to 71 specify the training arguments, the parameters like learning rate, and epochs are specified here. The 16-bit floating-point datatype is specified here for the training process, which are used for reducing the memory footprints, `fp16=True` tells it to use FP16, and `bf16=True` to use BFLOAT16 or BF16 datatype, see Section 4.7. However, in this example, unfortunately FP16 causes overflow, and BFLOAT16 is not supported by the hardware at Google Colab with T4 GPU.

During the training, the training and validation losses are displayed for each epoch:

```
Epoch     Training Loss     Validation Loss
1         28.916100         30.461964
2         20.689100         17.516727
```

3	7.724800	5.802479
...		
79	0.064200	0.170041
80	0.157500	0.170037

Figure 5.2 shows the curves of train and evaluation loss during the fine-tuning:

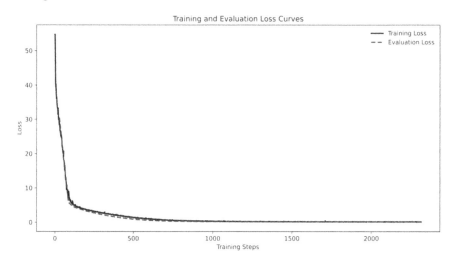

Figure 5.2 Fine-tuning Loss Curves

The solid line shows the training loss, and the dashed line is evaluation loss, both are converged at about 0.16.

It's important to evaluate the model after fine-tuning to make sure it meets the requirements. Use `trainer.predict()` method to do a prediction on the test subset:

```
78   pred = trainer.predict(tokenized_datasets["test"])
79   pred.metrics
```

Print out the metrics of the prediction:

```
{'test_loss': 0.1901451200246811,
 'test_runtime': 2.3994,
 'test_samples_per_second': 11.67,
 'test_steps_per_second': 1.667}
```

Save and load the fine-tuned model:

```
80    model_path="outputs/flan-t5-small_finetune"
81    trainer.save_model(model_path)
82    fine_tuned = T5ForConditionalGeneration
83                        .from_pretrained(model_path)
```

Line 81 saves the fine-tuned model to a path in the local machine, and Line 82 and 83 load the model into memory.

Again, we do a human assessment with the `fine_tuned` model:

Prompt:
*Summarize: AmericanAir I need to change my last name to my married name on my AAdvantage acct. Help.
 Our specialists are available to help. Give them a call at 8008828880. ...*

Target:
The customer is asking to change their name. The agent asked the customer to call them at 800-882-8880 for further assistance.

Predict:
Customer is requesting to change their last name to their married name on their AAdvantage acct.

Compared with the previous prediction, it significantly improves the predicted output after the fine-tuning on this data sample. However it still different from the target label, the reason could because the model we selected is a small one, and the dataset is relatively small, there are only 218 data sample in train set. It might perform well on a bigger model with a larger dataset, although extensive computational resources are required. Budget considerations are important for an organization to plan the fine-tuning of LLMs.

In the above example, we loaded the FLAN-T5 Small model from Hugging Face hub, and loaded the TweetSum dataset in csv format for text summarization, and tokenized the dataset for training purpose, the tokenizer is loaded together with the model. Here we load a relatively small model of about 77M params and slashed the data to a quarter, in order to make it in a manageable way for our running environment.

There is a phenomenon that often observed after fine-tuning of Large Language Models (LLMs), called **Catastrophic Forgetting**, it means the model forgets previously learned information after learning new data. The process of Fine-tuning is to train the model with a set of new data, the model updates its weights to minimize the loss on the new data. If the new data is significantly different from the original data on which the model was pre-trained, the updated weights may alter or overwrite the original weights. As a result, the model may forget what previously learned, and its performance on the original task may degrade substantially. This happens not only on LLMs, but also on all neural networks.

There are some aspects that cause catastrophic forgetting, if the fine-tuning is performed on very specific, or narrow, dataset, the model might become good at the new task but forget the originally pre-trained tasks.

If the fine-tuning is on imbalanced data, meaning too simple or too complex compared with the original dataset, the model's weights might be overwritten and lose its ability to perform well on the original tasks.

If the fine-tuning is on the similar data to the original dataset, it's not likely to have catastrophic forgetting.

It's essential to conduct a continuous monitoring and evaluation on the model's performance to make sure it's capable of doing the specialized tasks while retaining its generic capabilities. It's a significant challenge in the field of language processing especially in the continual learning scenarios, such as fine-tuning for new tasks.

5.2   Parameter Efficient Fine-tuning (PEFT)

In the previous section we have introduced the Transfer Learning and Fine-tuning, which take a pre-trained LLM and perform a full training on a smaller and specific dataset to repurpose the model to a particular task or domain.

As the parameters of most LLMs are hundreds of billions, even reaching trillions as introduced in Section 4.6, a full fine-tuning on the entire model is computationally expensive and sometimes impractical for organizations from cost perspective, it requires enough memory not only for storing the model and dataset but also for optimizer, gradients, activations and so on. In addition, the catastrophic forgetting often results from the full fine-tuning, the models "forget" what they originally learned while acquiring the new domain-specific knowledge due to the weights are altered or overwritten during the full fine-tuning.

The Prompt Engineering and In-Context Learning, on the other hand, do not require extensive computational powers as they do not update the model's weights with big amount of corpus, however, they are inefficient and do not render good performances due to the fact that the limited learning is performed by the prompt within the context window.

Here comes **Parameter-efficient Fine-tuning (PEFT)**, as an alternative to full fine-tuning and prompt engineering. It only updates a small subset of model's parameters, aiming at comparable performance to full fine-tuning while significantly reducing computational requirements. Different from Prompt Engineering, it does update model's weight, but only a small fraction.

PEFT will freeze most of the model's weights, and the fine-tuning is performed on the remaining, or a subset, of the weights, for example particular layers of components of the transformer architecture.

PEFT might not touch the original model weights at all, instead add a small number of new parameters or layers and fine-tune only the new layers. Therefore, the model can learn the new tasks with less computational resources and fewer labeled data, as the number of trained parameters is much smaller than that in the original LLM.

Remember in the previous section, we loaded the smallest FLAN-T5 model and used a very small amount of data in order to keep them manageable on the limited computing environment, in our case Google Colab free tier with a single T4 GPU. With PEFT only a small fraction of parameters is touched, it's much easier to manage it for the limited computing environment, and in fact, in most cases PEFT can be performed on a single GPU.

In addition, the catastrophic forgetting is less likely to happen because PEFT only modifies a small fraction of the original LLM's weight, or sometimes leaves them unchanged.

What are the differences of Fine-tuning vs PEFT?

Figure 5.3 shows the process of full Fine-tuning on various tasks:

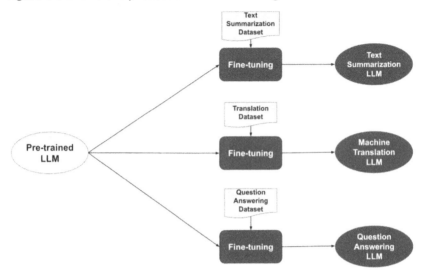

Figure 5.3 Full Fine-tuning for Various Tasks

The pre-trained LLM is fine-tuned on text summarization dataset, we get the LLM for text summarization task; fine-tuning with translation dataset gets a machine translation LLM, and so on.

The size of each resulting LLM is same as the original one, if the original one is a big one, say 100B params, then each resulting LLM is also a big one.

On the other hand, PEFT will freeze most of the weights of the original pre-trained LLM, or even freeze all of the weights, the training is performed against a small fraction of the weights, the result is a small amount of PEFT weights. The PEFT weights plus the original pre-trained LLM will be used to perform the specialized tasks, as shown in Figure 5.4.

For example, the text summarization dataset is PEFT-trained on top of the original pre-trained LLM, resulting the PEFT weights for text summarization. Similarly, the translation dataset is PEFT-trained, resulting the PEFT weights for translation; and question-answering dataset resulting another PEFT weights. The original model plus the PEFT weights will be able to do the specific tasks. Usually the sizes of PEFT weights are in a few hundred MBs, which is much smaller than the original LLM.

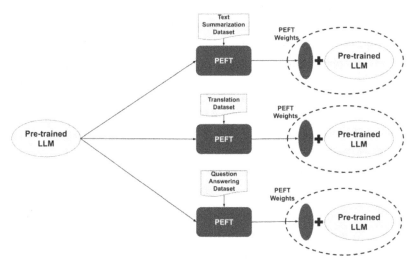

Figure 5.4 PEFT for Various Tasks

Different techniques or methods are employed in PEFT, ongoing research is underway to explore and develop new methods. Here are some widely used ones:

Adapter: adds new trainable layers to the transformer architecture, typically inside the encoder or decoder components after the multi-head attention or feed-forward layers. The fine-tuning updates only the parameters in the adapters, the newly added layers, while keeping the rest of the model's parameters frozen. This approach can save computational resources while still rendering good performance.

LoRA (Low-Rank Adaptation): similar to the Adapters, LoRA is also the small trainable layers that are inserted into the transformer architecture, and only these layers are trained. It's a lightweight training technique that significantly reduces the number of trainable parameters. The training is much faster, memory-efficient, and produces smaller weights which are easier to store and share.

Prompt tuning: different from the Prompt engineering, the Prompt tuning adds some vectors to the beginning of the input sequence, and feeds to the input layers of the transformer model. These vectors become additional embeddings which are prepended to the input sequence embeddings. In this case all weights of the original pre-trained model are frozen, the model takes this input with prefix embeddings as normal input sequence and performs the training process. As we explained earlier the embeddings are learnable parameters, only these prefix embeddings are updated during the training, all the weights of the model keep unchanged.

As a summary, a full fine-tuning takes a pre-trained language model and continue the training process on a new dataset with specific task, it applies to all the parameters of the model.

PEFT, on the other hand, is to adapt only a portion of the model's parameters to the new task. It can be advantageous because it typically requires fewer computational resources and can reduce the risk of catastrophic forgetting. It can also be more efficient to deploy the PEFT-finetuned models/weights quickly.

5.3   Low-Rank Adaptation (LoRA)

When we want to employ an existing LLMs, say GPT-3 with 175B params, for a task in specific domain such as healthcare, we will need to fine-tune it on the dataset in that domain. A full fine-tuning as explained earlier will update all 175 billion params, which requires extensive computational resources.

LoRA, one of the techniques of PEFT (Parameter Efficient Fine-tuning), is an alternative to the full fine-tuning, it applies the concept of **low-rank approximation** to fine-tune a small portion of parameters to achieve the same goal. LoRa is proposed by the paper *LoRA: Low-Rank Adaptation of LLMs*[20], *Hu et al, 2021, https://arxiv.org/abs/2106.09685*.

The math concepts used behind LoRA are explained in Section 2.12 and 2.13. To recap, a rank of matrix indicates the maximum number of linearly independent column/row vectors in the matrix. A full rank matrix means all columns and/or rows are linearly independent. If consider the 175B params of GPT-3 is a full-rank matrix, all parameters are independent, meaning any columns/rows can not be calculated from others.

The low-rank approximation of a matrix can be obtained by an operation called SVD (Singular Value Decomposition, see Section 2.13), it reduces the rank of the matrix to a smaller value but produce the same size of the matrix, meaning some columns/rows (parameters) are dependent on others and can be calculated by others.

Let's start with a simple example of Linear Transformation:

$$y = Wx$$

W is the weights that pre-trained with a dataset, say W is $m{\times}n$ matrix. Now freeze the weights and introduce a same-sized matrix ΔW:

$$y = (W+\Delta W)\,x$$

Then do a fine-tuning on the model with a dataset of the specific task, since W is frozen then the updates happen on ΔW only.

ΔW can be factorized with SVD:

$$\Delta W = U\,\Sigma\,V^T$$

As introduced in Section 2.13, we can choose a lower rank r to construct ΔW, then introduce two matrices:

$$B = U\Sigma$$

$$A = V^T$$

The size of B is $m{\times}r$, and the size of A is $r{\times}n$, then:

$$\Delta W_{(m,n)} = B_{(m,r)}\,A_{(r,n)}$$

As shown in Figure 5.5:

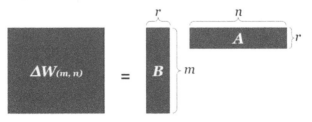

Figure 5.5 Weights for LoRA

Therefore:

$$y = (W+BA)\,x$$

Where W is the original weights of the model, which is frozen during fine-tuning. B and A are two new matrices, which are updated by the fine-tuning.

The total number of parameters of original W is:

Total params $= m \times n$

The number of parameters of B plus A is:

Fine-tuning params $= m \times r + r \times n = r\,(m+n)$

If r is chosen much smaller than the original rank, the parameters for fine-tuning will be greatly reduced. For example: $m = 512$, $n = 64$, $r = 16$, the number of parameters in the original model is:

$m \times n = 512 \times 64 = 32{,}768$

The number of parameters for fine-tuning is:

$r\,(m \times n) = 16 \times (512 + 64) = 9{,}216$

This is a 72% reduction in the parameters for fine-tuning. And this is the idea of LoRA.

As the transformer architecture is not simply a single matrix for trainable parameters, LoRA will be applied to each layer to reduce the number of parameters. Based on the paper:

> *We propose Low-Rank Adaptation, or LoRA, which freezes the pretrained model weights and injects trainable rank decomposition matrices into each layer of the Transformer architecture, greatly reducing the number of trainable parameters for downstream tasks.*
>
> *From LoRA: Low-Rank Adaptation of LLMs [20], https://arxiv.org/abs/2106.09685*

Figure 5.6 is the illustration of LoRA from the paper, the originally pre-trained weights is W in the left, its size is $d \times d$, it's frozen during training.

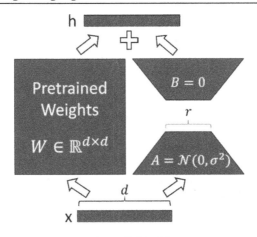

Figure 5.6 LoRA
Source from: LoRA: Low-Rank Adaptation of LLMs[20],
https://arxiv.org/abs/2106.09685. Modified by Author

A and B in the right are introduced by LoRA, r is the reduced rank. The size of A is $d \times r$, and B is $r \times d$, then $A \cdot B$ is also $d \times d$, which is same as W. The fine-tuning is to update the parameters in A and B.

For the implementation, we use the same things as what we did for fine-tuning in Section 5.1, the model is `flan-t5-base`, and the dataset is `tweetsum`.

First install `peft` package, and load the related libraries:

```
1   !pip install peft --quiet
2   from peft import LoraConfig, get_peft_model, TaskType
```

Then use the exact same codes to load the model and dataset, prepare and tokenize the dataset, as Section 5.1.

After that, configure LoRA with `LoraConfig()`

```
3   rank = 16
4   lora_config = LoraConfig(
5     r=rank,
6     lora_alpha=32,
6     lora_dropout=0.05,
7     bias="none",
8     task_type=TaskType.SEQ_2_SEQ_LM )
9   lora_model = get_peft_model(model, lora_config)
```

The rank is specified as `rank=16`. Line 9 obtains `lora_model` from the original `model` and `lora_config`.

For this example, we load `google/flan-t5-base` model, print out the total parameters and the learnable parameters for LoRA:

```
11    total_parameter = sum(p.numel() for p in
12                         lora_model.parameters())
13    lora_parameter = sum(p.numel() for p in
14                         lora_model.parameters() if p.requires_grad)
15    print(f"Total Parameters: {total_parameter:,}")
16    print(f"LoRA Parameters: {lora_parameter:,};
17            Percentage: {lora_parameter/total_parameter}")
```

```
Total Parameters: 249,347,328
LoRA Parameters: 1,769,472; Percentage: 0.007096
```

The total parameter is 249M, the LoRA trainable parameter is 1.7M, only 0.7%.

The train loop is pretty much the same as what we did in fine-tuning, the difference is `max_steps` is used instead of epochs, and the target model is `lora_model` obtained in Line 9,

```
21    max_steps = 300
22    lora_training_args = TrainingArguments(
23        learning_rate = 1e-3,
24        auto_find_batch_size = True,
25        logging_steps = 1,
26        max_steps = max_steps,
27        output_dir = 'outputs'
28    )
29    lora_triner = Trainer(
30        model = lora_model,
31        args = lora_training_args,
32        train_dataset = tokenized_datasets['train'],
33    )
34    lora_triner.train()
```

The training loss is displayed during the process for each step:

```
Step Training Loss
1      43.000000
2      42.250000
```

```
3      37.750000
...
299    0.238300
300    0.283200
```

The training process is visualized in Figure 5.7, the loss curve is converged in around 0.2 to 0.3. It's worthwhile to note that when we choose `google/flan-t5-small` as the base model, the loss curve is converged around 1.8 to 2.0, the reason might be a smaller LLM is less capable of capturing new data effectively compared to a larger one.

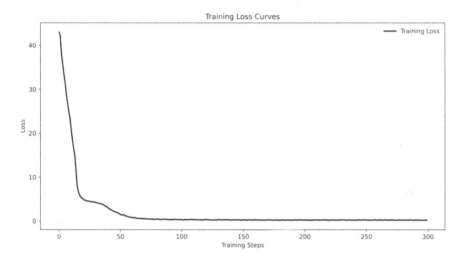

Figure 5.7 Loss During Training for LoRA

After the training, save the LoRA model:

```
35    lora_triner.save_model("outputs/flan-t5-base_lora")
```

The size of LoRA model in this example is only 3.5MB, which is much smaller than the original model.

Multiple LoRA models can be trained in the same way, each for a specific task, for example text summarization as a LoRA model, machine translation as another LoRA model, text classification, etc. as separate LoRA models, as Figure 5.4.

In order to load the LoRA model back to memory, we should load the original `flan-t5-base` as the base model, and load the LoRA model on top of it.

```
36    from peft import PeftModel, PeftConfig
37    tokenizer, base_model = load_model('google/flan-t5-base')
38    lora_model = PeftModel.from_pretrained(base_model,
39                        "outputs/flan-t5-base_lora",
40                        torch_dtype=torch.bfloat16,
41                        is_trainnable=False)
```

Line 37 loads the original `flan-t5-base` model as we did before, this should be the model that LoRA is trained on top of.

Line 38 to 41 is to load LoRA model together with the base model, Line 39 specify the path of the LoRA mode, which is saved in Line 35.

Line 40 is optional, it specifies the datatype of the loaded model to be `bfloat16`. Remember in Section 4.7 we introduced various datatypes for saving computational costs, `bfloat16` is one of the 16-bit datatype that compatible with 32-bit floating-point datatype (FP32) in data range and save the memory by half. This is how to specify the model to be loaded in this datatype.

Line 41 disables training mode, meaning the model is loaded not for training purpose. In this case there are no trainable parameters.

After the LoRA model is loaded, we can do the inferences, or predictions, on the test dataset as we did before. And also, can apply ROUGE or BLEU to evaluate the results. As an example of the inference on the LoRA model:

```
Target: Customer is waiting over 3 weeks for compensation
that was promised. Agent informed that he will get back to
him with further information.

Predict: Customer is complaining that they are still waiting
for compensation that was promised on 1Nov. Agent is asking
for an additional gesture of goodwill.

{'rouge1': Score(precision=0.416667,
                 recall=0.434782,
                 fmeasure=0.425532)}
```

The value of rank is important in the practice of LoRA, how to select an appropriate rank? Figure 5.8 lists the experimental results from the paper *LoRA: Low-Rank Adaptation of LLMs[20], https://arxiv.org/abs/2106.09685.* Various of rank values are evaluated on GPT-2 Medium model against different matric, such as val_loss, BLEU, ROUGE etc.

Rank r	val_loss	BLEU	NIST	METEOR	ROUGE_L	CIDEr
1	1.23	68.72	8.7215	0.4565	0.7052	2.4329
2	1.21	69.17	8.7413	0.4590	0.7052	2.4639
4	1.18	**70.38**	**8.8439**	**0.4689**	0.7186	**2.5349**
8	1.17	69.57	8.7457	0.4636	**0.7196**	2.5196
16	**1.16**	69.61	8.7483	0.4629	0.7177	2.4985
32	**1.16**	69.33	8.7736	0.4642	0.7105	2.5255
64	**1.16**	69.24	8.7174	0.4651	0.7180	2.5070
128	**1.16**	68.73	8.6718	0.4628	0.7127	2.5030
256	**1.16**	68.92	8.6982	0.4629	0.7128	2.5012
512	**1.16**	68.78	8.6857	0.4637	0.7128	2.5025
1024	1.17	69.37	8.7495	0.4659	0.7149	2.5090

Figure 5.8 Evaluation on Various Ranks on GPT-2
Source from: LoRA: Low-Rank Adaptation of LLMs[20],
https://arxiv.org/abs/2106.09685

It shows r=16 gets the best validation loss, or val_loss; r=8 for the best ROUGE_L result; r=4 for the best results on other matric.

If you are using LoRA on other models, it's a good idea to do the similar test and find a best rank.

Model & Method	# Trainable Parameters	MNLI	SST-2	MRPC	CoLA	QNLI	QQP	RTE	STS-B	Avg.
RoB$_{base}$ (FT)*	125.0M	**87.6**	94.8	90.2	**63.6**	92.8	**91.9**	78.7	91.2	86.4
RoB$_{base}$ (BitFit)*	0.1M	84.7	93.7	**92.7**	62.0	91.8	84.0	81.5	90.8	85.2
RoB$_{base}$ (Adpt^D)*	0.3M	87.1$_{\pm.0}$	94.2$_{\pm.1}$	88.5$_{\pm1.1}$	60.8$_{\pm.4}$	93.1$_{\pm.1}$	90.2$_{\pm.0}$	71.5$_{\pm2.7}$	89.7$_{\pm.3}$	84.4
RoB$_{base}$ (Adpt^D)*	0.9M	87.3$_{\pm.1}$	94.7$_{\pm.3}$	88.4$_{\pm.1}$	62.6$_{\pm.9}$	93.0$_{\pm.2}$	90.6$_{\pm.0}$	75.9$_{\pm2.2}$	90.3$_{\pm.1}$	85.4
RoB$_{base}$ (LoRA)	0.3M	87.5$_{\pm.3}$	**95.1**$_{\pm.2}$	89.7$_{\pm.7}$	63.4$_{\pm1.2}$	**93.3**$_{\pm.3}$	90.8$_{\pm.1}$	**86.6**$_{\pm.7}$	**91.5**$_{\pm.2}$	**87.2**
RoB$_{large}$ (FT)*	355.0M	90.2	**96.4**	**90.9**	68.0	94.7	**92.2**	86.6	92.4	88.9
RoB$_{large}$ (LoRA)	0.8M	**90.6**$_{\pm.2}$	96.2$_{\pm.5}$	**90.9**$_{\pm1.2}$	68.2$_{\pm1.9}$	**94.9**$_{\pm.3}$	91.6$_{\pm.1}$	**87.4**$_{\pm2.5}$	**92.6**$_{\pm.2}$	**89.0**
RoB$_{large}$ (Adpt^P)†	3.0M	90.2$_{\pm.3}$	96.1$_{\pm.3}$	90.2$_{\pm.7}$	**68.3**$_{\pm1.0}$	**94.8**$_{\pm.2}$	**91.9**$_{\pm.1}$	83.8$_{\pm2.9}$	92.1$_{\pm.7}$	88.4
RoB$_{large}$ (Adpt^P)†	0.8M	**90.5**$_{\pm.3}$	**96.6**$_{\pm.2}$	89.7$_{\pm1.2}$	67.8$_{\pm2.5}$	**94.8**$_{\pm.3}$	91.7$_{\pm.2}$	80.1$_{\pm2.9}$	91.9$_{\pm.4}$	87.9
RoB$_{large}$ (Adpt^H)†	6.0M	89.9$_{\pm.5}$	96.2$_{\pm.3}$	88.7$_{\pm2.9}$	66.5$_{\pm4.4}$	94.7$_{\pm.2}$	92.1$_{\pm.1}$	83.4$_{\pm1.1}$	91.0$_{\pm1.7}$	87.8
RoB$_{large}$ (Adpt^H)†	0.8M	90.3$_{\pm.3}$	96.3$_{\pm.5}$	87.7$_{\pm1.7}$	66.3$_{\pm2.0}$	94.7$_{\pm.2}$	91.5$_{\pm.1}$	72.9$_{\pm2.9}$	90.3$_{\pm.1}$	86.4
RoB$_{large}$ (LoRA)†	0.8M	**90.6**$_{\pm.2}$	96.2$_{\pm.5}$	**90.2**$_{\pm1.0}$	68.2$_{\pm1.9}$	**94.8**$_{\pm.3}$	91.6$_{\pm.2}$	85.2$_{\pm1.1}$	92.3$_{\pm.5}$	**88.6**
DeB$_{XXL}$ (FT)*	1500.0M	91.8	**97.2**	92.0	72.0	**96.0**	92.7	93.9	92.9	91.1
DeB$_{XXL}$ (LoRA)	4.7M	**91.9**$_{\pm.2}$	96.9$_{\pm.2}$	**92.6**$_{\pm.6}$	**72.4**$_{\pm1.1}$	**96.0**$_{\pm.1}$	**92.9**$_{\pm.1}$	**94.9**$_{\pm.4}$	**93.0**$_{\pm.2}$	**91.3**

Figure 5.9 LoRA Experiments Results
Source from: LoRA: Low-Rank Adaptation of LLMs[20],
https://arxiv.org/abs/2106.09685

The paper also lists the results of experiments on some LLMs with various fine-tuning methods. Figure 5.9 shows that LoRA is performed on RoBERTa Base, RoBERTa Large and DeBERTa XXL models together with some other fine-tuning methods, it seems LoRA achieved better results than full Fine-tuning, and required much fewer parameters to train.

The validation accuracy for various fine-tuning methods on GPT-3 (175B params) is shown in Figure 5.10:

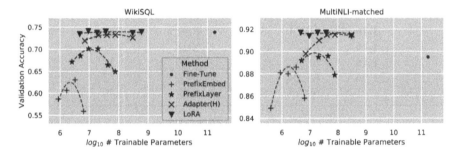

Figure 5.10 Validation Accuracy of LoRA vs Other Methods
Source from: LoRA: Low-Rank Adaptation of LLMs[20],
https://arxiv.org/abs/2106.09685

Compared with other Fine-tuning methods, LoRA achieved the best validation accuracy.

As a summary, LoRA, as one of the techniques of PEFT (Parameter Efficient Fine-tuning), stands out for delivering commendable overall results compared with other fine-tuning strategies, making it a robust and resource-friendly option for fine-tuning LLMs.

Its ability to optimize the number of learnable parameters leads to significantly lower hardware requirements and minimal increased inference latency compared with other fine-tuning methods.

LoRA allows for efficient adaptation of LLMs to specific tasks with trained weights that are both lightweight and rapidly shareable, facilitating quick transitions between tasks.

5.4 Adapter

Adapters is one of the first PEFT techniques released in the paper of *Parameter-Efficient Transfer Learning for NLP[21], Houlsby et al, 2019, https://arxiv.org/abs/ 1902.00751.*

In the Transformer architecture in Figure 3.1, the Adapter layers are added after the Multi-head Attention and Feed Forward Layers, and before Add & Norm layers. All weights of the model are frozen, only the newly added Adapter layers are fine-tuned and updated, as Figure 5.11:

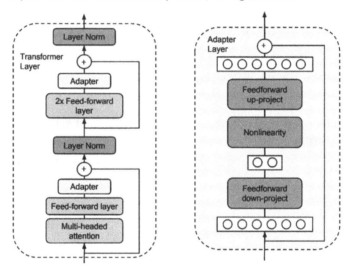

Figure 5.11 Adapter Architecture
Source from: Parameter-Efficient Transfer Learning for NLP [21], https://arxiv.org/abs/1902.00751

The left of Figure 5.11 shows part of the modified transformer architecture with the newly added Adapters.

And the right shows the Adapters' architecture, which is basically a bottleneck architecture of neural networks. The output from Attention or Feed Forward Layers become the input vector of the Adapter, it passes through a feedforward layer which performs a linear transformation, where the input vector is multiplied by a weight matrix and adding a bias term. The purpose of this layer is dimensionality reduction, which compresses the input data into a smaller and denser representation with reduced dimension.

Then a non-linear activation function is applied, the purpose is to learn and represent complex patterns. Common choices for activation functions include Sigmoid, ReLU (Rectified Linear Unit), or Tanh, which allows the lower-dimensional representation to capture non-linear relationships in the data.

Finally, the data passes through another feedforward layer to transform it back to the original dimension. This part is trying to reconstruct the input data from the lower-dimensional form. Then the data connect to the Add & Norm layer of the Transformer architecture.

The bottleneck architecture is a design where the network narrows in the middle which is the bottleneck layer. This design can significantly reduce the number of learnable parameters and here's how it works:

Suppose the input vector x with size n, and the bottleneck dimension, or the lowered-dimension, size is d, then the first part of the Adapters' architecture can be denoted as a linear transformation with an activation function:

$$y = f(W_e x + b_e)$$

Where:

W_e is the weight matrix in size $d \times n$.

b_e is the bias vector in size d.

$f()$ is a non-linear activation function, such as Sigmoid, ReLU or Tanh.

The second part of the Adapters' architecture is another linear transformation:

$$x' = W_d y + b_d$$

Where:

W_d is the weight matrix in size $n \times d$.

b_d is the bias vector in size n.

x' is the output of the Adapter that transformed back to the original size of x.

The learnable parameters can be calculated as:

The first part: $n \times d + d$ (weights and biases)

The second part: $d \times n + n$ (weights and biases)

Therefore, the total learnable parameters:

$$2 (n \times d) + n + d$$

Adopting the Adapter is a straightforward process, insert Adapter layers after the Multi-head Attention and Feed Forward Layers in the transformer architecture. By refining the adapter's parameters only, the pre-trained model's efficacy can be enhanced for a specific task without the necessity of modifying the entire model. This method is efficient, and saving both time and computational cost, yet it often yields more robust outcomes than a full fine-tuning.

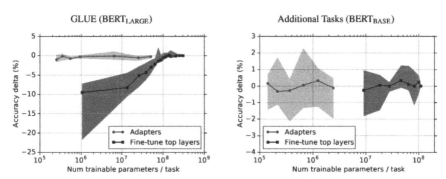

Figure 5.12 Adapter Accuracy vs Number of Trained Parameters
Source from: Parameter-Efficient Transfer Learning for NLP [21],
https://arxiv.org/abs/1902.00751

Figure 5.12 shows the experimental results of Adapter with accuracy vs number of trainable parameters by the paper.

5.5 Prompt Tuning

Prompt tuning is another technique of PEFT (Parameter Efficient Fine-tuning) used to fine-tune LLMs. The same concept is applied, keep the pre-trained model's parameters fixed while only adjust a small set of additional parameters.

Prompt tuning is different from Prompt Engineering introduced in Section 4.8, where users try different textual prompts with zero-shot, one-shot or few-shot learning to guide the model in generating the best possible outputs. Prompt tuning introduces soft prompts that are learned during the training process for specific tasks.

Unlike the Adapter approach which injects trainable modules between the layers of the transformer architecture, or full fine-tuning approach which updates all weights in the model, the soft prompts are vectors of learnable parameters that are prepended to the input embeddings. These are not human-readable texts, but rather sequences of parameters that are optimized during the fine-tuning process.

As we explained in the chapter of Transformer architecture, the input tokens are embedded to vectors of the dimension of d_{model} = 512, the soft prompt is a vector added in front of the embedded vector, as shown in Figure 5.13:

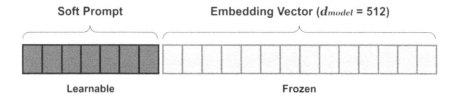

Figure 5.13 Soft Prompt

The embedding vector is the one that embedded from the input tokens and fed into the model, it is originally trainable parameters in the model. Now freeze these parameters and prepend soft prompt vector in front of the embedding vectors.

During the fine-tuning process, these soft prompts are adjusted to encode the task-specific information that influences the LLM to generate the desired outputs. While the parameters of the pre-trained model remain frozen, and only the soft prompts are updated based on the task-specific dataset.

Same as other techniques of PEFT, the Prompt tuning only updates a small fraction of parameters, which are the soft prompt vectors, therefore requires less computational resources than the traditional full fine-tuning.

The soft prompts learn to guide the LLM to produce the appropriate outputs for a specific task without the need to alter the model's inherent capabilities which acquired from the initial pre-training, thus it reduces the risk of catastrophic forgetting.

One of the research papers discussing Prompt Tuning is *Prompt Tuning: Better Sample Efficiency than Fine-Tuning for Pre-Trained Language Models* [22], *https://aclanthology.org/2022.findings-emnlp.401.pdf*, it examined this technique on LLMs and demonstrated its effectiveness and sample efficiency compared to the full fine-tuning methods.

In practice, Prompt Tuning can be effective, especially for tasks that do not deviate significantly from what the model was originally pre-trained on. It represents an approach for parameter efficient fine-tuning and customizing LLMs for specific tasks while leveraging their large pre-trained knowledge bases, at the same time minimizing the computational costs.

5.6 Evaluation

The evaluation of a LLM plays an important role in its lifecycle, especially after the fine-tuning process. It ensures that the model not only retains its general language processing capabilities but also acquires the skills in the specific domain or task it has been trained for.

Figure 5.14 shows the evaluation steps in the LLM's lifecycle. Step #4 is after the model is pre-trained, or an existing pre-trained model is selected. Step #6 is after the fine-tuning process.

The purpose of evaluation is to examine the LLM's capabilities in understanding and producing human-like text by measuring the efficiency of the model in various tasks such as translation, textual classification, summarization, and question-answering, etc.

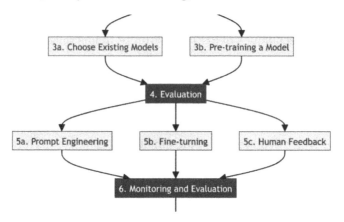

Figure 5.14 Evaluation Steps in LLM Lifecycle

After the fine-tuning process, the evaluation is to ensure the model has successfully adapted to the specialized vocabulary, style, and nuances of the target domain. At the same time, ensure the model is not over-specialized and loses its general language understanding and generation capabilities – known as Catastrophic forgetting.

In addition to the human assessments on the model, which we have done in the previous example, there are several automated metrics, such as ROUGE, BLEU, F1 Score, etc. This section will introduce these metrics.

ROUGE (Recall-Oriented Understudy for Gisting Evaluation), primarily used for text summarization, compares the overlap of unigrams, bigrams and N-grams word sequences, and word pairs between the system output and reference summaries. Then it calculates the Recall, Precision and F1 score.

Section 2.10 introduced the concepts of bigram and N-gram, to re-cap the concepts, as shown in Figure 5.15:

Figure 5.15 Unigram, Bigram and N-gram

Unigram is a single word or token in a sentence or a sequence. It is simplest form of N-gram where N is 1.

Bigram is two adjacent words or tokens in a sentence or a sequence. In other words, it consists of pairs of consecutive words. It's a form of N-gram where N is 2.

N-gram is N adjacent words or tokens in a sentence or a sequence, it can consist of any number of adjacent words or tokens.

ROUGE-N measures the overlap of N-grams between the model's generated text and the reference texts. For example, ROUGE-1 refers to the overlap of Unigrams, ROUGE-2 refers to Bigrams and so on. It calculates recall, precision, and F1-score based on matched counts.

ROUGE-1 calculates the recall and precision as following:

$$\text{Recall} = \frac{\text{number of overlapping unigrams}}{\text{unigrams in the reference text}}$$

$$\text{Precision} = \frac{\text{number of overlapping unigrams}}{\text{unigrams in the generated text}}$$

Recall assesses how many of the relevant tokens are captured by the model. Precision calculates how many of the generated tokens are relevant. F1-score is calculated based on both:

$$F_1\text{-Score} = \frac{2 \cdot \text{Recall} \cdot \text{Precision}}{\text{Recall} + \text{Precision}}$$

ROUGE-2 calculates the corresponding bigram numbers.

The Longest Common Subsequence (LCS) is a sequence that appears in both the reference and the generated texts in the same order, but not necessarily contiguously. **ROUGE-L** measures the longest matching sequence of words using LCS statistics. It is particularly useful because it does not require predefined lengths of word sequences. Longer subsequences are typically more meaningful than shorter ones, signaling better summaries.

For example, the generated text is:
Customer is requesting to change her name on their AAdvantage acct.

The reference text is:
The customer is asking to change her name, the agent asks her to call customer service.

Instead of counting the unigrams/bigrams manually, Python's `rouge_scorer` package can be used to calculate the metrics.

```
1    !pip install rouge_score
2    from rouge_score import rouge_scorer
3    scorer=rouge_scorer.RougeScorer(['rouge1','rouge2',
4                                'rougeL'],use_stemmer=True)
5    generated = "Customer is requesting to change her name on
6                their AAdvantage acct."
7    reference = "The customer is asking to change her name,
8                the agent asks her to call customer service."
9    scores = scorer.score(reference, generated)
10   print(scores)
```

Line 1 is to install `rouge_score` package, and Line 2 import it.

Line 3 creates an instance of the `RougeScorer` class to measure `rouge1`, `rouge2` and `rougeL`.

Line 5 and 6 is a sample generated summary text, Line 7 and 8 is a sample reference text.

Line 9 calculates the scores, Line 10 print it out:

```
{'rouge1': Score( precision=0.5454,
                  recall=0.375,
                  fmeasure=0.4444),
 'rouge2': Score( precision=0.4,
                  recall=0.26666,
                  fmeasure=0.32),
```

```
'rougeL': Score( precision=0.5454,
                 recall=0.375,
                 fmeasure=0.4444) }
```

We can calculate the ROUGE on each data item in test subset, this gives the quantitative results:

```
11    for item in tokenized_datasets['test']:
12        prompt = "Summarize: " + item['inputs']
13        output = generate_output(tokenizer, ft_model, prompt)
14        scores = scorer.score(item['summaries'], output)
15        print("Target:", item['summaries'])
16        print("Predict:", output)
17        print(scores)
18        print()
```

The results look like below for each item,

```
Target: Customer is complaining that the watchlist is not
updated with new episodes from past two days. Agent informed
that the team is working hard to investigate to show new
episodes on page.

Predict: The watchlist is not updating with new episodes
past couple days.

{'rouge1': Score( precision=0.9090,
                  recall=0.3125,
                  fmeasure=0.4651),
  'rouge2': Score( precision=0.7,
                   recall=0.2258,
                   fmeasure=0.3414),
  'rougeL': Score( precision=0.9090,
                   recall=0.3125,
                   fmeasure=0.4651) }
```

Consider running the same before the fine-tuning process and compare the results of before and after. It provides a quick, objective and quantitative measure of the model's performance.

In addition to ROUGE which is used primarily for text summarization, **BLEU (Bilingual Evaluation Understudy)** is commonly used for evaluating the machine-translated texts from one natural language to another. It quantifies how many words and phrases in the machine-translated output match reference translations.

Similar to ROUGE, BLEU also considers the N-grams (often up to 4-grams), it counts the maximum number of times a particular N-gram appears in any single reference translation. It then clips the count of those N-grams in the machine-translated text to this maximum value.

Precision is calculated for each N-gram by dividing the sum of the clipped counts by the total number of N-grams in the machine-translated text. The BLEU score ranges from 0 to 1, where 1 means a perfect match with the reference translation.

BLEU focuses solely on precision; it does not directly measure how fluent or how adequately the translated text conveys the semantic meaning. As such BLEU can serve as an approximate quantitative measure but should ideally be supplemented by human evaluation, especially when assessing the model's translation quality.

Here is the code snippet to calculate BLUE using `nltk` library, one of the most commonly used libraries for this purpose. It has a built-in BLEU score calculator.

```
1    from nltk.translate.bleu_score import sentence_bleu
2    from nltk.translate.bleu_score import SmoothingFunction
3    reference_text = "Ein Boston Terrier läuft über saftig-
4                      grünes Gras vor einem weißen Zaun."
5    output_text = "Ein Fan sitzt auf einer grünen Wiese vor
6                   einem weißen Zaun"
7    reference = tokenize_de(reference_text)
8    output = tokenize_de(output_text)
9    score = sentence_bleu([reference], output,
10           smoothing_function=SmoothingFunction().method1)
11   print(f"BLEU Score: {score}")
```

Consider this code snippet is part of the previous example codes of English to German machine translation, Line 7 and 8 uses `tokenize_de()` which is defined in that example codes.

Line 9 and 10 calculate the BLEU using `nltk` functions.

The result is:

```
BLEU Score: 0.22652
```

In summary, the continuous and comprehensive evaluation of LLMs is essential to ensure their efficacy, reliability, and safe integration into real-world applications. While automated metrics provide a quick and objective measure of model capabilities, combining these with thoughtful human evaluations and robustness tests provides the most complete picture of an LLM's overall performance and applicability.

The problem is that the LLMs are complex, the simple evaluation using automated metric like ROUGE and BLEU might be good for evaluating the individual output, they can not give the overall picture of the models. In order to holistically evaluate the LLMs, the AI researchers and communities have established benchmarks and datasets to better evaluate the model's overall performances.

Here are some well-known benchmarks:

GLUE (General Language Understanding Evaluation) and SuperGLUE: both are general benchmarks designed to measure the performance of LLMs on a variety of natural language understanding tasks. SuperGLUE is the successor to the original GLUE benchmark, they are collections of diverse NLP tasks designed to evaluate the understanding of language, including tasks such as question answering, sentiment analysis, and textual entailment.

To evaluate a LLM with SuperGLUE or GLUE, the first thing is to collect test data from the benchmark for each task, some might require pre-processing depends on the dataset.

Then use the model to make inference on the test data, and compare them against the ground truth using the evaluation metric specific to each task. And analyze the results to find areas where the LLM excels or struggles. Selecting the right evaluation dataset is vital, so that you can accurately assess a model's performance and capabilities.

SuperGLUE provides leaderboards where you can submit the results for comparison against other models. Follow the submission guidelines and submit them to the appropriate leaderboard. SuperGLUE provides scripts for evaluation and a standard format for submitting predictions, so that model performance is consistent and comparable across different submissions.

SQuAD (Stanford Question Answering Dataset): is a benchmark for evaluating LLMs on the task of reading comprehension, specifically question answering (QA). It provides a way to measure how well models can understand a passage of text and provide accurate answers to questions. It comes in two versions at the time of this writing, SQuAD1.1 and the more challenging SQuAD2.0.

It consists of dataset of question-answer pairs based on Wikipedia articles. SQuAD2.0 also includes additional questions that are intentionally unanswerable based on the provided passages. This is designed to require models not only to find answers but also to mimic a more realistic scenario where not all questions have the answers.

The models are evaluated against two main metrics: F1-score as explained earlier, and Exact match (EM) which measures the percentage of the model's outputs that match the ground truth exactly.

Due to its high-quality dataset and widely used in the communities, SQuAD has become an important tool in the evaluation of NLP models for question answering and reading comprehension. Models that perform well on SQuAD have proven to be sophisticated in understanding and processing natural language.

HELM (Holistic Evaluation of Language Models) is a comprehensive benchmark for evaluating the capabilities of large language models (LLMs). Rather than focusing on a single specific metric such as accuracy, a holistic evaluation recognizes the multifaceted nature of language understanding and generation.

HELM assesses LLMs across a diverse range of tasks and abilities, including but not limited to:

- Linguistic Understanding: evaluate a model's grasp of grammar, syntax, semantics, and pragmatics, etc.
- Performance on Diverse Tasks: such as translation, question-answering, summarization, and more specialized tasks like legal or medical document analysis.

- Robustness and Generalization: evaluate how well a model can handle edge cases or adapt to domains and tasks it was not explicitly trained for.
- Bias and Fairness: evaluate the model's performance in terms of ethical considerations, such as avoiding the reinforcement or amplification of societal biases.
- Resource Efficiency: evaluate the computational resources required for training and deploying the model.

Figure 5.16 shows the ideas of HELM, based on the paper of *Holistic Evaluation of Language Models* [19], *https://arxiv.org/abs/2211.09110*:

> *Previous language model benchmarks (e.g. SuperGLUE, EleutherAI LM Evaluation Harness, BIG-Bench) are collections of datasets, each with a standard task framing and canonical metric, usually accuracy (left). In comparison, in HELM we take a top-down approach of first explicitly stating what we want to evaluate (i.e. scenarios and metrics) by working through their underlying structure. Given this stated taxonomy, we make deliberate decisions on what subset we implement and evaluate, which makes explicit what we miss (e.g. coverage of languages beyond English).*
>
> *from Holistic Evaluation of Language Models* [19], *https://arxiv.org/abs/2211.09110*

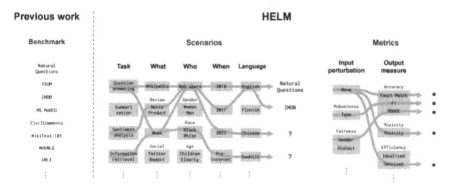

Figure 5.16 HELM Approach
Source from: Holistic Evaluation of Language Models [19],
https://arxiv.org/abs/2211.09110

HELM framework would incorporate tools, metrics, and qualitative assessments that cover these aspects and possibly more. It aims to provide a comprehensive picture of the strengths, limitations and risks of a language model from a multi-dimensional perspective, and offer guidance on which models perform well for specific tasks.

HELM takes a multi-metric approach, measuring seven metrics across the core scenarios, ensuring that trade-offs between models and metrics are clearly exposed. Figure 5.17 shows the multiple metrics of HELM:

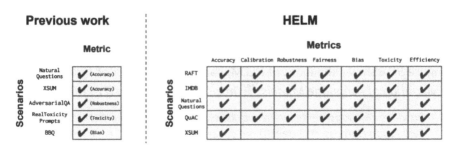

Figure 5.17 Multiple Metrics in HELM
Source from Holistic Evaluation of Language Models [19],
https://arxiv.org/abs/2211.09110

Based on the paper:

> *In comparison to most prior benchmarks of language technologies, which primarily center accuracy and often relegate other desiderata to their own bespoke datasets (if at all), in HELM we take a multi-metric approach. This foregrounds metrics beyond accuracy and allows one to study the tradeoffs between the metrics.*
>
> *from "Holistic Evaluation of Language Models"* [19], *https://arxiv.org/abs/2211.09110*

The metrics in HELM framework include:

1. **Accuracy**: measures the proportion of predictions that a model gets right.
2. **Calibration**: measures the percentage of a model's predicted probabilities reflect the true likelihood of an event.
3. **Robustness**: assesses a model's ability to maintain its performance when facing with new, noisy and challenging data.
4. **Fairness**: measures how outputs of a model are unbiased and equitable across different groups, it ensures that the model does not favor one group or discriminate against another. Usually the imbalanced training data can result in unfair outcomes.

5. **Bias**: evaluates the extent to which the model's predictions are prejudiced in favor of or against certain groups or outcomes.

6. **Toxicity**: measures the degree to which model's outputs can be harmful, offensive, or inappropriate, it ensures LLMs not generate harmful language or content.

7. **Efficiency**: quantifies the computational resources required by the model to perform a task, such as memory usage, energy consumption, speed of inference, and the needs for specialized hardware.

The HELM benchmark provides a comprehensive and rigorous framework for evaluating the capabilities of LLMs, enabling researchers to gain a deeper understanding of the strengths, limitations and risks of these models and to track their progress over time. It is intended to be a living benchmark for the community, continuously updated with new scenarios, metrics, and models.

It's worth noting that implementing such a comprehensive evaluation is complex and requires the methodologies from different research areas and may need cross-disciplinary collaborations to establish testing protocols that can fairly and effectively measure LLM's performance across the numerous facets of language.

5.7 Reinforcement Learning

Fine-tuning LLMs offers the advantage of significantly enhancing their performance on specific tasks by adapting them to the nuances and unique requirements of the target domain.

However, there are several challenges and problems that must be addressed to ensure they provide reliable and appropriate outputs when deployed in various scenarios.

The majority of data for pre-training or fine-tuning comes from internet and websites, in some cases the data might contain biases, the LLM can learn and even amplify these biases, which could lead to fairness issues and ethical concerns when the model makes predictions. They can generate unethical or harmful content if not properly overseen. Making a balance between model freedom and societal norms is tricky and requires careful consideration.

LLMs often perform well on the types of data they have been trained on, but they might not generalize well to new or specific tasks that were not included in the training data. Especially when fine-tuning on a narrow set of data can cause the model to overfit to that dataset, resulting in poor generalization to new types of data or domains it hasn't seen before.

Fine-tuning LLMs on specific tasks often relies on self-supervised or unsupervised learning objectives, such as next-token prediction or masked language modeling. These objectives may not align well with the desired real-world goals or behavior, leading to suboptimal performance.

As examples, an LLM could produce descriptions that make derogatory comments about specific ethnic groups, like race, gender, age, or religion. It could potentially generate content such as hate speech, extremism, or conspiracy theories, if their training data contained such content or if they are prompted in certain ways. It might also inadvertently reproduce copyrighted or plagiarized content, violating intellectual property rights.

Reinforcement Learning (RL), particularly together with human feedback, presents a solution to address these challenges. It's a type of machine learning where an Agent learns to make decisions by taking Actions in an Environment to achieve some goal. The Agent receives feedback through rewards or penalties, which are contingent on the actions taken. In simple terms, reinforcement learning is all about trial and error and learning from past experiences.

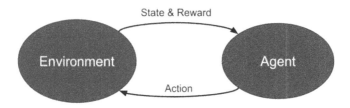

Figure 5.18 High-level Overview of Reinforcement Learning

As shown in Figure 5.18, there are several main components for the reinforcement learning,

- **Agent**: The decision-making entity that perceives the environment and takes actions to achieve a goal.
- **Environment**: The settings in which the agent operates and interacts with. The environment provides observations and rewards to the Agent based on its actions.
- **State**: A representation of the current situation or condition of the environment.
- **Action**: The choices or decisions made by the agent that cause a change in the environment's state.
- **Reward**: A feedback signal, typically a numeric value, that indicates how good or bad the agent's action was in a given state. The agent's objective is to maximize the cumulative reward over time.

Figure 5.19 illustrates a detailed view of Reinforcement learning.

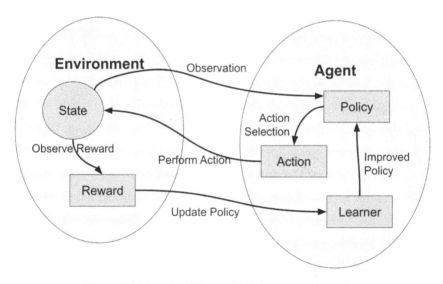

Figure 5.19 Detailed View of Reinforcement Learning

In the Environment on the left:

- The State node represents the current state of the environment.

- The Reward node represents the reward signal provided by the environment based on the agent's action.

In the Agent on the right:

- The Policy node represents the strategy or set of rules the agent follows to determine which action to take in a given state.
- The Action node represents the action chosen by the agent based on the current state and policy.
- The Learner node responsible for updating the agent's policy based on the experience (state, action, reward).

The goal of the agent is to learn a policy, a strategy for selecting actions based on the current state, which maximizes the sum of rewards over time. This is done through a trial-and-error process, taking actions in the environment, observing the resulting rewards or penalties, and gradually adjusting its behavior to maximize the cumulative reward over time.

Figure 5.20 depicts the workflow of Reinforcement learning.

1. Initialization: Define the environment, the agent, and the state and action spaces, initialize the policy to determine the agent's behavior.
2. Observation: The agent observes the current state of the environment.
3. Decision: Based on the current policy, the agent selects an action to perform.
4. Action: The agent performs the chosen action in the environment.
5. Reward: After the action is taken, the agent receives a reward or penalty from the environment based on the success of the action.
6. Learning: The agent updates its policy using the reward signal and the transition (considering both the current state and the next state) to learn better actions.
7. Evaluation: Periodically, the policy's performance is evaluated, and adjustments are made if necessary.
8. Adjust Policy: Update the policy, if necessary, based on the evaluation results.

9. Convergence: Over time and after many iterations, the agent's policy converges to a strategy that ideally maximizes the cumulative reward it receives from the environment.

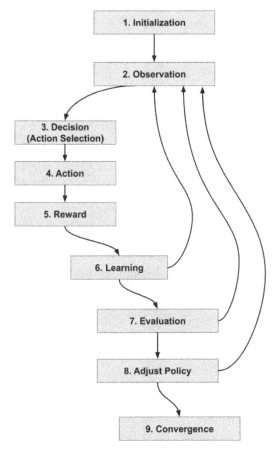

Figure 5.20 Workflow of Reinforcement Learning

This process repeats, with the agent continuously interacting with the environment, observing new states, taking actions, learning from the rewards, and adjusting policy until convergence.

Here we introduce Q-learning algorithm, which is a model-free reinforcement learning technique used to learn the quality of actions, denoting how beneficial it is to take a certain action in a given state.

The code begins with importing the libraries:

```
1    import torch
2    import torch.nn as nn
3    import torch.optim as optim
4    import random
5    import numpy as np
```

Initialize some parameters, as below:

```
6    state_size = 6
7    action_size = 2
8    epochs = 1000
9    gamma = 0.6
10   epsilon = 0.1
11   alpha = 0.1
```

`state_size` represents the size of the environment's state space, allocated as one-hot encoded vectors.

`action_size` is the number of possible actions the agent can take, there are two actions in this example, 1 is for moving right, 0 is moving left.

`epochs` are the number of episodes we will run the training for.

`gamma` is the discount factor for future rewards, which influences their present value.

`epsilon` is used for ε-greedy policy, determining how often the agent will explore rather than exploit.

`alpha` is the learning rate, which affects how strongly the network weights are adjusted during training.

Define an Aagent, `QNetwork`, which is a simple neural network that extends `nn.Module`. It is defined with a single fully connected linear layer `self.fc` with input size `state_size` and output size `action_size`:

```
12   class QNetwork(nn.Module):
13       def __init__(self, state_size, action_size):
14           super(QNetwork, self).__init__()
15           self.fc = nn.Linear(state_size, action_size)
16       def forward(self, state):
17           return self.fc(state)
```

Next step is to setup the environment by instantiating the `QNetwork` with the initial random weights in Line 18.

```
18    net = QNetwork(state_size, action_size)
19    optimizer = optim.Adam(net.parameters(), lr=alpha)
20    loss_fn = nn.MSELoss()
```

Then, Line 19 sets up the `optimizer`, choosing `Adam` as the optimization algorithm, and providing it with the network's parameters and the learning rate.

Line 20 defines the loss function as Mean Squared Error (MSE), which is commonly used for regression tasks.

Here is the main training loop:

```
21    for epoch in range(epochs):
22        state = torch.zeros(state_size)
23        state[0] = 1
24        done = False
25        while not done:
26          if random.random() < epsilon:
27            action = random.randrange(action_size)
28          else:
29            q_values = net(state)
30            action = torch.argmax(q_values).item()
31
32          next_state = torch.zeros(state_size)
33          if action == 1 and
34            torch.argmax(state).item() < state_size - 1:
35            next_state[torch.argmax(state).item() + 1] = 1
36          else:
37            next_state[torch.argmax(state).item()] = 1
38          reward = 0
39          next_state_max = torch.argmax(next_state).item()
40          if next_state_max == state_size - 1:
41            reward = 1
42            done = True
43          predicted_q_values = net(state)
44          target_q_value = reward + gamma *
45                            torch.max(net(next_state)).detach()
46          target_q_values = predicted_q_values.clone()
47          target_q_values[action] = target_q_value
48
```

```
49          optimizer.zero_grad()
50          loss = loss_fn(predicted_q_values, target_q_values)
51          loss.backward()
52          optimizer.step()
53          state = next_state
54    print("Training complete")
```

A state tensor is zero-initialized to represent the one-hot encoding in Line 22, and the first element is set to one, representing the initial state in Line 23.

Line 25 starts the inner loop, which repeatedly selects an action using the ε-greedy policy, observes the next state and reward after taking the action, computes the target and predicted Q-values, performs a gradient descent step, and then moves to the next state.

Line 26 to 30 makes decision, or select actions, by the ε-greedy policy. With chance `epsilon`, a random action is taken; otherwise, the action with the highest Q-value (as predicted by the Q-network from the current state) is chosen.

Line 32 to 39 simulate taking the chosen action and receiving the next state and reward. In a real environment, this would interact with the environment. Instead, this code simulates the next state and reward.

Line 43 to 47 calculate target Q-values for training using the Bellman equation.

As the learning process, Line 49 to 52 update the neural network weights using backpropagation.

After the training, print out the results -- the policy which is simply the best action for each state as determined by the maximum Q-value from the network's output.

```
Derived policy:
State 0: Move right
State 1: Move right
State 2: Move right
State 3: Move left
State 4: Move right
State 5: Move right
```

This code demonstrates a simplified version of Q-learning algorithm, it should be noted though, this example does not include all aspects of reinforcement learning such as an actual environment to interact with (it would usually use an API). The update logic, therefore, is a simulation rather than a real environment update.

5.8   Reinforcement Learning Human Feedback (RLHF)

RLHF (Reinforcement Learning Human Feedback) is a machine learning technique used to train large language models like GPT in a way that tries to align the model's behavior with human preferences and values.

The idea is to first pre-train a large language model, or choose a pre-trained LLM, then perform the fine-tuning on it.

After the model has acquired the capabilities of both broad knowledge and domain specific information, humans provide feedback on samples of text generated by the model, scoring them based on how well the outputs align with the desired behavior (e.g. being Helpful, Harmless, Honest). This is corresponding to step 5c in lifecycle of LLMs in Figure 1.2.

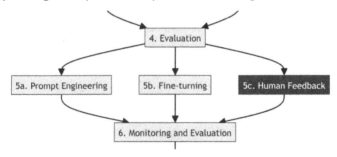

Let's look at some examples of **Helpful**, **Harmless** and **Honest**.

When you ask an LLM a question:

How can I quickly get to the community center?

The LLM's answer:

You'll have to figure it out on your own.

This answer is not **Helpful** because it ignores the user's request entirely. We expect the LLM answers it like this:

> The quickest way to get there is to take the highway and exit on Main St. Let me know if you need turn-by-turn directions.

When a user asks an LLM a question:

> Tell me which stock is going up next month?

The LLM's is expected to answer with **Honest**, something like:

> I don't have that specific piece of information during my training. Consider consulting with a financial advisor who can provide guidance based on your financial goals and risk tolerance.

When a user wants to chat with an LLM on some offensive or unethical topics about individuals or groups, the LLM is expected to give a **Harmless** response, like:

> I don't tell offensive or hateful language towards any groups.

In a standard Reinforcement learning scenario as introduced in Section 5.7, an agent learns by interacting with an environment according to a reward module. The environment provides rewards (or punishments) based on the agent's actions, and the agent's objective is to maximize the sum of these rewards over time. However, defining an appropriate reward module that aligns with complex or nuanced human values can be very challenging, and certain desired behaviors might be difficult to specify programmatically. This is where RLHF (Reinforcement Learning Human Feedback) comes into play.

RLHF will address the above issues especially related to legal and ethical. By observing the LLM's behavior, humans can provide additional signals that help to adjust the reward module or directly influence the learning process. RLHF takes the humans feedbacks on what kinds of outputs are considered acceptable vs problematic, and integrates the complex human values into the model's behaviors. Therefore, the model learns to avoid generating outputs that violate ethical norms or laws based on the human preferences.

As shown in Figure 5.21, three actions are integrated to the standard Reinforcement Learning.

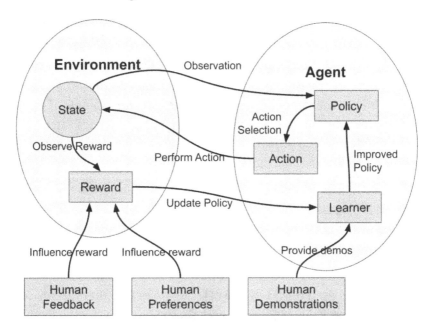

Figure 5.21 Reinforcement Learning with Human Feedback

Human Feedback: humans provide signals or inputs to influence the reward module. The data of human feedback is used to fine-tune the model's parameters using Reinforcement learning algorithms introduced in the previous section. The goal is for the model to learn to generate outputs that receive high scores from the human raters.

A human operator can provide binary feedback on the outputs of the LLMs, for example, when asking an LLM the question:

How can I quickly get to the community center?

The LLM gives two answers:

1. *You'll have to figure it out on your own.*

2. *The quickest way to get there is to take the highway and exit on Main St. Let me know if you need turn-by-turn directions.*

The human operator can give #1 a negative feedback, and #2 a positive. Or alternatively the humans can give score-based feedback, for example range the score on a scale from -5 to 5 based on the relevance and helpfulness of each response.

The humans can also rank different outcomes that an LLM has produced, the rankings can then be translated into numerical reward signals, with higher-ranked outcomes receiving larger rewards.

Human preferences: Humans can provide feedback on the appropriateness of content generated by the LLM, for example, if the LLM generates a response that includes biased language, humans can label them as undesirable. The model would receive a reward signal based on how well it avoids such language in the future.

For educational or information retrieval applications, human feedback can be based on the clarity, completeness, and correctness of the answers provided by the LLM. The model then uses these preferences to produce better-quality answers.

When an LLM is being used to assist with moral or ethical decision-making, human preferences can be collected to ensure that the advice or suggestions it provides are aligned with shared human values and ethical norms.

In tasks requiring creativity, such as storytelling or poetry writing, humans can provide feedback on which generated pieces are the most creative, original, or emotionally evocative.

Human Demonstrations: humans directly showing the desired behavior as examples for the model to learn from, based on actual human behavior or responses. For example, a LLM is presented with examples of high-quality writing including drafts, edits, and final versions. By studying these demonstrations, the LLM can learn how to suggest improvements to text, correct grammar, and adjust the style of writing to suit different contexts.

Human educators might provide demonstrations in the form of well-structured tutorials on a subject, including explanations, examples, and methods used to solve problems. This helps the LLM to learn not just the content but also effective techniques for teaching complex concepts.

Software developers might provide examples of good coding practice, including writing, testing, documenting conventions. By following these demonstrations, an LLM that assists with programming can learn to generate not only functional code but also code that is clear, maintainable, and well-documented.

In terms of ethical and harmless, humans can provide examples of appropriate responses that avoid potential harm.

The RLHF will be refining the initial model built on these demonstrations with reward signals that reinforce the generation of similar high-quality outputs in line with the demonstrated examples.

In summary, RLHF is a powerful technique for aligning the behavior and outputs of LLMs with desired characteristics and human preferences. By incorporating the insights and judgments of human raters, the RLHF process enables LLMs to internalize human values, ethics, and expectations, ensuring that these powerful models remain aligned with the human expectations and preferences.

5.9   Implementation of RLHF

This section will explore the implementation of RLHF using TRLX (Transformer Reinforcement Learning X), which is an open-source framework, developed by CarperAI, for training LLMs with RLHF.

The process is shown in Figure 5.22, there are several components involved here:

Pre-trained/Fine-tuned LLM is the one that we discussed earlier, the model is pre-trained or fine-tuned with the datasets.

Reward model is a separate model used to predicts how good an output is according to human judgements. Its role is to provide a reward signal that guides the reinforcement learning process. The reward model is trained using supervised learning on human feedback data.

Proximal Policy Optimization (PPO) is basically a reinforcement learning algorithm to update the weights of LLM. The LLM generates outputs, and these outputs are scored by the reward model. Then, PPO updates the parameters of the LLM to improve the reward of generated outputs.

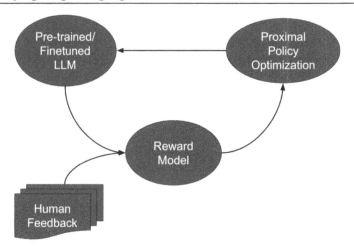

Figure 5.22 Implementation of HLHF

The paper of *Learning to summarize from human feedback[24], Stiennon et al. 2020, https://arxiv.org/abs/2009.01325* introduced a practice of applying RLHF on the GPT models. The researchers at OpenAI present their approach to fine-tuning the GPT models using Reinforcement Learning with Human Feedback (RLHF).

The key innovation is using RLHF as the reward signal, rather than just supervised learning on a fixed dataset. This allows continually adapting the model outputs towards what humans prefer through an iterative process of sampling, scoring, and reinforcement learning.

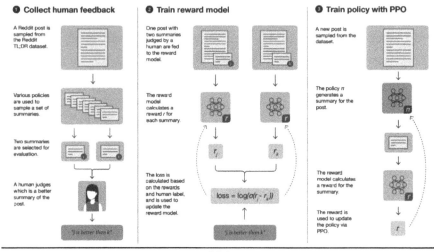

Figure 5.23 Steps of Implementation of RLHF
Source from Learning to summarize from human feedback[24],
https://arxiv.org/abs/2009.01325

The paper describes a text summarization task. The steps of gathering the human feedback, training the reward model and training PPO are illustrated in Figure 5.23.

1. **Collect human feedback**: Human raters are presented with a source text and two summaries, and are asked to choose which one they think is better. Some quality standards are defined to guide the human raters, such as how well the summary captures important points from the input text, how accurately the summary reflects the content, and how well-written and logically structured the summary is, and so on. The human raters are also trained with an initial set of examples and explanations of the quality criteria, and how to align their ratings with the standards. In order to mitigate individual rater's biases and inconsistencies, multiple raters' judgments are collected per pair of summaries.

2. **Train the Reward model**: These human rated pairwise preferences are used as labels to train a binary classifier. The inputs to the classifier are features extracted from the pairs of summaries, and the label indicates which of the two summaries was preferred by the human raters. The loss is calculated based on the human labels, and then is used to update the Reward model. The Reward model is designed to output a probability indicating the likelihood that a certain summary would be preferred over another in a pairwise comparison.

3. **Train policy with PPO**: the policy model π is the pre-trained or fine-tuned LLM that has been trained on the supervised learning task. π generates summaries from the input text, the reward model generates a score for the summary, the reward is used to update the policy model. PPO allows the model to gradually learn to take actions (generate outputs) that maximize rewards from the reward model, while maintaining a proximity constraint to the previous policy for stability.

TRLX is a framework developed by CarperAI which facilitates the training of Reinforcement Learning (RL) agents for LLMs, keeping the focus on scalability and efficiency. It is designed to work with models of different sizes and architectures, providing an extensible tool to the community for advancing RL methods, especially in natural language processing tasks.

TRLX provides an implementation of PPO (Proximal Policy Optimization) algorithm, which is robust and reliable for training policies in complex environments.

The framework is compatible with transformer-based language models, such as GPT, BERT, FLAN-T5 and so on, most of them are available in Hugging Face's transformers library. This allows users to leverage pre-trained language models and fine-tune them for specific tasks using RLHF.

TRLX is available at *https://github.com/CarperAI/trlx*.

Follow the instructions to install TRLX, please note, due to the fact that TRLX project is under active development at the time of this writing, the code snippets in this section are intended to show the concept only, they are not tested in a specific environment. Here is to install TRLX:

```
1   !git clone https://github.com/CarperAI/trlx.git
2   %cd trlx
3   !pip install -r requirements.txt
```

The process starts with fine-tuning a pre-trained transformer model on a dataset, say text summarization dataset.

```
4    import trlX
5    from transformers import T5Tokenizer
6    from transformers import T5ForConditionalGeneration
7    from datasets import load_dataset
8    model_name = 'google/flan-t5-base'
9    def load_model(model_name):
10       tokenizer = T5Tokenizer.
11                   from_pretrained(model_name)
12       model = T5ForConditionalGeneration.
13                   from_pretrained(model_name)
14       return tokenizer, model
15   tokenizer, model = load_model(model_name)
16   # Load dataset
17   dataset = load_dataset(summarization_dataset)
```

```
18    # To do: tokenize the dataset following previous examples.
19    # Fine-tune the model with TRLX
20    trainer = trlX.trainer(
21        model=model,
22        tokenizer=tokenizer,
23        train_dataset=dataset['train'],
24        val_dataset=dataset['val'],
25        train_batch_size=8,
26        gradient_accumulation_steps=2,
27    )
28    trainer.train()
```

Load a pre-trained LLM, here we use `google/flan-t5-base`, and obtain both the `model` and its `tokenizer`.

Then load a dataset for fine-tuning, the data should be tokenized before training. So far it's exactly the same as what we previous did for fine-tuning an LLM.

Line 20 to 27 define a `trlx.trainer()` with the loaded model, tokenizer, train dataset, validation dataset, and other parameters. This step is similar to what we have done for training a LoRA model, but the `trainer` is from the `trlx` library.

Like 28 performs the training with the `trainer.train()` method.

This above step is for setting up the libraries, loading the pre-trained model and dataset, then instructing the training tool (the trainer from TRLX) to fine-tune the model for the summarization task.

Then move on to train the Reward model, which is step #2 in Figure 5.23. We will also use TRLX library for this purpose:

```
31    from trlX import RewardModel, RewardTrainer
32    reward_model = RewardModel(model, tokenizer)
33    human_rating_dataset = load_dataset('human_rating_dataset')
34    # Train the reward model
35    reward_trainer = RewardTrainer(
36        reward_model=reward_model
37        args=training_args,
38        train_dataset=human_rating_dataset,
39    )
40    reward_trainer.train()
```

Line 32 is to create a reward model from TRLX library. Line 33 brings in the human rating dataset, which consists of pairs of summaries along with scores indicating how good they are.

Line 35 to 40 create a `reward_trainer`, and use it to train the reward model.

Finally, use PPO to further fine-tune the LLM:

```
41   ppo_trainer = trlX.PPOTrainer(
42       model=model,
43       tokenizer=tokenizer,
44       reward_model=reward_model,
45       train_dataset=train_dataset,
46       train_batch_size=8,
47   )
48   ppo_trainer.train()
```

`trlX.PPOTrainer` is used to put everything together, the original model, tokenizer, reward_model and train dataset, its `train()` method starts the training process.

In summary, TRLX framework provides a powerful platform for RLHF, where the LLMs learn from a reward signal that is generated based on human judgment. TRLX aims to unite advancements in scaling RLHF with powerful, iterative, and customizable design. The framework is designed to make the process of scaling of RLHF techniques on LLMs more accessible, efficient, and safer.

Because things are changing week by week, make sure to reference the documentation of the latest version of the framework, and also investigate for any similar tools and frameworks for the purpose of RLHF.

5.10 Conclusion

In this chapter, we have explored the depths of fine-tuning LLMs, unveiling various techniques and methodologies that empower us to adapt these models to specific tasks and domains. From the foundational concept of transfer learning to the hands-on implementation of full fine-tuning of the

LLMs, we have gained a solid understanding of the process and its practical applications.

Moreover, we deep-dive into PEFT (Parameter-Efficient Fine-Tuning), an advancement in adapting LLMs to specific tasks of domains, which presents alternatives to the computationally intensive full fine-tuning approach. PEFT encompasses techniques such as LoRA, Adapters, and Prompt Tuning, that prioritize updating a minimal subset of a model's parameters to achieve results comparable to full fine-tuning with significantly less computational overhead.

Evaluating the performance of fine-tuned LLMs is important, and we covered a range of evaluation techniques and benchmarks to assess model quality and effectiveness. The ROUGE and BLEU metrics, along with their code implementations, equip you with the tools to evaluate text summarization and machine translation tasks. We also discussed comprehensive benchmarks like GLUE, SuperGLUE, SQuAD and HELM, which serve as holistic evaluation frameworks for LLM's capabilities.

Finally, we ventured into the realm of reinforcement learning, exploring the Reinforcement Learning with Human Feedback (RLHF) methodology and the TRLX framework. By incorporating human preferences and feedback into the fine-tuning process, we can iteratively refine and improve the behavior of LLMs, unlocking new possibilities for effective language models.

Wrapping up this chapter, by traversing the landscape from the foundational pre-training processes, to fine-tuning techniques such as PEFT (including LoRA, Adapters, and Prompt Tuning) and RLHF, we've dived deep into how language models learn and get better without needing a ton of power behind them.

With the knowledge and skills acquired throughout this chapter, you are now equipped to embark on your own fine-tuning journey, adapting large language models to meet the unique demands of your organization and applications. Whether you seek to enhance text summarization, improve language understanding, or develop custom language models, the techniques and methodologies presented here will serve as a solid foundation for your endeavors.

One of the key points is that there's a way for the AI researchers and developers to improve their skills without spending too much computer hardware resources. And the best part, it's not just for the big players in tech anymore; it's stuff that anyone who's into AI can get their hands dirty with.

6. Deployment of LLMs

n today's data-driven world, the usage of Large Language Models (LLMs) has escalated rapidly. These powerful models, trained on vast amounts of data, have demonstrated remarkable capabilities in understanding and generating human-like text, making them invaluable across numerous industries. However, unlocking their potential requires not only developing and fine-tuning these models but also successfully deploying them in real-world environments.

Deployment, the process of integrating a developed model into an existing production environment to make inferences, is a critical yet often overlooked aspect. Ensuring the efficient and scalable delivery of LLM-powered services while maintaining high performance, security, and ethical standards is a complex endeavor. It involves a series of complex steps that, when executed well, unleash the LLM's potential to impact operations significantly.

As the adoption of LLMs continues to grow across industries, it has become increasingly important to understand the methods and techniques of deploying these models in real-world environments. This chapter explore the various aspects of LLM deployment, providing a comprehensive guide to navigating the challenges and leveraging the full potential of these cutting-edge language models.

Deployment is the step 7 in the lifecycle of LLMs in Figure 1.2

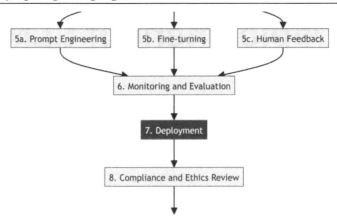

Figure 6.1 Deployment in Lifecycle of LLMs

This chapter explores the key considerations and best practices involved in deploying LLMs at an enterprise scale, that include the following:

Challenges and Considerations: An overview of the technical and ethical hurdles of operationalizing LLMs, including computational demands, safety risks, alignment with human values, and legal implications.

Pre-Deployment Optimization: Strategies for optimizing LLM performance, efficiency, and cost through techniques like model compression, quantization, pruning, and hardware acceleration.

Security and Privacy: Robust security controls, differential privacy safeguards, and information risk assessments to protect LLM systems and mitigate abuse or unintended exposure of sensitive data.

Deployment Architectures: Architectural patterns for scalable, reliable, and secure model deployment, including on-premises, cloud deployment, and containerization approaches.

Scalability and Load Balancing: Autoscaling frameworks, load balancing methodologies and distributed serving strategies to handle unpredictable traffic demands and burst capacities at scale.

Compliance and Ethics Review: Frameworks to evaluate LLM deployments through a compliance viewpoint across areas like bias mitigation, intellectual property risks, truth/disinformation, and ethical principles.

Model Versioning and Updates: Versioning schemes, safe rollout practices, and performance optimizations to manage the full lifecycle of LLM deployments as new model checkpoints are released.

LLM-Powered Applications: A quick overview of developing the applications that powered by LLMs, together with hands-on code examples for chatbot, webui and so on.

Future Trends and Challenges: Emerging trends like multimodal models, safer generation techniques, AI governance, and testing complexities that will shape the future LLM deployment landscape.

6.1 Challenges and Considerations

Deploying Large Language Models (LLMs) involves navigating a range of challenges and considerations to ensure the models are effective, reliable, and ethically in real-world applications. Here are several key challenges and considerations:

Model size, computational and memory requirements: LLMs can be extremely large, often billions of parameters, and may require significant computational resources for both deployment and inference. Deploying them on standard hardware can be challenging, it typically requires specialized hardware (e.g., GPUs, TPUs) or distributed computing setups. Organizations must consider whether they have the appropriate hardware or cloud infrastructure to handle these demands efficiently.

Latency and throughput: Even with powerful hardware, efficient inference is crucial for serving LLM-powered applications with low latency and high throughput. It's important to ensuring the model responds quickly enough to meet user expectations and handles the volume of requests for good user experience. As the demand for LLM-powered applications grows, ensuring scalability and load balancing becomes essential.

Monitoring and maintenance: Deploying LLMs requires monitoring various performance metrics (e.g., latency, throughput, resource utilization) and optimizing the deployment pipeline accordingly.

Continuous monitoring is important to quickly identify and resolve any performance issues, bugs, or unexpected behavior of the deployed models.

Continuous learning and updating: LLMs are constantly evolving, the deployed LLMs may need regular updates to maintain their performance, adapt to new data, and prevent model drift. Implementing a system for continuous learning without service disruption is challenging and requires careful planning.

Security and privacy: LLMs might process and generate sensitive data, protecting sensitive information is important. The data security and privacy are critical concerns. Deployment strategies must include robust security measures to prevent data breaches, like data encryption, secure communication, access control, and comply with data protection regulations.

Regulatory compliance and ethical considerations: Since LLMs learn from large datasets mostly from internet, they can exhibit biases, generate harmful or offensive content. It's essential to assess and mitigate biases that could lead to unfair outcomes or discrimination, ensuring that the use of LLMs adheres to all applicable laws and consider the broader ethical implications of their use.

Integration with existing systems: The LLM often needs to be integrated with existing business processes and systems, APIs, and user interfaces, which may cause significant changes to workflows or existing infrastructure. Ensuring seamless interoperability and compatibility is an important consideration.

Cost management: Deploying and maintaining LLMs can be costly. Organizations should balance the costs of computing resources, development, and ongoing operations against the value provided by the model.

Deployment architecture: Choosing the right deployment architecture (on-premises, cloud-based, hybrid) based on factors like data privacy, scalability, and cost requirements is important for successful deployments.

Addressing these challenges requires a proactive and comprehensive approach that involves technical know-how, strategic planning, and ethical governance, etc. By understanding and addressing these challenges and considerations, organizations can effectively leverage the power of LLMs while ensuring efficient, scalable, and secure deployments in production environments.

6.2 Pre-Deployment Optimization

Deploying Large Language Models (LLMs) in production environments requires careful consideration and optimization to ensure efficient performance and resource utilization. Before the full-scale deployment, it's important to optimize them to ensure they operate efficiently within the constraints of a production environment.

The optimization process comprises model refinement strategies aimed at reducing computational burden while preserving, or even enhancing, model performance. Careful attention during this phase can lead to significant improvements in speed, cost-effectiveness, and user experience.

Computational and Memory Requirements of LLMs

As mentioned in previous chapters, LLMs can have billions of parameters, they are resource-intensive, often requiring substantial computational power and memory. The specific requirements vary based on the model architecture, size, and the hardware used for deployment. For example, the GPT-3 with 175 billion parameters requires tens of gigabytes of memory and substantial computational resources for inference. This can lead to challenges when deploying LLMs on limited hardware or in cost-sensitive environments.

To mitigate such issues, understanding and optimizing the model's architecture and operations is required for efficient resource utilization. Strategies include simplifying the model, reducing precision, or using specialized hardware accelerators.

Specialized hardware accelerators, such as GPUs, TPUs, or other AI-specific processors, are often employed. These accelerators are designed to efficiently handle the parallel computations required for deep learning models, resulting in significant performance improvements compared to traditional CPUs.

In addition to the specialized hardware accelerators, several techniques can be employed to optimize LLMs for deployment, including model quantization, model pruning and sparsity, and knowledge distillation and model compression.

Model Quantization

Model quantization is a process of reducing the precision of model weights from 32-bit floating-point to lower-precision formats, which can reduce the model size and speed up inference operations. For example, as discussed in Section 4.7, the default data format for LLMs is **FP32** (32-bit single-precision floating-point format), by converting it to **FP16** (half-precision floating-point) or **BFLOAT16** (Brain floating point), or even **INT8**, quantization can lead to less memory usage and faster processing, although sometimes at the expense of slight decreases in model accuracy or stability.

Several quantization techniques can be applied to the model:

Post-training quantization, this is to quantize the model weights after training is completed. In the code example in Section 5.3, we load the model with `torch_dtype=torch.bfloat16` for inference, that is to convert the weights to BFLOAT16, which is compatible with 32-bit FP32 in data range and reduce the size of the weights by half.

Quantization-aware training, the model is trained with quantized weights from the start, allowing the model to adapt to the quantized representation during training. For example BFLOAT16 is used when initially loading the pre-trained LLM, then perform the fine-tuning with the same datatype.

Mixed-precision quantization, different parts of the model can be quantized to different precision levels, balancing model size and performance.

It worthwhile to note that quantizing with FP16 might potentially lead to issues of data overflow, information loss or numerical instability because FP16 has a smaller value range compared to FP32. It might not be able to accurately represent the full dynamic range of the model's weights and activations. BF16 might be a better alternative in this case since it has the same range with FP32, reference Section 4.7 for details.

Knowledge Distillation and Model Compression

Knowledge distillation and model compression techniques aim to transfer the knowledge from a large, highly accurate "teacher" model to a smaller, more resource-efficient "student" model. By doing so, it captures the essential information the larger model has learned, and mimic its outputs or behavior, but with less computational overhead and effectively compressing the knowledge into a more compact representation. This approach not only helps ease deployment but also can make the model more interpretable and easier to update.

For example, Section 4.6 introduces some existing popular LLMs, one of them is DistilBERT, it's distilled from BERT and retains most of BERT's knowledge with 40% fewer params, so it's a smaller, faster and lightweight version of BERT.

There are several approaches to knowledge distillation, including:

Response-based distillation: the student model is trained to match the output distributions (e.g., logits or probabilities) of the teacher model.

Feature-based distillation: in addition to matching outputs, the student model is trained to mimic the intermediate feature representations of the teacher model.

Attention-based distillation: the student model learns to mimic the attention patterns of the teacher model. Reference Chapter 3 for the details of attention mechanism of the transformer architecture.

Knowledge distillation and model compression techniques can significantly reduce the size and computational requirements of large language models, making them more suitable for deployment in resource-constrained environments.

Model Pruning and Sparsity

Model pruning is a process of identifying and removing redundant or less important weights (usually close-to-zero values) from the model, setting those weights to zeros, aiming at reducing the computational burden without significantly impacting performance. Pruning can be achieved through various techniques, such as Magnitude-based pruning, which removes weights of small values; or more sophisticated methods that consider the importance of weights based on their contribution to the model's output.

Sparsity refers to the model structure having a large number of zero-valued weights. Sparse models can be more computationally efficient, as operations involving zero values can be skipped or optimized, especially when combined with hardware and software designed to leverage sparse matrix operations. Model pruning often leads to increased sparsity.

One of the widely used pruning technique is called Wanda (pruning by Weights AND Activations), which can prune LLMs to high degrees of sparsity thus to reduce the computational requirements while maintaining its performance without an expensive re-training.

Wanda is proposed by *A Simple and Effective Pruning Approach for Large Language Models* [25], Sun et al, 2023, *https://arxiv.org/abs/2306.11695*.

The traditional Magnitude-based pruning works as Figure 6.2:

$$S = |W|$$

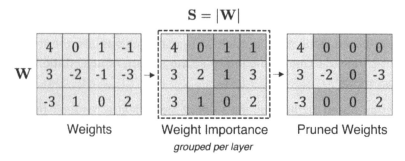

Weights   Weight Importance   Pruned Weights

grouped per layer

Figure 6.2 Magnitude-based Pruning

Source from: A Simple and Effective Pruning Approach for Large Language Models[25], https://arxiv.org/abs/2306.11695, modified by Author

The weights of a neural network are grouped by layers, and the importance of the weight is determined by their magnitude, in the middle in Figure 6.2:

$$S = |W|$$

All the weights with the magnitude ≤ 1 are replaced with zeros. As the result, the sparsity is increased in the weights of the neural network.

On the other hand, Wanda works differently, as shown in Figure 6.3,

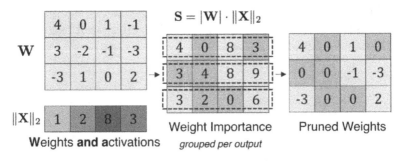

Weights **and** activations   *grouped per output*

Figure 6.3 Wanda (pruning by Weights AND Activations)
Source from: A Simple and Effective Pruning Approach for Large Language Models[25], https://arxiv.org/abs/2306.11695, modified by Author

The importance of the weights is calculated not only from the weights W, but also from the input activations X. The importance is computed as the elementwise product between the weight magnitude and the norm of input activations:

$$S = |W| \cdot \|X\|_2$$

Here the L2 norm of X is used to measure the magnitudes of input activation. And the importance is grouped by output, instead of the entire weight matrix as magnitude-based pruning. The smaller elements in the weight importance S are replaced by zeros, as shown in the right of Figure 6.3.

The below code snippet is proposed by the paper to calculate Wanda weights:

```
1    # W: weight matrix (C_out, C_in);
2    # X: input matrix (N * L, C_in);
```

```
3    # s: desired sparsity, between 0 and 1;
4
5    def prune(W, X, s):
6        metric = W.abs() * X.norm(p=2, dim=0)
7        _, sorted_idx = torch.sort(metric, dim=1)
8        pruned_idx = sorted_idx[:,:int(C_in * s)]
9        W.scatter_(dim=1, index=pruned_idx, src=0)
10       return W
```

The paper also lists some experimental results, as shown in Figure 6.4, Wanda is evaluated on two most widely adopted LLM model families: LLaMA 7B/13B/30B/65B and LLaMA-2 7B/13B/70B, against two prior pruning techniques, Magnitude pruning, and SparseGPT.

Method	Weight Update	Sparsity	7B	13B	30B	65B	7B	13B	70B
			LLaMA				LLaMA-2		
Dense	-	0%	59.99	62.59	65.38	66.97	59.71	63.03	67.08
Magnitude	✗	50%	46.94	47.61	53.83	62.74	51.14	52.85	60.93
SparseGPT	✓	50%	54.94	58.61	63.09	66.30	56.24	60.72	67.28
Wanda	✗	50%	54.21	59.33	63.60	66.67	56.24	60.83	67.03
Magnitude	✗	4:8	46.03	50.53	53.53	62.17	50.64	52.81	60.28
SparseGPT	✓	4:8	52.80	55.99	60.79	64.87	53.80	59.15	65.84
Wanda	✗	4:8	52.76	56.09	61.00	64.97	52.49	58.75	66.06
Magnitude	✗	2:4	44.73	48.00	53.16	61.28	45.58	49.89	59.95
SparseGPT	✓	2:4	50.60	53.22	58.91	62.57	50.94	54.86	63.89
Wanda	✗	2:4	48.53	52.30	59.21	62.84	48.75	55.03	64.14

Figure 6.4 Wanda Results Compared with Other Pruning Techniques
Source from: A Simple and Effective Pruning Approach for Large Language Models[25], https://arxiv.org/abs/2306.11695

The experiment is to perform zero-shot inference with 7 tasks on pruned LLaMa and LLaMA-2 models, the table in Figure 6.4 lists the mean accuracies (%) in the 7 columns in the right. Three pruning methods are used for comparison, Wanda, Magitude and SparseGPT (which requires weights update by re-training).

The results show that Wanda outperforms the Magnitude pruning approach by a large margin, and rivals with SparseGPT, which was the previous best approach but requires weights update by re-training.

With Wanda, the majority of the parameters removed are activations, while a significantly lower proportion are weights. This divergence from traditional magnitude-based pruning can result in benefits such as faster inference time, lower energy consumption, and reduced memory usage. This approach may be particularly beneficial for deploying LLMs on resource-constrained devices and platforms where computational efficiency and power usage are significant concerns.

An implementation of Wanda is available at:
https://github.com/locuslab/wanda

In summary, pre-deployment preparation is important for the successful operationalization of LLMs. Through optimization, computational and memory demands are reduced, enabling smoother integration and operation within various infrastructure limits. Techniques such as model quantization, pruning, sparsity, and knowledge distillation are tools that aid in the compression and acceleration of LLMs. By employing these strategies, organizations can achieve the dual objectives of maintaining high performance and managing deployment costs effectively.

6.3   Security and Privacy

When deploying LLMs, it is essential to classify the data used for training and inference based on its sensitivity level to ensure the appropriate level of security and privacy protections are applied.

Data Sensitivity Classifications

In an organization, the sensitivity levels are typically categorized into four classifications:

High sensitivity: This includes data that contains personally identifiable information (PII), such as names, addresses, social security numbers, social insurance numbers, financial information, healthcare records, or other information that could lead to drastic consequences if disclosed. Strict security measures and access controls are required for handling and processing this data. Access to data in this category is extremely restricted and heavily monitored.

Medium sensitivity: This category includes data that is less critical but still confidential, it may not directly identify individuals but could be used in combination with other information to do so. Examples include email addresses, user identifiers, or demographic information. Unauthorized access could impact the business or individuals to a substantial extent. It requires strong access controls to prevent leaks.

Low sensitivity: This data is not highly confidential but is not intended for public distribution. It could include internal communication that mentions business practices.

Public sensitivity: This data is intended for public consumption and distribution, such as news articles, public reports, or open-source datasets. Such data requires minimal security measures.

The classification of data sensitivity levels should be based on a thorough risk assessment, considering factors such as the potential harm to individuals or organizations if the data were exposed or misused, as well as regulatory requirements and industry standards.

The controls and measures should be put in place to protect the data based on the above classification, often mandated by organizational policies and legal frameworks.

Data Encryption and Secure Communication

To protect sensitive data during transfer and storage, it is important to implement robust encryption mechanisms and secure communication protocols. Encrypting data ensures that even if an unauthorized party gains access to it, they cannot interpret the content.

Data encryption at rest: Sensitive data stored in databases, file systems, or cloud storage should be encrypted using strong encryption algorithms, such as AES256, and key management practices. TDE (Transparent Data Encryption) is a technology used primarily in databases, it encrypts data at the database or storage engine level, providing encryption of data at rest automatically and transparently to the applications accessing the database.

Data encryption in transit: When transmitting data over networks, secure communication protocols such as Transport Layer Security (TLS) or Secure Sockets Layer (SSL) should be used to encrypt the data stream.

Secure communication channels: Communication between LLM components (e.g., model servers, data pipelines, and user interfaces) should occur over secure channels, using authenticated and encrypted connections. VPNs (Virtual Private Networks) can be used to securely access cloud services and APIs for LLMs, ensuring the traffic is encrypted and protected from eavesdroppers.

Key management: Encryption keys should be securely generated, stored, and managed using industry-standard key management practices, such as hardware security modules (HSMs) or key vaults. HSMs are physical devices that handle encryption keys securely, providing a hardware barrier against unauthorized access.

Access Control and Authentication

Implementing robust access control and authentication mechanisms is essential to ensure that only authorized individuals or systems can access sensitive data and LLM components.

Access control is the selective restriction of access to the data, it ensures that only authorized personnel can interact with the LLM or the data it processes. Authentication is equally important—it ensures that users are who they claim to be.

Role-based access control (RBAC): Defining roles and permissions based on the roles of individual users within an organization, ensuring that users and systems have access only to the resources and data they need to perform their tasks.

Multi-factor authentication (MFA): Requiring multiple authentication factors, such as passwords, biometrics, or hardware tokens, to verify the identity of users or systems.

Auditing and logging: Maintaining comprehensive audit logs and monitoring access attempts to detect and respond to potential security incidents or unauthorized access.

Secure credential management: Implementing secure practices for managing and rotating credentials, such as passwords, API keys, and access tokens, across LLM components and associated systems.

Privacy-Preserving Techniques

To protect individual privacy and comply with data protection regulations, organizations can implement privacy-preserving techniques when training and deploying LLMs. These techniques include:

Federated learning: This approach enables training LLMs on decentralized data sources, without the need to centralize or share raw data. Models are trained locally on individual devices or data silos and then aggregated to create a global model.

Differential privacy: This technique introduces controlled noise or perturbations to the data or model outputs, ensuring that the presence or absence of any individual's data has a negligible impact on the overall results, thereby preserving privacy.

Secure multi-party computation (MPC): MPC protocols enable multiple parties to collaboratively train LLMs on their combined data without revealing their individual data to each other, preserving data privacy and confidentiality.

Homomorphic encryption: This encryption technique allows computations to be performed on encrypted data without the need for decryption, enabling privacy-preserving processing of sensitive data in LLM applications.

The above techniques can help in reducing the risks associated with handling sensitive data.

Compliance with Data Protection Regulations

Deploying LLMs often involves the processing and storage of personal or sensitive data, which is subject to various data protection regulations, such as the General Data Protection Regulation (GDPR) in the European Union or Health Insurance Portability and Accountability Act (HIPAA) in the United States. It is imperative to comply with local and global data protection regulations to avoid legal and financial penalties, as well as to maintain the trust of customers and users.

Organizations should ensure that their LLM deployments adhere to the following principles:

Data minimization: Collect and process only the data that is strictly necessary for the intended purpose, minimizing the collection and retention of personal or sensitive information.

Purpose limitation: Clearly define and communicate the specific purposes for which data is collected and processed and ensure that the data is not used for any other purposes without explicit consent. For example, using social security numbers (SSNs) as the primary keys for searching purpose might violate this principle, since it misuses the highly sensitive data.

Data protection impact assessments (DPIAs): Conduct DPIAs to identify and mitigate potential privacy risks associated with LLM deployments, especially for high-risk processing activities.

Data protection by design and default: Embed data protection principles into the design and architecture of LLM systems from the beginning, ensuring that privacy and security are integral components rather than afterthoughts.

International data transfers: Implement appropriate safeguards and mechanisms, such as standard contractual clauses or binding corporate rules, when transferring personal data across international borders to ensure compliance with cross-border data transfer requirements.

Adhering to these security and privacy considerations is not only a legal and ethical requirement for deploying LLMs, but also critical for maintaining public trust and protecting the integrity of the organizations. By implementing these security and privacy measures, organizations can deploy LLMs while maintaining the highest levels of data protection, privacy, and regulatory compliance.

6.4   Deployment Architectures

The foundation for deploying LLMs efficiently is selecting appropriate architecture that meets performance requirements and optimizes running costs. The deployment architecture depends on various factors, including the available hardware resources, scalability requirements, and the desired level of control and customization. This section explores different deployment architectures for LLMs, covering hardware considerations, on-premises, cloud-based, hybrid approaches, containerization, and scaling for high availability and redundancy.

Choosing the Right Hardware

LLMs typically require powerful hardware with substantial GPU resources for efficient training and inference. The choice of hardware depends on factors such as the model size, batch size, and the desired performance.

LLMs are highly parallelizable and benefit significantly from high-performance GPUs, such as NVIDIA's A100, H100 or AMD's Instinct GPUs, which are commonly used for LLM training and inference.

Some companies develop specialized hardware accelerators optimized for LLM workloads, such as Google's Tensor Processing Units (TPUs) or Graphcore's Intelligence Processing Units (IPUs), they can offer even more specialized performance benefits. The choice will depend on the model's size, the expected workload, the latency requirements, and the available budget.

CPU-based systems can also be used for smaller models or inference tasks with lower performance requirements.

On-premises Deployment

On-premises deployment is to host the LLMs on local servers or data centers within an organization's infrastructure. This approach provides maximum control over hardware resources, data security, and customization options. It is a preferred choice for those with strict data sensitivity or privacy requirements and those who require full control over their hardware and network.

However, the main challenges are the significant upfront investments in hardware and ongoing maintenance and upgrades.

Advantages:

- Full control over hardware resources and data security.
- Customization and fine-tuning of the LLM for specific use cases.
- No dependency on external cloud providers.

Disadvantages:

- High upfront costs for hardware and infrastructure.
- Ongoing maintenance and operational costs.
- Potential scalability limitations based on available resources.

Cloud-based Deployment

Cloud-based deployment leverages the resources and infrastructure provided by cloud service providers like Amazon Web Services (AWS), Microsoft Azure, or Google Cloud Platform (GCP). It offers flexibility, scalability, and reduced maintenance concerns.

Cloud providers often have specialized hardware for machine learning workloads, reducing the need for physical hardware investments and allowing organizations to pay for only what they use based on the pay-as-you-go pricing models, making it suitable for organizations with varying resource demands or limited on-premises infrastructure.

Advantages:

- Scalability and on-demand resource allocation.
- Managed services and reduced operational overhead.
- Pay-as-you-go pricing models.
- Access to specialized hardware accelerators provided by the vendors, e.g., Google TPUs.

Disadvantages:

- Potential data privacy and security concerns.
- Dependency on cloud provider's service availability and pricing.
- Potential vendor lock-in and limited customization options.

Hybrid Deployment

Hybrid deployment combines on-premises and cloud-based solutions, it can maximize the security and control of on-premises solutions with the scalability and resource availability of the cloud, and allows organizations to leverage their existing on-premises infrastructure while utilizing cloud resources for additional capacity or specialized workloads.

With hybrid deployment, LLMs can be kept on-premises for training with sensitive data and deployed in the cloud to scale out for handling unpredictable workloads.

Advantages:

- Flexibility to utilize both on-premises and cloud resources.
- Potential cost savings by leveraging existing on-premises infrastructure.
- Ability to handle bursts in demand or specialized workloads using cloud resources.

Disadvantages:

- Increased complexity in managing and integrating multiple environments.
- Potential data transfer costs between on-premises and cloud environments.
- Potential security and compliance challenges.

Containerization and Orchestration (e.g., Docker, Kubernetes)

Containerization packages the LLM and its environment into a container that can run reliably across different computing environments, the tools like Docker and orchestration platforms like Kubernetes can simplify the deployment and management of LLMs across different environments, making it easier to deploy and scale. Kubernetes manage these containers, automating deployment, scaling, and management of the application, thus ensuring the LLM's high availability and resource optimization across clusters of hosts.

Advantages:

- Consistent and reproducible deployments across different environments.
- Simplified management and scaling of LLM services.
- Improved resource utilization and efficiency.
- Easier integration with continuous integration and deployment (CI/CD) pipelines.

Disadvantages:

- Learning curve for container and orchestration technologies, e.g. Docker and Kubernetes.
- Potential overhead and complexity for small-scale deployments.
- Potential security concerns if containers are not properly configured.

The deployment of LLMs is a multifaceted endeavor, each aspect of which, from hardware selection to deployment strategies, demands careful attention. Organizations should thoroughly assess their needs, capabilities, and goals for a deployment architecture that not only aligns with their operational paradigm but also propels them towards achieving an optimized, robust, and responsive LLM environment. As the diverse deployment options illustrate, there is no one-size-fits-all solution, but rather a spectrum of architectures that can be tailored to best support the successful and strategic implementation of Large Language Models.

6.5 Scalability and Load Balancing

As the demand for LLM services increases, they often need to handle large volumes of requests, it's important to ensure an environment that provides high availability and redundancy to handle high load and potential system failures. Scalability and load balancing become critical considerations to ensure consistent performance, high availability, and efficient resource utilization. This section discusses various strategies for scaling and load balancing LLM deployments.

Horizontal Scaling (Adding More Instances)

Horizontal scaling, also known as scaling out, involves adding more instances or replicas of the LLM service across the available infrastructure to distribute the workloads more evenly thus handle increased load, as shown in Figure 6.5. This type of scaling is important for accommodating growing numbers of requests without degrading performance, allowing the system to handle a higher volume of requests and improve overall throughput.

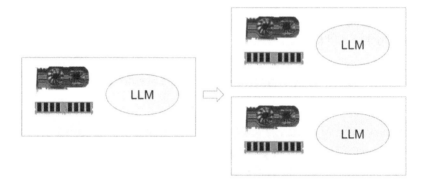

Figure 6.5 Horizontal scaling, aka. Scaling out

In practice, this could mean spinning up more virtual machines or containers that run instances of the LLM. Horizontal scaling enhances fault tolerance, as the failure of one instance leaves others unaffected and able to handle the incoming requests, ensuring continuous service availability.

Advantages:

- Increased capacity to handle more requests and higher concurrency.
- Better fault tolerance and high availability.

Disadvantages:

- Increased complexity in managing and coordinating multiple instances.
- Potential for increased networking overhead and latency.
- Potential for increased licensing or usage costs (if using commercial LLM services).

Vertical Scaling (Increasing Resource Allocation)

Vertical scaling, also known as scaling up, involves increasing the hardware resources (e.g., CPU, GPU, memory) allocated to individual instances of the LLM service, as shown in Figure 6.6. It can quickly provide more power to single instance which may be less complex than horizontally scaling, and it can improve the performance and throughput of each instance, allowing it to handle more requests or process larger models.

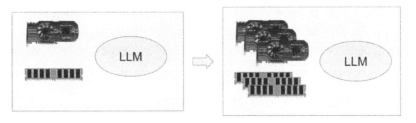

Figure 6.6 Vertical scaling, aka. Scaling up

However, vertical scaling has its limitations, there is a cap on how much a single machine can be upgraded before it's necessary to resort to horizontal scaling.

Advantages:

- Improved performance and throughput for each instance.
- Potential for better resource utilization and efficiency.
- Simpler implementation compared to horizontal scaling.

Disadvantages:

- Limited scalability due to hardware constraints.
- Potential for higher costs associated with upgrading hardware resources.
- Increased risk of single points of failure (SPOF), if not combined with horizontal scaling.

Load Balancing

Load balancing is to distribute incoming traffic and requests evenly across multiple instances of the LLM services to prevent any single node from becoming a bottleneck.

Various load balancing strategies can be employed to ensure efficient resource utilization and optimal performance.

Round-robin load balancing: A simple method where each new request is forwarded to the next instance across a list of available instances, ensuring an even distribution of load. This approach assumes all servers are equally capable of handling requests.

Least connections load balancing: A more dynamic approach where new requests are sent to the instance with the fewest active connections, ensuring better load distribution based on the current workload, and preventing any single instance from becoming a bottleneck. This can be more efficient than round-robin, as it accounts for the actual load on each server.

Weighted load balancing: Instances are assigned weights based on their capacity or performance, and requests are distributed proportionally based on these weights.

IP hash load balancing: Requests are distributed based on a hash of the client's IP address, ensuring that clients are consistently routed to the same instance for session persistence.

Different strategies may be employed depending on the specific performance characteristics and requirements of the deployment. They can be implemented using dedicated load balancers (hardware or software) or leveraging cloud-based load balancing services provided by major cloud providers.

Autoscaling and Elasticity

Autoscaling and elasticity are system's ability to automatically adjust the number of active instances up or down dynamically in response to the changing workload. They ensure efficient resource utilization and avoids over-provisioning or under-provisioning of resources.

Autoscaling ensures that the architecture can handle load surges without manual intervention and the resources are not being wasted during quieter periods. Elasticity ensures the system's capacity to scale resources quickly and efficiently in response to dynamic workloads. Together, autoscaling and elasticity make the system both responsive and cost-efficient. It requires careful configuration of scaling policies based on metrics that accurately reflect the system's load to avoid unnecessary scaling actions.

Horizontal autoscaling: Automatically adding or removing instances of the LLM service based on predefined rules or metrics (e.g., CPU utilization, request rates).

Vertical autoscaling: Automatically increasing or decreasing the hardware resources (e.g., CPU, GPU, memory) allocated to individual instances based on demand.

Elasticity: The ability to dynamically scale resources up or down in response to changing workloads, ensuring optimal performance and cost-effectiveness.

Autoscaling and elasticity can be implemented using cloud-based services (e.g., AWS Auto Scaling, Azure Virtual Machine Scale Sets, Google Compute Engine Autoscaler) or custom solutions integrated with monitoring and orchestration tools.

In summary, these concepts ensure that a deployed LLM can adapt to the workload demands placed upon it. Employing such scalability measures and load balancing strategies is essential for maintaining the responsiveness and reliability of LLM services, regardless of the fluctuations in traffic and demand.

6.6 Compliance and Ethics Review

The deployment of Large Language Models (LLMs) requires careful consideration of both compliance with legal standards and adherence to ethical guidelines. A thorough compliance and ethics review should be conducted together with the deployment of LLMs to identify and mitigate risks across key areas. This is step 8 in the lifecycle of LLMs in Figure 1.2.

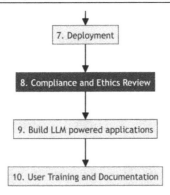

Figure 6.7 Compliance and Ethics Review in LLM Lifecycle

This section outlines the key aspects of Compliance and Ethics Review, which includes but not limited to:

Legal Compliance

Data protection laws: Ensure that the collection, storage, and processing of data by the LLM adhere to global data protection regulations like GDPR, CCPA/CPRA, PIPEDA, and others. Pay particular attention to the handling of sensitive information such as PII (Personally Identifiable Information).

Intellectual property and copyright: Verify that the LLMs do not generate content that infringes upon copyrighted materials or intellectual property rights of third parties.

Accessibility standards: Confirm that the deployment of LLMs is compliant with accessibility laws and guidelines, such as the Americans with Disabilities Act (ADA), or AODA Standards in Canada, ensuring that services are usable by people with disabilities.

Consumer protection laws: Ensure the LLM provides accurate information and does not mislead users, in compliance with Federal Trade Commission (FTC) guidelines and other consumer protection statutes.

Export control regulations: Review any export control implications if the LLM or associated data could be considered a dual-use item under jurisdictions like the U.S. Export Administration Regulations (EAR).

Sector-specific regulations: For LLMs applied within specific sectors, comply with industry-specific regulations, such as HIPAA for healthcare-related implementations or FINRA for financial services.

Ethical Guidelines

Transparency: Implement measures to be open about the capabilities and limitations of the LLM. Inform users about what kind of data the LLM processes and for what purposes.

Privacy by design: Integrate privacy considerations into the development process of the LLM. Use anonymization, pseudonymization, and encryption to protect users' personal information.

Fairness and bias mitigation: LLMs can reflect societal biases present in their training data. Rigorous testing should analyze the model outputs for evidence of harmful biases related to protected characteristics like race, gender, age, disability status, etc. Commit to fairness and the equitable treatment of all users by regularly evaluating model's outputs and updating the model to reduce biases.

Disinformation and misleading information: LLMs can generate fluent but entirely fabricated content that appears factual. Risk assessments should determine if model outputs could be interpreted as intentionally misleading or deceptive. Appropriate transparency around the artificial nature of generated text may need to be enforced.

Safety and misuse: Robust content filtering, usage monitoring, and misuse prevention controls are important for safe LLM deployment, especially for open-ended generative use cases. Policies restricting unsafe or unethical uses should be defined.

User Consent: Obtain explicit user consent for data collection and processing, wherever required, and provide users with clear options to opt-out or manage their data preferences.

The landscape of compliance and ethics in technology is continually evolving. As such, it is essential to have ongoing review processes in place to monitor and update the compliance and ethics frameworks guiding the deployment of LLMs. Regular training for staff, periodic risk assessments, and the implementation of feedback mechanisms are critical to maintaining the integrity and responsibility of LLM deployment.

6.7   Model Versioning and Updates

Large language models are actively researched and iterated, with new model checkpoints being periodically released, things are changing week by week. Thus, the deployment is a dynamic process that requires continuous monitoring and updates to maintain performance, accuracy, and efficiency. Having a robust strategy for versioning and updating the deployed LLM models is important for maintaining the health and relevance over time, keeping high performance and aligning with the latest advances.

Version control of LLMs after deployment is a systematic process designed to track changes to the models, and to manage its associated data and configuration settings over time. It ensures that updates and iterations to deployed models are handled in an organized manner, maintaining the integrity and performance of these models while allowing for continuous improvement, rollback, and auditability.

Model Registry

It's a good practice for an organization to establish a central model registry where all versions of LLMs are stored. This registry should include metadata about each version, such as the date of release, the author of the changes, and a summary of what was changed.

Each model version should be assigned unique identifiers, apply semantic versioning principles to model releases, whereby each version is marked with a number in the format of major.minor.patch. This allows users and developers to easily track changes and avoids ambiguity when discussing model performance.

Release Management

Separate environments should be established for development, testing, and production. Before a new version is rolled out, it should pass through stages where it is rigorously tested.

The organization should consider automating the deployment process to reduce the risk of human errors and to streamline the update process. Automation tools can handle the deployment of new versions and manage rollback if needed.

To further limit risk, consider using feature flags to toggle new features or models on or off without deploying new code, this allows the organization to perform A/B testing and canary releases, which is gradually rolling out the features to a small subset of users before to the entire platform or infrastructure.

Change Tracking and Rollback Planning

The organization should also maintain detailed changelogs that capture what changes have been made in each version, including fixes, improvements, and new features. Employ differences analysis tools to compare model versions and understand the exact changes made from one iteration to the next.

Take snapshots of the model state before each update. This allows for a quick rollback to the previous state if issues are detected post-deployment. Ensure that the model update process is reversible. Each new version should be deployable and removable with minimal downtime.

Monitoring and Evaluation

Comprehensive monitoring should track model performance metrics over time, including latency, throughput, resource utilization, and output quality to identify if an update has negatively impacted performance. Degradations in these metrics may signal the need for a model update.

Consider incorporating user feedbacks into version assessments as well, any user issues can signal the need for a model rollback or updates.

Monitoring Metrics

Below are the major monitoring metrics that should be monitored:

Latency: Monitor response times to ensure the model meets the required speed for interactions and transactions from various geographic locations.

Throughput: Track the number of requests processed by the model within a certain timeframe to manage load and optimize resource allocation.

Resource utilization: Continuously monitor GPU, CPU, memory, and storage usage to optimize for cost and efficiency, adjusting infrastructure as needed.

Error rates: Keep track of errors and exceptions raised by the LLM to quickly address potential issues in model performance or data processing.

In conclusion, a well-structured approach to model versioning and updates ensures that LLM deployments are maintained at the highest quality standards, providing reliability and value to users. A commitment to regular analysis with strategic improvements establishes a foundation for the ongoing success of LLM applications.

6.8 LLM-Powered Applications

Large language models (LLMs) are driving a wave of innovative and powerful applications across nearly every industry and domain. By pre-training and/or fine-tuning with vast datasets, these models develop an extensive knowledge base and strong language understanding abilities. LLM-powered applications are reshaping industries, streamlining workflows, and enhancing human-machine collaboration.

Building LLM-powered applications is step 9 in the lifecycle of LLMs.

Figure 6.8 LLM-Powered Applications in LLM Lifecycle

This section provides a bird's eye view of various applications that utilize the capabilities of LLMs to drive innovation and efficiency across various domains.

Customer Interaction

Customer service has been revolutionized by LLM integration, with chatbots and virtual assistants providing instant, informative, and personalized responses to customer inquiries.

LLMs power advanced conversational AI assistants and chatbots that can engage in more natural and contextual dialogue with customers. These AI agents can understand complex queries, provide relevant information, offer recommendations, and even complete tasks on behalf of the customer, all through natural language interactions.

The virtual agents powered by LLMs can handle a significant portion of customer service inquiries, questions, and support requests across various channels like websites, mobile apps, and messaging platforms. They can troubleshoot issues, provide product information, and guide customers through processes like returns, exchanges, or booking appointments.

By leveraging their language understanding capabilities, LLMs can analyze customer conversations, emails, or social media comments to detect sentiment (positive, negative, or neutral) and infer the underlying intentions or goals. This can help prioritize and route customer interactions appropriately.

LLMs can also act as intelligent knowledge bases, providing accurate and up-to-date information to customers by drawing insights from various data sources, including product manuals, support documentation, and past customer interactions.

With their multi-language generation capabilities, LLMs can power customer support experiences in multiple languages, enabling businesses to provide consistent service to a global customer base without the need for human translation.

Content Creation

In the area of content creation, LLMs have become invaluable for generating high-quality written material, stimulating creativity, and reducing repetitive workload for human creators. From creative writing and scripting to editing, paraphrasing, and content ideation, LLMs are augmenting human writers as co-creative AI collaborators.

For example, journalists and content marketers use LLMs to produce draft articles and personalized narratives; scriptwriters explore LLM collaborations to brainstorm dialogue options; while developers can use LLMs like GPT-3 to assist in generating code snippets based on natural language descriptions or partial code inputs.

LLMs can act as co-creative writing assistants, helping authors with tasks like generating story ideas, developing characters and plots, providing suggestions for descriptions or dialogue, and even assisting with full story or article drafts. They can help creating topics, generate brief outlines or structures for blog posts, articles, scripts, or other creative pieces. This can jumpstart the writing process and provide a framework to build upon.

LLMs can rephrase or rewrite existing content to match a desired style, voice, or tone, enabling content creators to adapt their work for different audiences or platforms. This includes capabilities like adjusting formality levels, translating idioms, or even translating between languages. They can also rephrase or expand upon existing text through techniques like paraphrasing or lexical substitution.

For long-form content, LLMs can generate concise summaries that capture key points and insights, enabling easier content repurposing into formats like social media posts, email newsletters, or video scripts.

Developers can use LLMs to generate code snippets or even entire functions/classes based on natural language descriptions, or generate documentation for existing code, making it easier to understand and maintain codebases, especially when working with legacy systems or unfamiliar libraries.

With their multi-language skills, LLMs can create content in multiple languages, enabling creators to reach broader global audiences without relying on human translation.

Education

Education technology leverages LLMs to create adaptive learning platforms that offer personalized educational experiences and tutoring systems. These models provide instant feedback, answer educational queries, and plan learning resources to suit individual student needs. Language learning is another area benefiting greatly from LLMs, facilitating language acquisition through conversational bots and immersive exercises.

LLMs can act as intelligent tutoring systems, providing personalized learning experiences by adapting to each student's level of understanding, learning style, and pace. They can explain concepts, answer follow-up questions, and provide step-by-step guidance across various subjects.

LLMs can also be integrated into writing assistants that provide feedback on grammar, style, word choice, and clarity. Instead of simply rewriting, they help students improve their own writing skills.

Educators can leverage LLMs to generate customized learning materials, lesson plans, and practice exercises tailored to the specific needs and skill levels of their students or classes.

Students learning different languages can leverage LLMs in conversational practice sessions, perform language translations, and improve their fluency and comprehension in the languages.

Healthcare

In healthcare, LLMs are transforming patient support and medical research. Conversational systems powered by LLMs offer preliminary health advice, symptom checking, and management of patient queries, easing the load on medical professionals. Analyzing medical literature and assisting in diagnostic data interpretation, LLMs are proving to be invaluable assistive tools for healthcare providers.

LLMs trained on vast biomedical literature can provide accurate answers to complex medical queries from researchers, physicians, and patients, serving as a valuable knowledge base.

They can also summarize and extract insights from large volumes of scientific papers and clinical studies, accelerating medical research and evidence-based practice.

Conversational LLM agents can interact with patients, gather medical histories, provide information about conditions and treatments, and guide them through care pathways or triage processes.

LLMs can assist physicians by automatically generating detailed clinical notes and documentation based on patient interactions and medical data, reducing administrative burdens.

In drug development, LLMs can analyze molecular data and biomedical knowledge to support drug discovery pipelines, such as identifying potential drug candidates or predicting therapeutic properties.

Business Analytics

Incorporating LLMs into business intelligence tools has led to advanced analytic capabilities, where companies leverage these models to distill insights from vast amounts of unstructured text data. Predictive analytics is another area seeing significant gains, with LLMs trained to predict market trends and consumer behavior from existing datasets.

LLMs can analyze large datasets, including unstructured data like reports, emails, and customer feedback, to generate concise summaries, extract key insights, and identify trends or patterns. This can accelerate data-driven decision-making by surfacing relevant information from vast amounts of data.

By analyzing data from sources like news articles, social media, industry reports, and company filings, LLMs can provide insights into market trends, competitor strategies, and consumer sentiments, informing strategic business decisions.

LLMs can automatically generate well-structured, narrative reports and presentations based on data inputs, reducing the manual effort required for data storytelling and communication. These reports can adapt their content and language based on the intended audience or stakeholders.

With their ability to identify patterns and relationships in data, LLMs can support forecasting models for activities like sales projections, inventory optimization, resource planning, and budget allocation.

LLMs can act as intelligent knowledge repositories, providing context-aware information and insights to business users by drawing upon various data sources, including internal documents, industry reports, and external data feeds.

Translation and Global Connectivity

Large Language Models (LLMs) can be highly beneficial in the areas of translation and global connectivity due to their ability to understand and generate human-like text in multiple languages. This capacity is particularly impactful in global customer support and has the potential to bridge language barriers like never before, fostering a more interconnected world.

LLMs can be fine-tuned on translation tasks, allowing them to translate text from one language to another with high accuracy. Unlike traditional machine translation systems that rely on phrase-based or statistical methods, LLMs can capture the context and nuances of the text, resulting in more natural and fluent translations.

Trained on multilingual data, LLMs can also facilitate communication between people speaking different languages. An LLM-powered application could allow users to converse in their native languages, while the LLM translates the messages in real-time, enabling seamless cross-linguistic communication.

They can power chatbots and virtual assistants that can communicate with customers in multiple languages, improving customer experience and ensuring seamless support across global markets.

Conclusion

From automating time-consuming tasks to assisting with complex decision-making, LLM-powered applications are omnipresent. The efficiency and adaptability of LLMs have led to broad adoption across fields, and their potential continues to grow as these models become more nuanced and capable. However, while reveling in the benefits, we should also be aware of the associated challenges and ethical considerations – a balance that must be actively managed to optimize the benefits of LLMs for society at large.

6.9 Vector Database

A vector database is a specialized type of database designed to store and query high-dimensional vector representations of data, such as embeddings generated by LLMs, as well as other machine learning models.

Vector databases are specialized types of databases designed to store, index, and manage high-dimensional vector embeddings efficiently. As we discussed in Section 2.8, embeddings are data points that represent objects in a high-dimensional vector space, where each dimension captures some aspect of the object's properties. These objects can be anything from images, text, or any data that can be translated into numerical form. In LLMs, vector embeddings are used to represent words, sentences, or entire documents as numerical vectors that capture semantic meaning.

Vector databases play an important role in efficiently storing and retrieving the vast amounts of embedded information learned by these models, allowing for efficient similarity search and retrieval operations.

Vector databases offer several benefits for LLMs:

Efficient similarity search: They are optimized for performing fast nearest neighbor searches in high dimensional spaces. This is particularly useful for LLMs that need to find the most similar text or word embeddings quickly, which is important for tasks like semantic search, duplicate detection, or recommendation systems.

Scalability: Vector databases are designed to scale with high-dimensional data and can handle the massive amount of vector data generated by LLMs. They can maintain performance even as the size of the data grows, which is essential for models dealing with large volumes of text.

Indexing and retrieval: Vector databases can index vectors in such a way that retrieval of relevant vectors is substantially faster than linear search. By using techniques like tree-based indexing, hash partitioning, or clustering, they can drastically reduce the search space and increase retrieval speed.

Flexibility: Vector databases can handle a wide range of data types, including text, images, audio, and video, making them versatile for a variety of applications.

There are several database systems that can be used as vector databases, for example, Pinecone, PostgreSQL with vector extensions, Elasticsearch, Milvus, FAISS (Facebook AI Similarity Search), and so on.

Vector databases complement the capabilities of LLMs by providing an infrastructure that supports the efficient storage, indexing, and retrieval of embeddings. Although they are not required for deploying LLMs, their use can significantly enhance the efficiency, scalability, and performance of LLM deployments, particularly in scenarios where rapid retrieval of relevant information from the model's knowledge base is essential for generating high-quality and contextually relevant outputs.

6.10 LangChain

LangChain is an open-source framework and set of tools that designed to empower developers to build LLM-powered applications that leverage large language models more effectively and efficiently. It focuses on abstracting the complexity involved in integrating language models into software applications, providing a structured environment for handling various tasks associated with language processing. LangChain was launched in October 2022, and available in both Python and Javascript.

Abstraction is a term in software development, it's the practice of simplifying complex systems or entities by focusing on their essential features and hiding the underlying complexities.

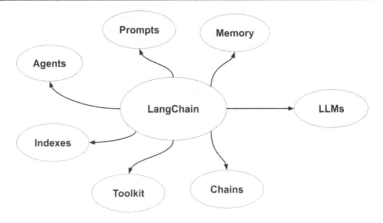

Figure 6.9 LangChain

Figure 6.9 shows the key components of LangChain:

Agents: are the core component in LangChain, it interacts with the large language models (LLMs) to accomplish tasks. Developers can build custom agents to suit their specific application needs. The agents can be combined into chains to create more complex workflows.

Chains: are used to connect LLMs with other components together, such as Agents or Prompt, allowing for more complex workflows and interactions. Chains provide a way to orchestrate the execution of agents in a structured manner.

Memory: includes built-in support for managing the memory of agents, enabling them to remember and refer to previous conversations or context. Normally LLMs are stateless, meaning not remember the previous conversations, unless the chat history is used in the prompt as input. Memory solves this problem by adding memory to the workflow, it can retain the entire previous conversation, or the summarization of the previous conversation. Memory helps Agents maintain state and continuity across interactions.

Prompts: are tools for creating, managing, and optimizing the prompts used to interact with the LLMs. Especially it simplifies the Prompt engineering process, see Section 4.8.

Indexes: are tools and utilities that facilitates retrieving and organizing relevant information from a corpus of data, helping the framework to effectively handle data-intensive tasks. It includes Document Loaders to load data from various sources; and Text Splitters to break the documents down into chunks; then Vector Stores to access the vector databases for storing the embedded data; Retrievers retrieve the data and integrate into chains to build the workflows.

Toolkits: The framework includes a variety of pre-built "toolkits" that provide functionality for common use cases, such as question answering, text generation, and knowledge retrieval. These toolkits help developers leverage the capabilities of LLMs more easily.

One of the common use cases for LangChain is integrating LLMs with vector databases, which are used for efficient similarity-based retrieval of information, as introduced in the previous section. It allows developers to build more powerful, scalable, and context-aware applications that can leverage the strengths of both LLMs and Vector databases to deliver better user experiences and insights.

LangChain is a versatile framework that can enable a wide range of use cases for LLM-powered applications. Some key use cases include:

- **Chatbots**: can be built with LangChain's Agents and Chains, and integrated into existing communication channels and workflows with their own APIs. The Memory and Prompt management can help create more natural and contextual conversations.
- **Multimodal Applications**: By integrating with various LLMs and data sources, LangChain can support the development of multimodal applications that can understand and generate content across text, images, audio, and other formats.
- **Knowledge-Intensive Applications**: LangChain's ability to connect LLMs with vector databases and other information sources makes it well-suited for building knowledge-management systems, research tools, and decision-support applications that require accessing and reasoning over large knowledge bases.

Let's look at some examples of how LangChain work in different cases. First install the package:

```
1    !pip install langchain
```

Use Prompt template to build prompts:

```
2    from langchain import PromptTemplate
3
4    template = """
5    The customer review is: {review}
6    Please classify it as Positive, Negative, or Neutral.
7    """
8
9    prompt = PromptTemplate(
10       input_variables=["review"],
11       template=template
12   )
13   review = "The shipping was quick and the item was perfect.
14   Totally satisfied!"
15   prompt_text = prompt.format(review=review)
16   print(prompt_text)
```

Line 2 imports `PromptTemplate` from the package.

Line 4 create a prompt template, and Line 9 to 12 build a `PromptTemplate` object the template text.

Line 13 is to use the prompt template by defining a `review` text. And Line 15 creates the prompt text from the text and the template.

Line 16 print out the prompt text:

```
The customer review is: The shipping was quick and the item
was perfect. Totally satisfied!
Please classify it as Positive, Negative, or Neutral.
```

Although it might not help too much for a single prompt, the benefit is significant when dealing with lots of different prompts. It helps developers to build more robust, maintainable, and scalable prompts, especially perform prompt engineering for one-shot or few-shot learnings.

Use LLMChain to connect to an LLM in HuggingFace hub, which is an open-source platform that provides access to many pre-trained LLMs. A token-based authentication system ensures secure access to the hosted models.

To access and use the LLMs hosted on the Hugging Face Hub, users need to create an account and obtain an API token from its website. This token authenticates the user and grants them the necessary permissions to interact with the models. The token should be securely stored and included in the requests made to the Hugging Face API when interacting with the hosted models.

Below code configures the access token for the request, the access token should be set in the environment variable as below, replace the `access token` with yours,

```
21    import os
22    os.environ['HUGGINGFACEHUB_API_TOKEN'] = 'access token'
```

Then we create a Chain to connect the prompt to google/flan-t5-large model in the HuggingFace hub,

```
23    from langchain import HuggingFaceHub, LLMChain
24    # initialize Hub LLM
25    hub_llm = HuggingFaceHub(
26                     repo_id='google/flan-t5-large' )
27    # create prompt template > LLM chain
28    llm_chain = LLMChain(
29                     prompt=prompt,
30                     llm=hub_llm  )
31    # ask the user question about NFL 2010
32    print(llm_chain.run(review))
```

Line 23 imports `LLMChain` and `HuggingFaceHub` libraries.

Line 25 and 26 specify the model name, here we use `flan-t5-large`, the default HuggingFace environment do not have enough space for larger models for inference, like `flan-t5-xxl`, etc.

Line 28 to 30 creates an `LLMChain` that connects the prompt we created above in Line 15 to the LLM in Hugging Face hub.

Line 32 run the `LLMChain` to perform inference and print out the result:

```
Positive
```

We can also run multiple prompts in one go:

```
33    reviews = [
```

```
34      {'review': "The shipping was quick and the item ..."},
35      {'review': "The restaurant was terrible, and the ..."},
36      {'review': "The new update is almost useless, the ..."} ]
37   results = llm_chain.generate(reviews)
38   print(results.generations)
```

Use the prompt template to create multiple prompts like Line 33 to 36.

Line 37 invokes `generate()` function to send the prompts to the LLM, and obtains the results.

Line 38 print out the results:

```
[[Generation(text='Positive')],
 [Generation(text='Negative')],
 [Generation(text='Negative')]]
```

Similarly, you can use LangChain to connect OpenAI's model, where a paid OpenAI API key is needed for this purpose.

In conclusion, LangChain is a powerful and versatile open-source framework that simplifies the development of LLM-powered applications by providing a set of abstractions and tools. It enables developers to focus on building innovative solutions, rather than getting bogged down by the complexities of LLM workflows.

6.11 Chatbot, Example of LLM-Powered Application

This section will showcase the development of a chatbot as an illustrative example of an LLM-powered application, leveraging the capabilities of large language models to build a conversational agent.

In the last chapter, we used `flan-t5-base` as the base model and performed LoRA (Low-Rank Adaptation) fine-tuning on `tweetsum` dataset, a collection of tweet-summary pairs. This process involved adapting the pre-trained model to the specific task of summarizing tweets, while maintaining the base model's general language understanding capabilities.

After the fine-tuning process, we saved the resulting LoRA model, which encapsulates the task-specific knowledge and adaptations.

In this section, we will explore three examples of chatbots using local LLM, using LangChain and using OpenAI provided LLM service.

Chatbot with local flan-t5-base plus LoRA

In this example, we will leverage the fine-tuned LoRA model as the backend for building a simple chatbot application. We will load the saved LoRA model and integrate it into a conversational framework, allowing users to interact with the chatbot through natural language inputs. By combining the base model's general language understanding with the task-specific fine-tuning on the `tweetsum` dataset, our chatbot will be capable of generating concise and relevant responses, particularly in the context of summarizing tweets or short text snippets.

This example showcases the versatility of LLMs and the power of fine-tuning techniques like LoRA. By starting with a strong base model and adapting it to a specific task, we can create specialized applications tailored to various domains or use cases. In our case, the chatbot will leverage the fine-tuned model's ability to summarize tweets, providing users with a convenient and interactive way to obtain concise summaries from lengthy or complex tweets.

As we did before, first install the necessary packages and import the libraries,

```
1    !pip install torch torchvision torchaudio --quiet
2    !pip install transformers --quiet
3    !pip install peft --quiet
4    !pip install sentencepiece --quiet
5
6    import torch
7    from transformers import T5Tokenizer
8    from transformers import T5ForConditionalGeneration
9    from transformers import GenerationConfig
10   from peft import PeftModel, PeftConfig
```

Next, load the base model together with the LoRA model,

```
11   base_model_name = 'google/flan-t5-base'
```

```
12    lora_model_name = 'outputs/flan-t5-base_lora'
13
14    def load_model(base_model_name, lora_model_name):
15      tokenizer = T5Tokenizer.from_pretrained(
16                          base_model_name)
17      base_model = T5ForConditionalGeneration.from_pretrained(
18                          base_model_name,
19                          torch_dtype=torch.bfloat16)
20      model = PeftModel.from_pretrained(
21                          base_model,
22                          lora_model_name,
23                          torch_dtype=torch.bfloat16,
24                          is_trainnable=False)
25      return tokenizer, model
26
27    tokenizer, model = load_model(base_model_name,
28                                  lora_model_name)
29    total_parameter = sum(p.numel() for p in model.parameters())
30    print(f"Parameters of the model: {total_parameter:,}")
```

The function load_model() from Line 14 to 25 will load the base model and LoRA model. Line 15 and 16 load `tokenizer` and Line 17 to 19 load `flan-t5-base` as the `base_model`. Then Line 20 to 24 load the LoRA model on top of it.

In Line 19 and Line 23, the datatype of the loaded models is specified as `torch.bfloat16`, this is model quantization technique where a 16-bit floating-point format is used instead of 32-bit one, the purpose is to reduce the model size in memory and speed up inference operations.

Line 29 and 30 print out the number of the model's parameter:

```
Parameters of the model: 249,347,328
```

Next, create a function to generate output from the model:

```
31    def generate_output(tokenizer, model,
32                          input_text, max_length=200):
33      input_ids = tokenizer(
34                          input_text,
35                          return_tensors="pt").input_ids
36      outputs = model.generate(
37                          input_ids=input_ids,
38                          generation_config=
```

```
39                          GenerationConfig(max_length,
40                                          num_beams=1))
41      response = tokenizer.decode(outputs[0],
42                          skip_special_tokens=True)
43      return response
```

Line 33 to 35 tokenize the input text into tokens.

Line 36 to 40 send input tokens to the model and obtain the generated outputs.

Line 41 and 42 decode the generated output to human readable texts.

Then create a simple chatbot:

```
44   def chatbot():
45     print("Chatbot initialized. You can start chatting now
46          (type 'quit' to stop)!\n")
47     while True:
48       user_input = input("You: ")
49       if user_input.lower() == "quit":
50         break
51       response = generate_output(tokenizer, model, user_input)
52       print(f"Chatbot: {response}\n")
53
54   # Run the chatbot
55   chatbot()
```

Line 48 takes user input from the UI, Line 49 and 50 check if user inputs "quit" to break the loop.

Line 51 generates the output from the model.

Since we have fine-tuned the model with text summarization dataset, we will ask it to perform some similar tasks, something like below:

```
Chatbot initialized. You can start chatting now (type 'quit'
to stop)!

You: How are you doing today
Chatbot: I am doing well today.

You: Summarize: Tesco please bring security back to the Hall
Green store. The store is getting a more and more
uncomfortable vibe, not alone on this either...
```

```
Chatbot: Customer is complaining about the security of the
store. Agent is asking for the customer to contact the
store.

You: Summarize: LondonMidland you didnt even. Ask me to pass
on an apology to my friend for this farce <LINK> <BR> Im
sorry if your tweet was missed and for the problems
yesterday evening...
Chatbot: Customer is complaining about the delay in the
service and the alleged to be a selfish and sod off home
like this TOC tends to do.

You: quit
```

The above code example is a very simple chatbot using a pre-trained base model plus a fine-tuned LoRA model. You can also build a similar chatbot using the open-source or commercial hosted large language models, for example, OpenAI's ChatGPT.

Chatbot with LangChain, Accessing LLMs in HuggingFace Hub

Last section introduced LangChain, an open-source framework facilitating the development of LLM-powered applications. This is an example of chatbot with LangChain accessing the flan-t5-large model from HuggingFace hub, same as the last section, an access token is needed from the HuggingFace.

Install the package and import libraries:

```
1    !pip install langchain
2    !pip install huggingface_hub
3    from langchain import PromptTemplate
4    from langchain import HuggingFaceHub, LLMChain
```

Configure the access token:

```
5    import os
6    os.environ['HUGGINGFACEHUB_API_TOKEN'] = 'access token'
```

Create a prompt template and a LLM hub:

```
7    template = """
8    Please answer question: {question}
9    """
```

```
10    prompt = PromptTemplate(
11        input_variables=["question"],
12        template=template
13    )
14    # initialize Hub LLM
15    hub_llm = HuggingFaceHub(
16        repo_id='google/flan-t5-large')
17
18    llm_chain = LLMChain(
19        prompt=prompt,
20        llm=hub_llm )
```

It's similar to the example in the previous section, we create a LLMChain to connect an LLM with a prompt template.

Then, create the chatbot:

```
21    def chatbot():
22        print("Chatbot initialized.\n")
23        while True:
24            # Get user input
25            user_input = input("You: ")
26            if user_input.lower() == "quit":
27                break
28            answer = llm_chain.run(user_input)
29            print(answer, '\n')
30    # Run the chatbot
31    chatbot()
```

Line 25 takes user input from screen, and pass it to the LLMChain in Line 28 to obtain the result from the model.

Then you can chat with the model, for example:

```
Chatbot initialized.
You: How are you
Chatbot: good

You: Which is the capital city of Japan?
Chatbot: tokyo

You: What do turtles eat?
Chatbot: mollusks

You: How much do elephants weight at birth?
Chatbot: 240-400 lbs
```

```
You: How much time to penguins spend on land?
Chatbot: a few hours
You: Thanks
Chatbot: thank you
You: quit
```

Chatbot interact with OpenAI

Here is another example of how to do it with ChatGPT. First, obtain an API key which a unique identifier provided by OpenAI to interact with the ChatGPT or similar AI models available through OpenAI's API service. It is essentially a token that allows authenticated access to the API, enabling developers to send requests to the AI model and receive responses.

To get the API key, create an OpenAI account, if you don't have it, from their website (https://www.openai.com/), login and navigate to the API section from its dashboard, create a new API key from there.

Once an API key is generated, make sure to store it in a safe place. It should be kept confidential since it grants access to your OpenAI account and services.

The below code snippets are referencing OpenAI's document at *https://platform.openai.com/docs/api-reference/introduction*

Install the official OpenAI Python library:

```
1   !pip install openai
```

Create an openai object:

```
2   from openai import OpenAI
3   client = OpenAI(
4       # organization='org-xxxxxx',
5       api_key='sk-xxxxxxxxx',
6   )
```

The API key is specified in Line 5. Alternatively, if your organization has an account with OpenAI, use the org ID as Line 4.

Then create `ask-chatgpt()` function to interact with the online model:

```
7   def ask_chatgpt(input_text):
```

```
8       stream = client.chat.completions.create(
9           model="gpt-3.5-turbo",
10          messages=[{"role": "You", "content": input_text}],
11          stream=True,
12      )
13      response = None
14      for chunk in stream:
15          if chunk.choices[0].message.content is not None:
16              response = chunk.choices[0].message.content
17      return response
```

Line 8 to 12 create a streaming request to the service, the model name is specified in Line 9, you can select any available models provided by OpenAI.

The response from the service is something like:

```
{    "id": "chatcmpl-abc123",
     "object": "chat.completion",
     "created": 1677858242,
     "model": "gpt-3.5-turbo-0613",
     "usage": {
         "prompt_tokens": 13,
         "completion_tokens": 7,
         "total_tokens": 20
     },
     "choices": [
         {
             "message": {
                 "role": "assistant",
                 "content": "\n\nThis is a test!"
             },
             "logprobs": null,
             "finish_reason": "stop",
             "index": 0
         }
     ]
}
```

The output is in `choices[0].message.content`, return it as the output of the `ask-chatgpt()` function.

Finally, create similar chatbot like below:

```
18      print("Chatbot: How can I help you? (type 'quit' to
19      stop)!\n")
```

```
20    while True:
21        user_input = input("You: ")
22        if user_input.lower() == "quit":
23            break
24        response = ask_chatgpt(user_input)
25        print(f"Chatbot: {response}\n")
```

Line 21 takes a user input, Line 24 retrieve the output from `ask-chatgpt()` function.

Line 22 and 23 check user input to terminate the loop.

In summary, we explored two approaches to building chatbots using LLMs. The first approach demonstrated how to create a chatbot with a locally hosted LLM model together with a fine-tune LoRA model. This allows for customization and personalization of the language model to suit specific domains or use cases. The second approach showcased the process of obtaining an API key from HuggingFace or OpenAI and leveraging their powerful online service to build a chatbot. This approach offers the convenience of accessing state-of-the-art language models without the need for extensive computational resources or model training.

6.12 WebUI, Example of LLM-Power Application

In this section we introduce a project that provides a web-based user interface for running LLMs locally for text generation. The project is available at: *https://github.com/oobabooga/text-generation-webui*.

It aims to make it easier for users to interact with and utilize powerful language models without requiring extensive coding or command-line expertise.

There are some key features and details about this project:

Web UI: The project includes a web-based user interface built with Python and Gradio, allowing users to interact with the language models through a graphical user interface.

Language Models Support: The project supports various language models, including GPT-2, GPT-J, GPT-Neo, and OPT models. Users can load these models from HuggingFace (https://huggingface.co/), and run them directly from the web interface.

Text Generation: The primary use case is for text generation tasks, such as generating stories, articles, code snippets, or any other textual content based on user prompts or inputs.

LoRA Fine-tuning: The project also includes functionality to load fine-tuned models, allowing users to adapt the models to specific domains or tasks.

Extensions: The repository supports various extensions, including extensions for image captioning, text-to-image generation, and more.

Local Deployment: Users can run the web UI locally on their machines, which is particularly useful for those working with large language models that may require data security and privacy.

Docker Support: The project provides Docker instructions for easy deployment and containerization of the web UI and language models.

Community-Driven: The project is an open-source project with an active community of contributors, who continuously improve and add new features to the project.

It supports both GPU and CPU modes, which means that even without a graphics card, you can still run the webui. The hardware requirements are:

- Operating System: Windows/Linux/MacOS
- GPU/CPU: At least 6GB GPU or a minimum of 4 cores
- RAM: At least 16GB
- Hard disk space: 30GB

The author provides one-click installation packages for three operating systems: Windows, Linux, and macOS. You can git clone the repository into your local directory, alternatively download the appropriate package for your system, extract the files from the downloaded archive.

The installation and deployment processes are fully automated. In a terminal window, type the command for your OS to start the installation:

- `start_linux.sh` for Linux
- `start_macos.sh` for MacOS
- `start_windows.bat` for Windows

During the installation, you will be prompted to choose one of the following hardware options:

```
A) NVIDIA
B) AMD (Linux and MacOS only)
C) Apple M Series
D) Intel ARC (IPEX)
N) None (CPU-only mode)
```

Select one based on your GPU type, you can choose to run it on CPU-only mode if no any GPUs.

Wait for a while for the installation process, which will install all required libraries. After the installation is finished, a URL address will be displayed: *http://127.0.0.1:7860*.

Open a browser and navigate to that URL, the web user interface will appear in the browser.

You will need to download a model before using it, HuggingFace has a variety of LLMs, navigate to its website at *https://huggingface.co/*, and look for a model, and copy the model name.

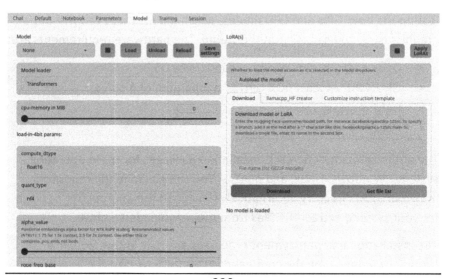

Figure 6.10 Download and Select Models

In the webUI, navigate to the model tab, in "Download model or LoRA" section, paste the HuggingFace model name there, and click "Download" button, see Figure 6.10.

Alternatively, this project comes with a command-line utility for downloading, for example to download `TheBloke/wizard-mega-13B-GGUF` model, in the terminal window type:

```
python download-model.py TheBloke/wizard-mega-13B-GGUF
```

This command will download the model and place it under the `models` folder. It could take a while depends on the size of the model.

If download any LoRA models, or if you fine-tune the models with LoRA, they will be placed under `loras` folder.

After downloading the models, navigate to the model tab, refresh the model list, and select one from the dropdown list and load it.

Then you can go to Chat tab to interact with the model, as shown in Figure 6.11

Figure 6.11 Interact with the Model

Overall, `text-generation-webui` project aims to make it more accessible for researchers, developers, and enthusiasts to leverage the power of large language models for various text generation tasks, without the need for extensive coding or command-line expertise. The web-based interface and the ability to run models locally or in containerized environments make it a valuable tool for those working with language models, especially when dealing with sensitive data that requires local processing for security and privacy reasons.

6.13 Future Trends and Challenges

As the field of artificial intelligence (AI) continues to evolve, LLMs are becoming increasingly sophisticated and integral to a variety of applications. However, rapid advancement brings both exciting possibilities and challenges.

This section is a discussion of the future trends and potential hurdles that may influence the deployment of LLMs.

Future Trends

Advancements in model architecture: LLMs are likely to become even more powerful with advancements in neural network architectures, potentially leading to models that understand context and subtleties even better.

Personalization and contextualization: There will be a push towards personalized LLMs that can adapt to individual user preferences and contexts, delivering more relevant and customized interactions.

Multimodal capabilities: LLMs will increasingly incorporate other forms of data, such as images and sounds, enabling them to understand and generate multimodal content.

Increased efficiency: There will be significant emphasis on creating more efficient models that require less computational power, addressing concerns about the environmental impact of training large models.

Explainability and transparency: The trend towards building models that can explain their reasoning and decisions will continue, enhancing trust and usability.

Robustness and generalization: LLMs will be developed to be more robust against adversarial attacks and capable of generalizing across a wider array of tasks without task-specific fine-tuning.

Challenges

Scalability: As models become larger and more complex, the challenge to scale them efficiently while managing costs and environmental impact increases. Deploying such massive models will require continued innovation in areas like model parallelism, systems design, hardware acceleration, and efficient data/memory management.

Bias and fairness: Mitigating bias and ensuring fairness in LLMs remains a critical challenge, especially as models are deployed globally across diverse populations.

Data privacy: Adhering to strict data privacy and protection laws when collecting and using data to train LLMs will become more complex but increasingly necessary.

Ethical use: The risk of misuse of LLMs in creating fake content or misinformation presents a challenge in developing ethical guidelines and use policies.

Security: Ensuring the security of LLMs against hacking and unauthorized access is vital, especially as they become core components in critical applications.

Regulatory compliance: Keeping pace with and adhering to international and regional regulations that govern AI application will be a continuous challenge.

Human-AI collaboration: Balancing between automating with LLMs and the need for human expertise and oversight will be a continuing challenge.

Overcoming these future trends and challenges will require continued research, interdisciplinary collaboration between fields like deep learning, systems design, and deployment best practices.

6.14 Conclusion

The deployment of large language models (LLMs) is a complex and multifaceted process that requires careful consideration of various factors. Throughout this chapter, we explored the challenges and considerations in deploying LLMs, including pre-deployment optimization, security and privacy concerns, deployment architectures, scalability and load balancing, compliance and ethics reviews, and model versioning and updates.

The development of LLM-powered applications, such as chatbots and web-based interfaces, will continue to gain traction, enabling more accessible and user-friendly interactions with these powerful language models. The examples we discussed, including LangChain, OpenAI-powered chatbot and the text-generation-webui project, demonstrate the potential of LLM-powered applications to revolutionize various industries and use cases.

However, as LLM-powered applications become more prevalent, it is crucial to address ethical concerns and ensure responsible deployment. Maintaining transparency, accountability, and fairness in these systems will be essential to building trust and fostering widespread adoption.

As we look towards the future, the deployment of LLMs is likely to face new challenges and trends. The increasing demand for real-time, personalized, and context-aware language models will necessitate advancements in edge computing and on-device deployment strategies. Additionally, the need for privacy-preserving techniques, such as federated learning and secure multi-party computation, will become more pressing as LLMs handle sensitive data.

Overall, the deployment of LLMs presents both exciting opportunities and significant challenges. By carefully navigating the considerations outlined in this chapter and staying informed about emerging trends and best practices, organizations and individuals can leverage the full potential of LLMs while mitigating risks and addressing ethical concerns. Continuous research, collaboration, and innovation will be key to unlocking the transformative power of LLMs in various domains.

Index

V

Vector databases, 314
Vertical scaling, 300, 301

W

Wanda, 288

Wavelength, 92
Weight, 37

Z

Zero-shot learning, 207, 223

References

1. *Attention Is All You Need, https://arxiv.org/abs/1706.03762*
2. *Layer Normalization, https://arxiv.org/abs/1607.06450*
3. *Machine Learning and Deep Learning With Python, by James Chen, ISBN: 978-1-7389084-0-0, 2023*
4. https://web.mit.edu/15.053/www/AMP-Appendix-A.pdf
5. https://web.stanford.edu/~boyd/vmls/vmls.pdf
6. https://arxiv.org/pdf/1609.04747.pdf
7. https://pytorch.org/docs/stable/optim.html
8. Dropout: A Simple Way to Prevent Neural Networks from Overfitting, https://www.cs.toronto.edu/~rsalakhu/papers/srivastava14a.pdf
9. https://nlp.seas.harvard.edu/annotated-transformer/
10. https://github.com/jadore801120/attention-is-all-you-need-pytorch
11. https://github.com/JayParks/transformer
12. https://www.freecodecamp.org/news/how-to-build-a-large-language-model-from-scratch-using-python/
13. A Learning Rate Tuner for Deep Neural Networks, https://arxiv.org/abs/2105.14526
14. Multi30K: Multilingual English-German Image Descriptions, https://arxiv.org/abs/1605.00459
15. A Survey of Large Language Models, https://arxiv.org/abs/2303.18223
16. Scaling Instruction-Finetuned Language Models, https://arxiv.org/abs/2210.11416v5
17. Language Models are Few-Shot Learners, https://arxiv.org/abs/2005.14165
18. Efficient Large-Scale Language Model Training on GPU Clusters Using Megatron-LM, https://arxiv.org/abs/2104.04473
19. Holistic Evaluation of Language Models, https://arxiv.org/abs/2211.09110
20. LoRA: Low-Rank Adaptation of LLMs, https://arxiv.org/abs/2106.09685
21. Parameter-Efficient Transfer Learning for NLP, https://arxiv.org/abs/1902.00751
22. Prompt-Tuning Can Be Much Better Than Fine-Tuning …, https://aclanthology.org/2022.findings-emnlp.401.pdf
23. Learning to summarize from human feedback, https://arxiv.org/abs/2009.01325
24. Learning to summarize from human feedback, https://arxiv.org/abs/2009.01325
25. A Simple and Effective Pruning Approach for Large Language Models, https://arxiv.org/abs/2306.11695

About the Author

James Chen, a highly accomplished IT professional with a solid academic background, holds a degree from Tsinghua University, one of China's most prestigious universities, and has developed a deep understanding of computer science theory and practices. With his extensive technical background, James has played key roles in designing and developing cutting-edge software solutions for a variety of industries including technology, financial, healthcare, e-commerce, etc. He has been working with all aspects of system design and development and actively contributed as the lead implementer of complex multi-clients and multi-tiered systems such as web systems, traditional n-tiered systems, mobile applications, and mixed software/hardware systems. He has a talent for identifying key business problems and designing customized solutions that are both efficient and effective.

His wide-ranging technical interests led him to the emerging fields of computer vision and machine learning since 2016, James has a passion for artificial intelligence and has honed his skills in this area through a combination of academic study and practical experiences. He has developed an in-depth understanding of the latest tools and techniques in computer vision and machine learning and is always looking for new ways to apply this knowledge to real-world problems.

DEMYSTIFYING LARGE LANGUAGE MODEL

by James Chen, 2024

www.ingramcontent.com/pod-product-compliance
Lightning Source LLC
Chambersburg PA
CBHW071102050326
40690CB00008B/1088